A Second Helping of Gumbo for the Soul: More Liberating Stories and Memories to Inspire Females of Color

A Volume in:
Contemporary Perspectives on Multicultural Gifted Education

Series Editors

Donna Y. Ford
Malik S. Henfield

Contemporary Perspectives on Multicultural Gifted Education

Series Editors

Donna Y. Ford
The Ohio State University

Malik S. Henfield
Loyola University Chicago

*Understanding the Intersections of Race, Gender, and Gifted Education:
An Anthology By and About Talented Black Girls and Women in STEM* (2020)
Nicole M. Joseph

*A Second Helping of Gumbo for the Soul:
More Liberating Stories and Memories to Inspire Females of Color* (2019)
Michelle Trotman Scott, Nicole McZeal Walters,
Jemimah L. Young, & Donna Y. Ford

*Gumbo for the Soul III: Males of Color Share Their Stories, Meditations,
Affirmations, and Inspirations* (2019)
Brian L. Wright, Nathaniel Bryan, Christopher Sewell,
Lucian Yates III, Michael Robinson, & Kianga Thomas

*Gumbo for the Soul:
Liberating Memoirs and Stories to Inspire Females of Color* (2016)
Donna Y. Ford , Joy Lawson Davis, Michelle Trotman Scott, Yolanda Sealey-Ruiz

A Second Helping of Gumbo for the Soul: More Liberating Stories and Memories to Inspire Females of Color

Edited by

Michelle Frazier Trotman Scott
Nicole McZeal Walters
Jemimah L. Young
Donna Y. Ford

≡IAP

INFORMATION AGE PUBLISHING, INC.
Charlotte, NC • www.infoagepub.com

Library of Congress Cataloging-In-Publication Data

The CIP data for this book can be found on the Library of Congress website (loc.gov).

Paperback: 978-1-64113-870-3
Hardcover: 978-1-64113-871-0
E-Book: 978-1-64113-872-7

Printed in the United States of America

CONTENTS

CHAPTER 1

PERSONAL PRESS OF PERFECTIONISM

Liberated from Victimization

Cynthia Alexander Mitchell

Key Challenges: family issues; rejection; sexual abuse; excessive self-pressure; manipulation; perfectionism; academic challenges

GENESIS: BEGINNING IN THE MIDDLE

When we think about the genesis or the beginning, typically we are referring to the initial day or start of an occurrence, act, or existence. Biblical scholars equate all of the initial foundations of the existence of (wo)man and major changes in the course of humanity around the beginning or genesis of our existence. Birth, in most cases, is the beginning of existence, but in my case, the genesis of an altered existence occurred early in my childhood. Even as I write, there is a nervousness about outlining the how in who I am as a woman of color. In reading my story, you will see how my *who* aligns with my *how* in a way that I stubbornly refused to allow the sporadic circumstances of life to dictate the narrative assigned to my preordained destiny.

A Second Helping of Gumbo for the Soul: More Liberating Stories and Memories to Inspire Females of Color, pages 1–4.

As a child, I remember the story of the *Little Red Riding Hood.* Although this story was and is still widely read to children, this children's book has a hidden meaning for me. The main character in the childhood fable starts out with Red going on a seemingly routine trip to her Grandma's house. However, on this particular day, there was nothing routine about this visit. She was taking the same route as always. She was carrying the same basket. She even wore the same red hooded cape. Yet, on this day, this trip would become a journey.

A trip to grandma's house in many cultures is a time, in most cases, cherished. This celebration is a way to connect with extended relatives through sharing moments missed due to the absence of day-to-day presence. When most children reflect on a visit to grandma's house, the smell of fresh baked cookies, the warm embrace, and the love that can only come from grandma's house are among the common expectations for most. Unfortunately, the four-hour drive to my grandma's house proved to be pure torture for me as a child. Each mile that we drove closer to Jackson caused an anxiety that had I been mischievously convinced not to share. In the mind of a then six-year-old, I became overly calculated about where I would or would not go when visiting Grandma. I even found myself announcing where I was in the house and who was around me.

In the fictitious child story, there was a wolf that was associated with deception that decided to disrupt the normalcy of a visit to grandma's house. In my story, the wolf did not dress up in grandmother clothes, but instead a loving and supporting uncle who greatly deceived me. Because he was my mother's youngest brother, he was perceived as innocent; however, he was anything but innocent. The lessons that we learned about good touch, bad touch, at his hand, totally blurred the lines for me, creating an altered reality.

SELF-CRUCIFIXION: A WINLESS COMPETITION

Sexual abuse is far too common in many of our families. Children who have been victimized respond in several ways. My response was framed around the fact that I felt like I had allowed this predator permission to violate me. Over and over, I would replay how I could have stopped him. These internal battles lead to the need to get it right. Not just get it right, but seek the approval of my parents and others to constantly validate everything that I did. More dangerously, I took on the self-inflicted charge to do the best and make whatever the situation or assignment flawless and faultless. Little did I know, by age seven, I would reconcile that my solution or coming to grips with the trauma, was to sentence myself to endure a level of internalized presser that was an impossible task—even for an adult.

For years, I wrestled with how to tell my parents that a trip to grandma's house was not in my best interest. I mentally grappled with how he could feel like he had the right to disrupt my existence by violating me. The struggle caused an illusion that I had to even protect my parents and extended family from the truth, despite the fact that I could tell my very openly loving family anything. The most damaging product of the violation was the newness of a forced silence due to predatory manipulation.

The birth of self-doubt manifested as a blind spot in my life. It is one thing to question and doubt others, but the ongoing questions, evaluation, and assessment in retrospect were mentally exhausting, especially for a child. The internal struggle indirectly taught me that I had to question in some cases; over think every detail of every action in my life. I defined this blind spot as the seed of reverse rejection. Outside rejection is normal and sometimes expected. Self-rejection is like living in a self-erected torture chamber where you are the prosecutor and emancipator interchangeably.

REDEMPTION: A STORY REWRITTEN

Redemption came for me as my predator eventually received the ultimate repayment for the abuse inflicted that secretly altered my entire childhood. Yet, the remnants of the seeds planted that drove my desire to succeed at everything and fail at nothing spilled into to every area of my life. Naturally strong-willed, I was determined not to let the actions of others define me as a person. There is both a good and bad side to making such a dominant stance. The good part was that I refused to play the victim. The bad side is that I created obstacles, with extreme barriers between anyone outside of my familial circle and me. In my mind, this barrier served as a buffer that could protect me from any cause pain or disappoint.

This was a dangerous position in that while a protective coat separated me from others with potential malice intent, I also missed the opportunity for the right people to gain tangible and beneficial positions in my life. The strict process to go beyond this self-erected barricade was virtually impossible to penetrate. As if this barrier was not enough, by doing this, I also created an unspoken contractual agreement for anyone that was allowed in my personal fortress. That contract obligated them to operate with little room for error. In many instances, even the smallest infraction that deviated from the expected behaviors, support, or treatment time would be punishable by permanent removal from the safe zone beyond the unseen barrier.

PERFECTLY IMPERFECT

The expectation of perfection was inflicted on my family, relationships, career, but most impactful, myself. The energy channeled in overcoming the pain caused by a feeling of having so little control of a situation fueled a fire that indicated that I would never lack the level of control over my life again. This was both dangerous and debilitating. Nothing is perfect, and there are so many things that we do not have control over in this life. The energy given to this self-redemptive, yet self-created strategy caused more frustration than solutions. The challenge with perfecting anything is that there is no perfect prototype in this thing that we call life. As frustrating as it can be, the ability to predict the outcomes and the actions of others is impossible. Nothing that we do can ever control the actions, responses or actions of others, good or bad. Within my elementary to college experiences, there was always the ongoing challenge that made me feel like I was competing with a ghost. The ghost was the loss of my former self. Before the abuse occurred, I remember being a part of a conversation with my kindergarten teacher about promoting me from kindergarten to second grade; however, unfortunately, the fall out also affected my academic progress. Within a year, I went from being advanced to temporarily struggling as a first grader. I can even remember the threat of Special Education used as an attempt to motivate me.

The burden of my secret had invaded a space that caused me to struggle to recapture what was seemingly easy for me just months earlier. This may sound eerie, but the reality is and was that I was always trying to make every effort not to fail or cause anyone else pain, while constantly reaching for an existence that was nonexistent. This was equivalent to running on a human hamster wheel. This pursuit proved to be exhausting, unfruitful and never-ending. For years, this was the testament to my story. As women, particularly of color, we need to learn to release ourselves from the pressures of assuming that the weight of the world is assigned to us.

RESURGENCE OF A NEW SELF

My awakening and release from the exhausting frustration came during my junior year in college. I remember the day that I realized that as a child, I could not control the bad decisions of others. I then knew that while the situation produced a victim, ultimately I had to heal. My emancipation occurred when I was able to see the potential that was ahead of me versus the distractions that occurred behind me. As shameful and stressful as my experience was, I released the weight of the guilt that haunted me. The perceived participation of the act by a six-year-old was not at all the reality. I realized that if had my choice, I would not have to heal from, deal with, nor reconcile the blatant misbehavior of anyone outside of myself.

In an ideal world, this would not be the case for any of us. The only choice that we have is to press forward. As women of color who must succeed, we are required to own the pain that has occurred in our life, but we cannot cosign on the lifetime sentence associated with the remnants of our negative experiences. We have to be clear, knowing that going forward is the only option. With this new definition, we are now required to seize the right to live a healthy, whole, successful, and productive life. Paralysis in the past is not an option when we own the need to actively participate in our own narratives.

Finally, there is a need for reclamation of a destiny that will open the floodgate of a resurgence of energy, creative genius, and most importantly life! We are freed from the fear of not getting it right and a freed to fail forward. We are freed knowing that acknowledging is not owning. Yet, acknowledgment leads to self-acceptance that is accompanied by a reset on the course of our paused purpose. Ultimately, this reset leads to redemption, hope, and an immeasurable stream of self-love and future possibilities.

CHAPTER 2

THE ART OF LETTING GO

Haile Bennett

Key Challenges: depression; mental health; self-doubt

Have you ever died and come back to life? Has your heart struggled to pump life into you while you walk into work? Have you operated on autopilot for months or years on end without you or the people around you even noticing? Maybe you were like me shuffling from meeting to meeting every day exhausted, but pushing through the grind. Leaving doctor appointments still unclear as to why you always felt terrible and lifeless despite how hard you tried to fight it. Maybe you realized that all the spaces and places you found yourself in felt more like prisons than sanctuaries.

Today, I feel an inherent sense of stress. I'm so worried about pulling everything and myself together. Why must I always feel as if I'm struggling like a fish flopping around out of water? ... Mostly I am just afraid. That fear feels isolating and lonely. I've gone so long detached from my life that I'm afraid I don't know how to really engage and be fully present. I'm afraid that all of these fears and pains will control me and overpower everything positive in my life and slowly kill me as it has been.

I wrote these words in my journal during a quiet moment of reflection. It had become clear that mentally and spiritually I was struggling. These circumstances

A Second Helping of Gumbo for the Soul: More Liberating Stories and Memories to Inspire Females of Color, pages 5–8.

I faced were new, but I had been here before. Unfortunately, this mental space was familiar territory—unhappy, alone, smothered by the negativity enveloping my life, and ready to give it all up completely. My parents divorced when I was in fifth grade, and I experienced my first battle with depression. I learned quickly from my interactions with people at home and school that my level of sadness was unacceptable, so I hid it. The strong Black woman doesn't cry when she is upset, and that's what I was on track to become. As I grew into a young woman, these limitations on my emotions directed the narration in my head. I actively stifled my softness and vulnerability, thinking it was only a detriment to me. My depression and anxiety often translated as anger and aggression. The frustrated energy I emitted after being constantly misunderstood only cemented the labels I often garnered while at school and among peers: bitch; angry; intimidating; combative; and rebellious.

In my quest for understanding and acceptance in my family, I pushed myself to meet their expectations and created an image of the life I should lead in order to make them proud. In order to fit into this perception of an acceptable person, I focused on becoming a high achiever, but was constantly battling internally as well as the external world around me. Regardless of how I failed in my interactions with people, I managed to succeed as a student. Yet my curiosities and the realities of my identity always took me astray from what my relatively conservative religious family deemed acceptable or appropriate. I knew that I couldn't be transparent about the way I experienced certain aspects of my life—like my sexuality and spirituality, or even wanting to explore the arts. Eventually, I leveraged my commitment to academics to attend boarding school and create a distance from my family that allowed me to explore my identity in its totality. I was finally free to embrace myself more fully—except for when I shrank myself down to a palatable version of myself whenever I came back home.

This is how I existed until I reached the age of 23. I found myself wrapping up graduate school, struggling to wrap my brain around my grandfather's death, and preparing to move back into my old bedroom in a house that truly hadn't felt like home for longer than I cared to remember. I had about two months to settle in when my uncle had a heart attack; and my grandmother's heart would stop in another two months.

Somehow, I pushed through the surmounting grief to perform the role of the fully functional Strong Black Woman. I found a comfortable job that fit into the socially acceptable box and put riskier, creative ideas on the backburner. Instead of fully acknowledging the pain I was feeling, I tried to focus on how I could help everyone else in my family. Along the way, I turned to old unhealthy habits to suppress my emotions. But, the act would only last so long. No matter how hard I tried to prevent it, I found myself fighting off my anxiety every morning on the way to work. I would bounce back and forth from sleepless nights to sleeping the day away. I constantly felt ill, but no doctor could really explain what was wrong.

Circuits were broken in my system. I was no longer able to function with the same survival methods I had been using for years.

There I was, in the empty bathroom at work. Staring out the window down those 26 floors to the ground after what I came to know as my daily pre-work anxiety attack. I probed in my mind what I was doing wrong, often using what I had written in my journal as a mantra of sorrow or frustration for myself. Then a softer, calmer voice whispered to me that I didn't have to force myself to keep living this way. Suddenly, it hit me: the real problem was that I wasn't listening to myself. All those years of hiding from my truth were to my detriment. I stuffed so much of me away in so many different ways, that my voice—my real voice, not that negative voice that had been built over time to feed into my fears, insecurities, and shame—was stuffed down, too. My real voice was the one that called out faintly to me, pushing past the negative voice that constantly recited my flaws and wrongdoings all day and night. I took that as a sign and promised myself to listen to this voice more often, not knowing the changes it would bring about in my life.

> Today feels easier. Clarity seems more achievable. Things fall apart, but eventually, they come back together again into something better, more exciting, more beautiful, more real. There is beauty in the struggle... For now, I have to remember that my struggle is my own. I can't expect anyone to understand it. It's for me to figure out and me alone... All that matters is allowing myself to be me.

It's been amazing to witness the way my life has transformed since making that promise to myself. The change is evident in how I manage my energy to the level of patience I have on a daily basis. Even the reflections in my journal feel more positive. Slowly, I realized that my intuition was my connection to Spirit. Now I call upon the voice that is soft enough to soothe, but strong enough to be heard through the noise. I can call upon my *Goddess* voice. I know that as long as I let my *Goddess* voice guide me, I'll be just fine. Before, I was ignoring this voice and becoming too fixated on external factors. But, the more I focus on nurturing my *Goddess* voice, the closer I am to being my best self. No more unrealistic standards based on what "they" say life should be. No more unsustainable methods to achieve these unhealthy goals. Now, everything I give to the world comes from a place of love, and the way I engage feels more impactful. My *Goddess* voice reconnected me to parts of myself that were slowly dying as I tried to fit into the expectations of the world. I'm constantly finding opportunities to strengthen my artistic voice now, and have gained a renewed connection to the earth and the souls that inhabit it.

All of my old coping and survival habits prevented me from releasing negativity and living a life grounded in love. The more I held onto things like fear and shame, the more negativity I attracted into my life. I've since let go of all that negativity. I practice acknowledging and releasing my pain and anger, which allows me to operate from a positive place and manifest blessings big and small in my life. Releasing negative emotions surrounding the relationship with my previous academic institutions, made room for new opportunities. I left my job to prioritize my family and myself. I then enrolled in an Ivy League graduate program that caters to my unique interests in spirituality and wellness. I ended unhealthy relationships and habits that kept me stuck in unhealthy cycles. Instead of getting caught up in loneliness or the fear of change, I filled that space with positivity and found that healthier options took their place. It's clear now that if I make room for a life of happiness, it is mine for the taking.

I'm still a work in progress and remind myself regularly of how both challenging and fulfilling this journey has been. Some days, it's harder to listen to my *Goddess* voice than others. These are the days I step up my self-care. I do things like meditate a little longer, spend some extra time writing in my journal, do some extra pampering, spend time outside, exercise, or reconnect with a great friend. And sometimes I just need a good cry to release some negativity.

Although I used to feel isolated and alone in my struggles, I believe my *Goddess* voice when she reminds me that I'm not. The more and more I let go of the unhealthy, negative way I lived before, the more fulfilling and light-filled my life has become. My struggles with mental health are more manageable, and my relationships are easier to maintain. Most importantly, I feel happy. I'm confident that I can be strong without sacrificing the vulnerability that makes me human. I know that the more I nurture my soul and the Goddess within me, the more light I will be able to shine on this world so that other women of color can stand in the light with me.

CHAPTER 3

HIDDEN FIGURE NO MORE

A Black Girl's Journey Through STEM Education

Ansley A. Booker

Key Challenges: bullying; double minority; social isolation

Cooking good gumbo is similar to following the scientific method to conduct a successful scientific experiment. You have to follow each step carefully to replicate a "confident" outcome.

OBSERVATION

Understanding the mechanics of science and its connections to human existence has intrigued me since early childhood. At the age of 12, I can recall asking my parents for a compound microscope to help me make observations about the world using a laboratory kit and to complete home science experiments. After I received the kit, I used it to conduct independent tests and science fair projects, one of which led to my nomination for the Georgia Governor's Honors Program. However, with each of my scientific discoveries, I was trying to deal with being a Black girl intrigued by topics that society found to be strange. A keen interest in science led to a lot of social isolation and bullying during my fourth, fifth and

A Second Helping of Gumbo for the Soul: More Liberating Stories and Memories to Inspire Females of Color, pages 9–12.
Copyright © 2020 by Information Age Publishing

sixth grade school years. I was bullied a great deal during this time for being "different." During elementary school, I was tracked scholastically, which resulted in me being removed from academic groups with my peers. I later learned to trust my academic freedom, and during seventh grade, I was able to find more Black girls who enjoyed math and science just as much as me. I would utilize those friendships to compete in even more scientific and quiz bowl competitions. Our team, which consisted mostly of Black girls, would later become state champions. These friendships continued to support me throughout high school. During high school, I continued to seek challenging science and math courses because I wanted to pursue a career in the health field.

In retrospect, I realized how important Black Science, Technology, Engineering and Mathematics (STEM) role models and teachers were, as well as the need for a strong support system. During my sixth and seventh grade years, I was introduced to my first Black science teachers who became my mentors. These mentors helped to encourage me in science and math, as well as provided a visual of people of color in STEM disciplines and careers. They also provided me with great constructive feedback and academic support. My sixth-grade science teacher even helped stop the bullying. Other significant contributors to my success early on were my parents and high school science teachers. They always nurtured my love for science and my career path because, being raised in a small town, I had limited access to Advanced Placement courses, SAT prep and other catalysts that could help better prepare me for college. My mother, who was an elementary school teacher, provided me with great scholarly books on African American scientists and inventors. My father consistently helped me to practice, providing results from my scientific inquiry by repeatedly asking about them. My anatomy and geometry teachers taught at a neighboring college and would use their resources and teaching strategies to prepare me for collegiate studies.

HYPOTHESIS

Because of my keen interest in the sciences, I hypothesized that I would be better suited for a scientific career. Therefore, I earned a Bachelor of Science in Biology with a minor in Chemistry and a Master of Science in Pharmacy with certificates in Clinical Trials and Regulatory Affairs. In undergraduate school, I worked on research with my professors that focused primarily on living systems and chemical reactions, which gave me a strong foundation in biological sciences. In 2007, I became involved in the Ronald E. McNair Baccalaureate Program, which was designed to prepare low-income and potential first-generation college students for doctoral studies. As a participant, I worked with my faculty mentor to complete a literature review on the influence of bilingual education in Early Childhood Education. My participation in this program was very integral to my educational success. It exposed me along with a multitude of students to research opportunities and served as an avenue to conduct and present scholarly research as an undergraduate. This experience also helped to broaden my academic and career perspectives as well. For the first time, I began to contemplate how to marry my two passions, science and teaching, on a post-secondary level. Before this experience, I was committed to research and design or a career as a healthcare practitioner.

My zeal for teaching was initially ignited when I became an educator and research assistant. In my sophomore year, I worked with my chemistry instructor to determine the best delivery format for freshmen-level chemistry classes using data collected in freshman satisfaction surveys. Next, I was paired with my industrial chemistry professor to select labs delivered in her "Survey of Industrial Chemistry" course. By my senior year, I was able to collaborate with graduate assistants and teach biology labs. As the assignments increased in scale and importance, I progressively realized that I loved science and wanted to educate others in some capacity. This experience was significant to me because it allowed me to conduct more laboratory research, draft proposals for collegiate instruction, and present my findings. I learned how to work within research teams, as well as how to utilize grant funding to find logical solutions to educational problems. It was my first introduction to a mixed methods approach to a research design. It was also important to me because I was one of few Black women in my college major. I used this opportunity to form more peer and study groups for minority women, which would help foster academic success because sometimes, we were ostracized by our male counterparts ostracized us. I also utilized it to craft my relationships and networking opportunities with faculty and staff. These relationships and experiences with faculty were later integral to my success in life and academic pursuits.

PROCEDURES

Later, after working in a local pharmacy during a flu outbreak, my interest shifted to the pharmaceutical field. During this particular outbreak, there was a shortage of Tamiflu, which left thousands of people without medication. Many of the consumers either could not afford the medication or did not have coverage for the brand-named drug under their insurance policies. As a solution, the local pharmacists offered generic alternatives and over-the-counter medications to treat patients' symptoms. Realizing how cost, supply and demand, and the roles healthcare providers played during this event triggered my desire to improve patient care through pharmaceutical research and regulatory policies and procedures. This was my motivation for wanting to complete a master's degree in pharmaceutical science. During this time, I had multiple obstacles working against me. I was dually minoritized in my program, and did not have a background in quality control or regulatory affairs. I felt like a 'hidden figure.' I often questioned my place within my program due to my differences. Also, my student profile was very different from many of my classmates. Not only was I not employed in the pharmaceutical industry, but I also selected to complete a thesis for my degree, unlike most of my classmates who chose to complete a capstone project.

Nervous about this decision and the impact that it would have on my future career choices, I told my thesis committee chair that I wanted to pursue my doctoral degree. I feared that he would criticize me for my choice of study. Rather, he validated my decision to write a master's thesis and confirmed that this was the appropriate path to take to reach my goals of becoming a scholar/practitioner. Because I had minimal experience in conducting research or working in the pharmaceutical field, he was very patient with me and helped me untiringly through the entire research process. His immeasurable insight and valuable recommendations on conducting a qualitative study on healthcare providers reporting adverse events to MedWatch was remarkable and helped me when I was doubtful about my decision. With his guidance, I was able to present my research findings at various conferences and colleges and universities. My professor's unwavering support, expertise, and words of encouragement are the reasons that I was able to complete my thesis and graduate with a master's degree from graduate school promptly.

EXPERIMENT

Currently, I am a doctoral student in an educational leadership program. This program has afforded me the opportunity to develop my interests in higher education. I am particularly interested in researching Black women who have obtained STEM graduate degrees. My goal is to unearth barriers and catalysts to their graduate and career success to develop retention models that may improve the college persistence of women and minority students in STEM programs. I would also like to conduct research experiments on ways to improve student initiatives and academic advising in graduate programs.

CONCLUSION (LESSONS LEARNED)

- "Courage is like—it's a habitus, a habit, a virtue: you get it by courageous acts. It's like you learn to swim by swimming. You learn courage by couraging." -Dr. Marie M. Daly
- "Don't let anyone rob you of your imagination, your creativity, or your curiosity. It's your place in the world; it's your life. Go on and do all you can with it, and make it the life you want to live." –Astronaut Mae Jemison
- Find a mentor, learn from them, and become a mentor to other ambitious young women in STEM.
- We are no longer hidden figures!!! Don't let bullying or social isolation stop you from pursuing your dreams.
- Always seek opportunities to learn something new and avenues for growth.
- Embrace your feminism and your heritage it makes you unique not less than. Neither gender nor skin color can measure intellect.

CHAPTER 4

PORCH STEPS

Robin Brandehoff

Key Challenges: poverty; first generation college access; self-doubt

I was fortunate growing up. My family lived below the poverty line, but with the help of friends, neighbors, and food banks, we always managed to scrape by. My story begins in Kahului, a small town on the island of Maui, Hawaii. Known for our harbor and small community college, many tourists come to Kahului to shop or lay on our pristine beaches. But they rarely see the worn-out homes and housing projects just beyond the beautiful trees. I grew up beyond the trees. When people hear that I grew up in Hawaii, they exclaim how lucky I was to grow up in paradise; but they do not understand that their paradise was my imprisonment. Imprisoned by an ocean on all sides of the island, our goods were imported and taxed beyond what we could afford. My clearest memories center around our lack of food and basic resources, seasoned with a fear of counting items at the checkout line and having to choose which products to put back. That familiar bloat of hunger that came from eating only Top Ramen or rice, or of having to share a candy bar with my family because it was all we could afford to eat that night.

It was the kindness of our community and the Aloha spirit that truly sustained my family. Despite the pangs of hunger and oppressive tourism, my community of Ohana taught me what it was to hope and aspire to do great things regardless

A Second Helping of Gumbo for the Soul: More Liberating Stories and Memories to Inspire Females of Color, pages 13–15.

of what we appeared to lack. My elders and Kumus would talk with me, to help paint a picture of understanding that wealth stretched beyond the conveyor belt of the supermarket; that our wealth came from the generosity and love we offered each other, especially in times of distress. It was this wealth of love and hope that I lamented leaving when a family friend paid our dues to get us off the island and onto the mainland.

We moved from "America's paradise" to a city popularly chosen for movie sets depicting perfect suburban communities. Set apart from these locales is where I lived, with its tar-patched streets and Section 8 housing complexes. Gunshots and drug deals were common where I grew up, and it did not take long for me to be inducted into my new community. This new neighborhood was marked as gang territory, but surprisingly, our neighbors never came across as a threat to our family. Instead, it always seemed that they were looking out for us, and particularly for my brother Michael, who had Autism.

Again, even here, it was my community of elders that continually sat me down to navigate the obstacles I found myself in. When I started running with a different crowd in middle school, it was my neighbor, a drug lord of East L.A., who sat me down and tried to reason with me. He encouraged me to do well in school, which were words of wisdom that he never received growing up. He said that with my grades, I could probably go to college and get out of this neighborhood forever.

At that time, I just laughed. No one in my family ever went to college, and none of us had the credit line to get a used car or even furniture. As far as I was concerned, I had no right to even consider placing the burden of college on my family. Instead, I would follow in my sister's footsteps and work to support us. The alternative was to fall in line with the soldiers of my block and not see my 18th birthday. Either way, at that time, college was a laughable notion.

In high school, I was truant so much that my mother was almost arrested on my account. I was pushed into a private Catholic high school where I was removed from the influences of my neighborhood, and forced to study (after all, I was paying for it). I still did not think of college as a prospect for me—it was expensive, and I constantly worried about who would help to take care of my brother and pay the bills. The reality of my fears hit me like a freight train when halfway through my freshman year, my mother had a major stroke and was hospitalized for an extended period of time. So, I dropped out of school to take care of my family, and did not think twice about it...but my teachers did. That semester, the school suspended my tuition costs, and teachers drove class work to and from my home, braving the contemptuous looks of my protective neighbors when my teachers knocked on our door. I was able to return to school during my sophomore year and was mentored through the next few years of academia by the best teachers on campus. However, despite this success, I still did not feel as though I was good enough or worth the cost of college. In my senior year, it was the same neighbor who planted the seed about attending college who asked how my college applications were going. When I told him that I was not going to college, his face contorted, and he firmly told me to sit down.

We sat on his porch for two hours as he recounted the moments in his life that went wrong and what he would give to go back and change them. I told him why I was not going to college, and his face continued to sour:

"You're being stupid, mija" he began. "Don't you understand what it means if you don't go? You're the hope of this neighborhood. I want my kids to look up to you and see that they can do it too. You're going to college."

With the finality of that statement, he stood up, walked inside, and slammed the door. He left me sitting alone on his porch to allow his words to sink in. Through the mesh of the screen door, I could see his youngest daughter sitting on the couch and working on her homework—and suddenly his words took on more meaning.

That night, I stayed up late and submitted three applications to colleges in Southern California. With the academic help of my teachers and the emotional support of the community members of my neighborhood, I became a first-generation high school graduate and earned my place at Whittier College.

My neighbor was right. Education allowed me to thrive for the first time in my life. I attended college and graduated with distinction with a double major My GPA of 3.59 also lead to an invitation to return in the fall to begin studies for my Master's in Education. I thoroughly enjoyed my experiences, achievements, and struggles in academia, and knew that I needed to pay these opportunities forward. All I wanted was to enter a classroom on my own terms and inspire other students like myself...so, I did.

I chose to work with gang-affiliated and recently incarcerated high school students in East L.A. and focused on mentoring them to navigate the channels of societal oppression that were, and still are, built against marginalized students of color. Building off the mentorship I received from my Ohana elders, and neighbors, I centered my teaching on aspirations for success and happiness. As a classroom community, we approached our obstacles of doubt, poverty, and society's perception of our self-worth and fought the currents holding us back.

As a college-educated teacher, I have many mentors to attribute my success to, but it was my neighbor's words that inspired me to be the educator and emerging scholar that I am today. Through his actions, I came to realize my own dream of working with students lost in a sea of their own self-doubt...I aspire to motivate them.

CHAPTER 5

YOUNG, GIFTED, BLACK, AND HARASSED

Notes from a California Childhood

Lisa Bratton

Key Challenges: peer pressure, discrimination; race; empowerment

In 1961, the year I was born, Black America was focused on the Freedom Rides, sit-ins, boycotts, marches, voter education, and segregation—in schools and in housing. While this was a pivotal year in African American history, everything about my life was the opposite of what most Black folks were facing.

I was born and raised in Vallejo, California. My parents, sister, brother and I lived in an integrated neighborhood on Indiana Street. Our next-door neighbors on one side were the Mitchells; Mr. Mitchell was a Tuskegee Airman. Next door to them lived the Browns, an African American couple who were also our land-lords (my parents later bought the house that we rented). Our other next-door neighbor was a White man who looked like Jimmy Durante. Both African Americans and Whites inhabited the rest of the street.

Before I started school, we "moved up in the world— "to an all African American neighborhood now known as Lofas-Lakeside. In virtually every household on

A Second Helping of Gumbo for the Soul: More Liberating Stories and Memories to Inspire Females of Color, pages 17–20.
Copyright © 2020 by Information Age Publishing

our street lived a married couple. My mother was a graduate of Benedict College and worked as a teacher at Napa State Hospital. My father was a laborer at Mare Island Naval Shipyard, owned a laundromat, and invested in rental property.

I also later learned that our neighborhood was the first in California to be built by African Americans for African Americans. My piano teacher's husband, Mr. B. W. Williams, was a general contractor who organized a team of African American professionals, including a real estate agent and an insurance broker, to build the community in the late 1950s. He secured commitments from several African Americans renters to purchase the homes, but no White person would sell him the land. He went to Mr. Lofas, a White man who agreed to purchase the land in his own name—if Williams would name a street after him. Williams agreed. Hence, I grew up on Lofas Place.

Lofas Place was our African village. The Matthews lived across the street; Rev. Matthews was retired and earned the nickname "Double-0" (as in Secret Agent 007) because he would call my parents if my siblings or I did anything outside of our routine. Together, with neighbors, we had neighborhood potlucks, supported each other in emergencies, and always had each other's back. I was also the neighborhood babysitter and made a small fortune during the summer season.

My parents usually told us about the news that would affect us, but almost never mentioned racial issues. We subscribed to *Ebony Magazine* and attended the all-Black Second Baptist Church, but that was the extent of the racial environment in our household. I was 6½ when Dr. King was assassinated. I remember that when I asked my mother what she was watching on TV, she said, "a funeral."

In 1969, my mother told us that we would soon have new neighbors in the house three doors away. The city was piloting a "Welfare House" (Section 8) and the people moving in were poor. Soon the neighbors did move in—and they were White. So, in 1960s, a segregated neighborhood was more desirable than an integrated one; African Americans were married homeowners, and White people lived in subsidized housing in stable Black communities.

My third-grade teacher, Ms. Rutherford, recommended me for the gifted program, but all I was told was that I was going to the school district office to take a test. As I waited in the lobby for my turn, I, of course, had a book. The secretaries commented, "Look how fast she is reading that book!" The next thing I knew, I was to be a part of the MGM program—Mentally Gifted Minors —and that I was told that I would have to change schools.

For the first few weeks of school, the school district sent a taxi for me. I thought nothing of this (except that it felt strange sitting alone in the back seat), but my older sister informed me that I was being pretentious. The taxi was temporary transportation until the bus logistics were worked out. There were times when I would miss the bus, but all I needed to do was call the school, and they would send a taxi for me.

I started out riding a "short yellow bus" with both MGM students and students with disabilities. I later rode the bus with other African American students who attended my new school, but did not live in my neighborhood. They would taunt me incessantly saying that I thought I was better than them because I was in "The Smart Class." Whenever anyone—child or adult—asked why I went to Cooper Elementary instead of Dan Mini, I usually said, "Because my mother said so." I never told anyone that I was gifted. I suppose it sounded pretentious.

I was the only African American girl in the gifted classes, which included Grades 4–6. The other boy in my class was so tall and big that no one dared bother him. Nonetheless, I experienced my first racial incidents as a 4th grader. I arrived at school early one morning and was on the playground with two White boys from my gifted class. I don't recall what we were discussing, but one boy, Kevin, said, "Well, at least he's White." This is the same Kevin who said, "Hail Hitler!" and gave the Nazi salute on more than one occasion.

Fortunately, my best friend Rena was in my class. She was Filipina, and we were often the targets of our teachers' racism and wrath. I also had a White friend, named Lisa, who was a student in my class. Our friendship was not as stable. She and I were friends one day and enemies the next. I recall one time when Rena and I were mad at Lisa, which happened from time to time, and we had some little girlish feud going on. Our teacher, Ms. Thurman, responded by calling my parents and telling them that Rena and I had a "Hate Club." I often wondered if she called Kevin's parents and told them he was a Hitler Youth....

The taunting that I had to endure from the other African American children on the bus and in my school continued until 6th grade when Gail, another African American girl, joined my class. Gail was a friend of the other African American children at the school. So, since I was her friend, I was in! The taunting stopped completely, and sixth grade was manageable.

My sister and brother were in private school, but since there was no opening in my grade, I remained in public school for Grades 7 and 8. I was still in the gifted program and was still bused across town. By the time I reached Grade 9, the private school, St. Vincent's, started high school and now had room for me. Off I went. Plaid uniform skirts. Nuns. Mass. No boys. And, overt racism.

Most of the girls were nice, but even some of those who were friendly exhibited racist behavior. We had to learn the map of the world, and as we were filling in our blank maps, one girl said "Nigger-ia" instead of "Nigeria" and "Nigger" instead of "Niger." Also, on a class trip to the beach, one girl, Dee Dee, got brown sand all over her legs. Her friend Liz screamed, "Dee Dee's a nigger!" I was in Liz's car one day, and she used the N-word as if I wasn't there. I didn't know how to handle these and other racist incidents, so I remained silent.

In 10th grade, I had a friend named David who was a year older than me and was very mature in his conversation. He asked me if I had read *The Autobiography of Malcolm X*. I thought it was a book about Madame X and I said "No. My sister has that book. I don't need to read it." Later, I got the book down from my sister's shelf and started to read it. I felt so empowered after reading it and felt that I really understood White people. It changed my life.

Soon after, in Religion class, our teacher, Sister Mariana, gave us some controversial topics and pictures, and we were to make statements about them. One of the words was "Africa." The White girls started chiming in, "Jungle!" "Monkeys!" "People don't wear clothes...." I let them all finish and raised my hand. I said, "Africa is a term that is misunderstood because of the high level of ignorance in this class." The class got quiet, and the nun got nervous. She changed the subject. This was a major turning point for me because I felt such a sense of empowerment that I stood up for my people and myself. And that was the last N-word I ever heard at school.

Surprisingly, my high school library had an extensive collection of books on African Americans, including *Seize the Time* by Bobby Seale. I checked out so many of those books that the librarian even made a comment to me. Throughout these books, Howard University was consistently mentioned...I was intrigued, and I was sold.

I got the highest grade of all 10th-grade students on the PSAT and was the only National Merit Scholar from St. Vincent's. As a result of my PSAT scores, I was invited to the University of California at Irvine for a weekend. I and other students were honored by California State University at Hayward. None of this mattered. No one could force me to apply anywhere else and attending Howard proved to be one of the best decisions I have ever made in my life.

I majored in Business with the intention of helping African Americans become entrepreneurs. I was able to do that at the Small Business Development Center, while a graduate student in the M.B.A. program at Atlanta University and worked in other aspects of business. In my 30s, I admitted to myself that I hated business. I began to think about what I liked and I knew that I liked Black people. At the time, Temple University had the only Ph.D. program in African American Studies in the world, so I applied, got in, and completed a second Master's and Ph.D. Today, as a history professor at Tuskegee University, I *do Black people* for a living. It seems now that my life has come full circle as it relates to race. My childhood represented the exact opposite experience from so much of the rest of Black America, but it is exactly that experience that has become my passion.

Ms. Thurman, Liz, Kevin, and the White girls from St. Vincent's helped teach me that empowering myself with self-knowledge is the best revenge. So, you should thank your haters for their hate and, in turn, use their hate to fuel the engine of your success.

CHAPTER 6

AGAINST THE ODDS

Building Efficacy and Shattering Threats

Kelly Bullock Daugherty

Key challenges: self-efficacy; academic efficacy; stereotype threat; mindset; low expectations

I was an average student. Early in my schooling, I recall truly enjoying learning. As I grew older and the content became more challenging, I began to struggle. The pace of learning proved too rigorous, the content too advanced, and my grades began to drop early on in high school. Don't get me wrong; I wasn't a failing student, but I wasn't the best student either. I was an athlete, and that helped to keep my grades at a level high enough to remain at least average, but I came to believe that this was ultimately my best. It was my normal, and I had become complacent. I assumed that if average was enough to play sports, then it had to be enough to get me to college. I would quickly learn differently.

I often wonder why it is difficult to remember the names of many of my teachers from way back then. I surmise it is because many of them lacked a genuine interest in my success. Their beliefs about my ability to thrive and succeed in college will forever be ingrained in my mind. I had dreams of attending a Division I college; however, after scoring below level on both my SAT and ACT,

A Second Helping of Gumbo for the Soul: More Liberating Stories and Memories to Inspire Females of Color, pages 21–24.

my counselor suggested I think about a smaller college or university—one with smaller professor-to-student ratios, and where I would receive more attention and assistance, if necessary. After receiving rejection letters from several Divisions I schools, I came to accept that my counselor was right. I would never survive at such distinguished, well-renowned colleges.

I decided that since academics were clearly not my strength, I would instead focus on my sports trajectory. I was an exceptional athlete. I was a state-ranked athlete in track, but volleyball was my first love. I decided that I wanted to attend the Olympic Trials to try out for the volleyball team. After all, since I wasn't academically strong, making the Olympic volleyball team would undoubtedly demonstrate I was a master at something. I shared my ambitions with my coach, and just as my counselor before him, he suggested I think again. "You're too short. You'd never make it," he told me. With the odds undoubtedly against me, I conceded. After all, they were my teachers and leaders. It was their job to know what was best for me and what was not.

I will not say that I settled, but I did end up attending a smaller college —a Historically Black College (HBCU) in Virginia, and I could not have hoped for a better experience. The class sizes were smaller, and the professors, specifically within my major, were challenging and attentive to my needs. I tried out for the volleyball team my freshman year and excelled quickly. What I did not expect was the realization that I was more than capable and that I could keep up with the pace and rigor of a collegiate curriculum. That first semester of my freshman year, not only was I able to keep up with a rigorous practice schedule, but I also earned a 4.0–grade point average. I had gone from average academic performance and a self-efficacy low enough to make me believe that average was the best I could do in high school, to earning straight A's in college.

During fall break, I reflected on how I was able to accomplish such a feat. I realized that I had allowed the low expectations of others to become my own. I had not realized that perhaps those educators had certain beliefs about me; that ultimately affected how they motivated me to pursue higher excellence and I unconsciously conformed to them. Now, I had broken through the obstacles I had managed to affix into my mindset. I was now able to see my full potential! Every semester, for the next four years of my college career, I would make the Dean's List. I was inducted into three honor societies and was awarded as one of the highest achieving student-athletes among all fall sports. The young woman that entered college as an average student had now graduated from college *Cum Laude* in 1994.

I suddenly had a newfound appreciation for academia. I had come to realize that I was indeed a scholar and I was motivated to learn more than ever. I went on to pursue a Master's degree in Counseling and Human Services, graduating again with a high-grade point average. Again, further confirmation that I was far from average. With an incessant love for children and a desire to influence their young lives in a broader capacity than counseling, I continued to further my education, pursuing a certification in teaching. I began my teaching career in 2000.

My career began in one of the largest urban districts in the state. Although I was certified, I was timid and ill-prepared for the experience. I knew that I had more to learn and was open to learning whatever I could to be an effective educator. My first principal was amazing, but she would leave soon after I was hired. Her replacement was a strong, Black woman whose intention was to regain order and refine teaching and learning in this failing school. I just knew she would be the one to teach me what it meant to be an effective teacher and educational leader. I was never more wrong.

As it turned out, I could do nothing right in her eyes. I was ineffective and lacked everything it took to make her believe otherwise. She spoke negatively about me to other staff and they, in turn, would relay these conversations back to me. In my last evaluation with her, she asked me about my long-term goals. I shared my desire to become an administrator one day, and her response to me was that I was an ineffective teacher and would be even more ineffective as an administrator. I was stunned. When I asked her what I needed to do to become a better teacher and a stronger leader, all she would offer is, "That's for you to figure out." I considered leaving education at that moment because I believed I was not good enough.

Fortunately for me, there was a reduction in force in 2003, and I was let go. That next fall, I received a position in a considerably smaller district. Somehow, the administrators there saw something in me that no one else did, not even myself. It is there that I was encouraged to pursue leadership positions and to learn more about what it meant to be an effective teacher. My practice began to change and so did I. Against all the odds, I decided I needed more and went on to pursue higher education once again. I was conferred my terminal degree, a Doctor of Education degree in Teacher Leadership, in 2013.

Today, as I enter my 18th year of teaching, my goals have changed. It is because of that first negative experience with my principal that I decided against becoming a principal. Instead, my sights have been set higher and broader because of my experience with her. While I am not an administrator, I sit on several leadership teams within my district. I am a member of a national leadership team for teacher efficacy and a national trainer for teacher effectiveness. I have mentored new and veteran teachers and led several professional development opportunities on instructional best practices, teacher efficacy, and stereotype threats.

How does one go from being average and ineffective to being an accomplished teacher and leader in her school, district, and beyond? What I came to realize is that my intrinsic motivation and effort level to complete a task is what would define my self-efficacy. Extraneous factors, in my case the stereotype threats and the low expectations placed on me, contributed to my perception that I was nothing more than just an average achiever. It is important for one to realize that success is a choice. Circumstances do not define success, nor do the people around you.

The belief you acquire about the level of success you will achieve begins with a growth mindset, the belief that hard work and asserted effort would produce the desired outcome, which nurtures and cultivates high levels of confidence in individuals, thus resulting in high levels of success.

It is equally important to be accountable for the choices you make toward your success. Blaming others for your failures, choices, and lack of productivity is detrimental to the development of self-efficacy. This is what ultimately led to my low achievement in high school and again early in my teaching career. I allowed my high school teachers, colleagues, and administrators to take control of my personal vision and my purpose. Because they did not believe in me, it didn't make sense to believe in myself. I depended on them to realize my purpose rather than defining my purpose for myself. It helps to have the support of others, but what I learned is that YOU are the most important person there is to believe in you.

Be attentive to the potential threats around you that could lead to your unwarranted functioning with a fixed mindset. In my case, stereotype threats led me to believe that I was unable to compete academically, unable to compete athletically, and unable to compete professionally. Looking back, I could have shattered all of those threats but, unfortunately, I did not believe in my own abilities enough to know any better.

Stereotype threats not only hinder one's growth mindset, but also cultural and academic development. What happens is that one begins to believe that the societal stigma placed on them are the norm. Do not allow the world to set your limits. You are an individual with a vision. It belongs to you, and no one can take it away from you. You will encounter many people who do not want to see you accomplish your goals and will place society's norms on you to keep you stagnant and complacent. You were intentionally created to be different; therefore, it is important for you to embrace your autonomy, uniqueness, and individuality. Honoring yourself in this way will shatter the threats that have been set before you and empower you to reach your full potential—against all the odds.

CHAPTER 7

AND BECAUSE OF THEM, I CAN FLY

Janice A. Byrd

Key Challenges: literacy; miseducation; death; single parent

Not many people know that when I was 11 years old, my favorite book was *The People Could Fly* by Virginia Hamilton (1985). I was one of the student library assistants, and each week I would check out this particular book. I'm pretty sure my name was the only one listed on the checkout card at one point in time. I, like the people in the story, oftentimes wished I could fly.

I grew up in a very rural area in South Carolina. We had a family farm that included hogs, chickens, and, at one point, horses. We also harvested crops like sweet corn, butter beans, string beans, peanuts, cucumbers, watermelons, and much more. During the summer, the family members (i.e., aunts, uncles, and cousins) would get up around 5 am to either plant crops or pick whatever was ready. A joyous day would end with me sitting on the swing eating a slice of freshly picked watermelon, which was not considered a racial stereotype at the time. I was just being a young girl enjoying southern, rural girl pleasures. Reading, riding my bike on the dirt road, and playing in the family garden were the things I found to be normal.

A Second Helping of Gumbo for the Soul: More Liberating Stories and Memories to Inspire Females of Color, pages 25–28.

Growing up poor, I didn't have cable, the Internet, or even access to many electronics. However, I did have books. During the summer, it was common for me to read two or three novels a day. Where we lived, door-to-door salesmen were frequent, and they sold vacuum cleaners and encyclopedias. I would always ask my parents to purchase the newest reference books and encyclopedias for my collection, and later my dad allowed me to subscribe to *National Geographic*. Reading about different cultures and places became my daily joy and was often looked upon as weird. Sometimes, I was even bullied in school because of my awkwardness. My teachers were aware of my book fixation and would recommend books for me.

Before "it" happened, a story involving my mom remains very vivid to me. I was in second grade and my teacher, Ms. Brown, taught a unit on slavery. Hearing about such an atrocity crushed my world. What hurt me the most was the idea that a group of people were hurt and treated differently, merely because of how they looked. What hurt even more was that these people looked like me and were related to me. I then felt a deep feeling of sadness, and then began to feel as if I was different from my White classmates. I somehow felt less than, different, and not good enough. I went home crying and told my mom, because I could not understand. She said, "a lot of bad things have happened to a lot of good people, but you will make a difference."

In addition to teachers, my elementary librarian, Mrs. Jackson, knew my heart and became a refuge for this awkward girl in elementary and middle school. She allowed me to work in the library as an aide, and that became my personal heaven. I would read on the job and was able to see the new books when they arrived. Mrs. Jackson, a stoic African American woman, was a positive influence on many girls like me and became even more important when "it" happened.

In addition to enjoying life on my dirt roads and reading, I also started sketching. It began with me imagining I was a fashion designer and I would sketch clothes. Later, with help in art classes, I learned how to sketch faces and recreate the beautiful paintings of Georgia O'Keeffe. I was a young girl very content in my own world and between reading, sketching, writing poetry, and enjoying the rustic outdoors, my life was beautifully simple until "it" happened. When "it" happened, the color in my world changed, I felt my first true pain, and I was introduced to loss.

The "it" was the death of my mom from the ultimate thief, cancer. My mom was diagnosed when I was about 9. I didn't completely understand what was going on, but I knew she was sick. I vividly remember her telling the story about finding the lump. She was in her room ironing clothes, and she reached back and felt something hard protruding from the side of her chest. After that, everything was a blur of doctors' visits, and neither she nor I were ever the same. I don't remember much of our relationship after the cancer diagnosis, except the stories she shared and me helping other family members care for her.

The day my mother died became an inerasable imprint in my mind. It was May 18th, and the doctors called the family to the hospital. My mom was in room 221, and I recall the hospital smell. It smelled like a weird mixture of alcohol and hydrogen peroxide. Even now, I become physically ill when going to a hospital. Me, an 11-year-old girl, sat in the hospital room and listened as the doctor say something to the effect of, "nothing else can be done, and we give her approximately X number of hours to live."

One of my older cousins took me out of the room, walked me to the end of the hall and asked, "Janice, are you okay?" I didn't respond because I didn't know what to say, but I felt an overwhelming need to pray. There was a window where I was standing, so I looked out, started crying, placed my hands together and asked God to save my mom. But, less than 24 hours later, I was brought back into the crowded hospital in a room crowded with family members only to be told to kiss mom goodbye because she was gone.

I am the youngest of four and have two older sisters and one older brother. They are all significantly older, and I was often called, "the surprise." Up until my mother's sickness, I wished I was a little closer in age with my siblings but, with them being older, I believed that they would help me understand and escape in many ways as I learned how to cope with my new reality after "it "happened. However, some were in college, and the others were working and living their own lives, so my 'understanding' never happened.

Considering neither my dad nor mom acquired much education, going to college was a big deal and education was something my parents taught us to value at an early age. After my mom died, my dad was helpful, but he was never an emotionally accessible person. Maybe he was that way because of how southern Black men were conditioned while growing up during his time or because he too was coping with his new reality after "it" happened. He grew up in a time and place where men were taught to work to take care of the home physically and financially, but leave the warm and fuzziness to the women. So, there I was, left to learn how to be a woman with an emotionally distant man trying his best to raise a young lady.

As I reflect upon this time, it's apparent that my current success has been greatly influenced by family and community members contributing at different times and in different places to help me develop into the woman I am now. From the aunts and uncles who loved me like their own, to cousins who would come over when I was home alone to keep me company, and also teachers who continued to remind me of my untapped potential. I may not speak with them often, or reaffirm the many ways they contributed to my development, but every day I make it my goal to uplift others as they uplifted me by excelling as an assistant professor, engaging in community service, teaching, and mentoring. And most importantly, because of my mother's words, I realize that, like Sarah in "The People Could Fly," told by Virginia Hamilton, I too can soar and, most importantly, I can encourage others to do the same:

Sarah flew over the fences. She flew over the woods. Tall trees could not snag her. Nor could the Overseer. She flew like an eagle now, until she was gone from sight. Remember, you too can fly!

REFERENCE

Hamilton, V. (1985). *The people could fly. American Black folktales* (vol. 1). News York, NY: Knopf Books for Young Readers.

CHAPTER 8

SHORT, SHY AND SMART

Determined to Excel in a
Desegregated Classroom

Theresa J. Canada

Key Challenges: segregation; bussing; discrimination; classism; peer pressure

Growing up during the 1960s in New York City was exciting yet difficult. This was a time where the nation's public schools were implementing the Brown vs. Topeka Board of Education decision of 1954. This chapter briefly describes my experience as a student leaving my neighborhood school in Harlem, a section of New York City, to attend a predominately White school away from my neighborhood. It describes how I was determined to succeed academically, despite the pressures of school desegregation.

FAMILY FOCUS

I am the second oldest daughter of four children (two sisters and one brother). My parents worked when I was a young child, which allowed me to have a very happy childhood. They sacrificed to make sure we had all that we needed, especially my mother. With both parents working, I can say that we grew up in a middle-class

A Second Helping of Gumbo for the Soul: More Liberating Stories and Memories to Inspire Females of Color, pages 29–32.
Copyright © 2020 by Information Age Publishing

environment. Of course, that changed once my mother stopped working full-time. When it came to education, my mother wanted us to have the best. She knew that the only option for schooling for her children was in the public education system.

I realized that sometimes it could be tough even growing up with both of your parents. My mother was adamant about her children having the best education possible. Therefore, when an opportunity presented itself to enhance our education, she took advantage of the situation. When it came to school, I (like so many of the children in my neighborhood) attended the local public school. But all that changed once I entered the 4th grade.

CLASSMATE SUPPORT

At some time during 3rd grade, my teacher identified me and a few other classmates to take a music test. Apparently, I passed this test and was selected to attend a school outside of my neighborhood.. The first few days, my mother rode with me on the bus so that I could learn the routine. Because my mother worked, she could not take off too many days to accompany me to school. Within the next few weeks, there I was, a short-statured little girl with a book bag and violin waiting for the bus each morning.

Catching the bus to school was not the most pleasant situation. Sometimes, the bus driver did not realize that I was actually waiting for the bus, and would pass by the bus stop. When I arrived at school, the real problems began. This was where the new teacher would ignore me and the other Black and Latino children when we raised our hands to answer questions. This was where the teacher segregated us based on seating patterns within the classroom. Although there were only five students of color in my 4th-grade class, we all were seated in the least desirable areas of the classroom. This was also the situation for the few White students who were transported into the district via a school bus. There were two other classmates who attended the new school who lived in my neighborhood. We would try to share a seat on the bus in the mornings, but we made sure that we shared a seat on the ride back home. One classmate's mother was a registered nurse at the hospital across the street from the apartment building where I lived. There was a local bus stop located in front of the hospital, and my classmate would wait for the bus at that particular stop. The location allowed her mother or one of her colleagues watch her daughter until the bus arrived. I caught the bus using an express bus stop, which, for many, was the preferred location. But, whenever I had time to walk to the local bus stop in front of the hospital, I would join my friend and wait with her, so that I would not have to make the 45-minute bus ride alone, all of which helped me adjust to the process of attending a new school.

The bus ride experience, which was also a part of my educational experience, was a rude awakening. As I rode 'downtown' to school, I watched as the type of housing, stores and people walking the streets changed. While my neighborhood was predominantly Black, the neighborhoods I saw while riding to school become increasingly White. However, it was not just the whiteness that was such a surprise, because there were a few White people who lived in my building, it was also the obvious affluence that was vivid. It became apparent that the people who lived 'downtown' were wealthier than those who lived in my neighborhood. This was when I realized that the socioeconomic status of a child could define the quality of education that they received.

People who know me as an adult probably cannot imagine that, as a young child, I was quite shy. Reflecting back on those early years, I can now say that I was more intuitive than shy. The image of shyness was a perfect fit for young Black and Latina girls in public schools. We were the ones who never gave the teachers any problems. More often than not, we were most likely considered the 'teacher's pet,' but this role led to both good and, at times, not so good results.

The relationship that one has with classmates could suffer due to the status she/he has with the teacher. In the classroom, the opposite role of 'teacher's pet' was the 'class clown.' In a majority of cases, the class clown was most likely a young Black male student. Of course, those of us who are now educators understand how that role evolved. But still, even at an early age, I knew that it was better to be the 'teacher's pet' than to be the 'class clown.'

EFFECT OF LEARNING ENVIRONMENT

Although I was shy, I was quite observant. I watched how classmates in my new school dressed and how they related to me and the other Black students. There was a distinct difference between the quality of the clothing that the White class-mates wore and what I wore to school. My mother was a stylish dresser, and my older sister and I were always well dressed. But the real difference was the cost of the clothing. I am sure that my classmates' parents spent much more on their clothes than my mother spent on ours. While we shopped at Gimbels and Macy's, my classmates shopped at B. Altman (now closed) and Lord and Taylor. I wanted to feel as if I belonged in my new school. Yet, I was faced with yet another factor that affected my classroom experience.

The type of learning environment that a child is in can affect how she/he learns. If your classmates treat you differently, it can impact how you learn. The interac-tion in the classroom can either make it a positive or negative experience. A few of the White students had no problem with speaking to me in class. Some even invited me to their birthday parties, while others wanted to avoid me like I was the plague. I learned to adjust and discern which children to stay away from. Fortu-nately, I had a best friend in my class who was Black. We sat next to and supported each other throughout the day. If it were not for her, I might not have been able to cope in this new learning environment.

Although I was short and shy, it was not until I entered to the 4th grade that I realized I was smart. I knew that I loved to read. Reading was my opportunity to learn about things that I could only imagine. Reading allowed me to dream of places I could visit and explore beyond where I lived. Reading was my escape from the realities of a mostly segregated society. I later learned that it was because of my reading level (and math level) that I was identified to attend the new school outside of my neighborhood. I was a 3rd grader who was reading on an 8th-grade level. So, while being smart provided an opportunity for a better public school experience, it also subjected me to an environment that was not as supportive as my neighborhood school.

Leaving my neighborhood to attend a new school labeled me as an outsider. The children who lived in my neighborhood saw me as 'different.' I was considered a 'bookworm'; someone who stayed inside and never came out to play. I had so much more homework that I rarely finished before bedtime. Not only was I ostracized because I was smart, but I was also ostracized because I appeared younger than my age. I did not seem to fit in at my new school nor in my neighborhood. Social interactions consisted mostly with my new Black friends who were part of this school desegregation experience. My neighborhood friends were limited, as was the interactions with them. However, the priority was schoolwork and not necessarily playing with neighborhood friends.

CONCLUSION

There were several factors that supported my focus on educational excellence. Of course, the primary factors were the home environment and parental support. As a young child, you are unaware of the importance of such factors. But as an adult and educator, I now know how important familial support and home values are for a child's development. Support from those you encounter each day in school also can encourage your academic success. Fortunately, I had great childhood friends who were also studious. The fact that my friends were similarly minded when it came to school made it much easier to persevere in a desegregated school setting.

Although it may not have been a requirement for other children, participating in church activities was essential to my survival in a newly desegregated school. During the 1960s, the Black church served many roles. In church, I was allowed to explore activities, such as recitations and readings. I was able to practice public speaking and socializing with peers. The church enabled me to grow and develop in a safe environment. It was in church and in the home that I found out that being smart was OK.

Despite the desegregation experience, I not only survived, but I also thrived. It was a combination of home, friends, and church that provided support to excel in school. The individuals in all of those settings saw the value in this short, shy, smart Black girl. Therefore, the message that I would like to share with other females of color is that if you keep the faith, have a few good friends and a family behind you, and then your smartness can never be overshadowed.

CHAPTER 9

STRENGTHENING MY CORE

Akilah R. Carter-Francique

Key Challenges: work-life balance; depression; wife-mother relationships; loss of self-identity; racism and microaggressions

I am approaching my 10th anniversary of earning my doctorate in Sports Studies from the University of Georgia, Athens (UGA). As I reflect on this moment, I find that, over the past few years, I was forced to strengthen my core to endure my work-life challenges and not lose my mind. Strengthening the core, from a sport and physical activity perspective, means to increase the strength and flexibility of the middle of the body. Strengthening of the abdominal muscles and back muscles promotes the improvement of physical skills and abilities, maintains the center of gravity, and enables the body to perform better. My core, well, my life core, consists of my faith, my family, and me. Now I know I am not the first Black woman, or woman for that matter, to experience challenges balancing life as a career person and mother. But for me, life as a Black woman raised to value herself and live proud as an educated Black female came under attack while working in higher education.

I spent the first 32 years of my life single with no dependents, achieving degrees at every level, and negotiating the world as a Black female who loves sports. I loved sports to the point that I began my participation at the age of five, compet-

A Second Helping of Gumbo for the Soul: More Liberating Stories and Memories to Inspire Females of Color, pages 33–36.

ing at the youth and interscholastic levels in track and field and volleyball through to the intercollegiate level in track and field in which I retired after the completion of my bachelor's degrees in Psychology and Kinesiology—Exercise Science. You see, following my undergraduate schooling and athletic participation, I journeyed through a couple of careers. I worked in K–12 education for an entire nine months as a counselor of sorts, and coached high school cross-country and track and field in the frozen tundra of Rockford, Illinois. In 2001, I went to work at UGA in the Department of Campus Recreation serving as staff administrator of the outdoor sports facility, supervising special events and student groups, and later managing the strength and conditioning facilities. While in this position, I decided to pursue my master's degree and did so successfully. One year later, I was inspired to pursue my doctoral degree. But I have to admit, I did not know when enrolling, nor did I fully know upon graduation, all that the doctorate entailed.

I would graduate covered by the blessings of an all-Black doctoral committee that, like my parents, encouraged me to bring my multiple selves to the academy. What I did not fully realize is that I would enter the ranks of academia, joining such a small number of Black females in sports and physical activity. Luckily, my committee gave me some insight regarding the potential hardships I may face based on the intersections of my race, gender, and marital status. However, I did not expect the rampant microaggressions and operation of covert racism coming from some of the White faculty, staff, and students to be as entrenched as it was. Nor did I expect some of my "Black" colleagues to support and excuse their behavior. As a junior scholar, I was simply enthused and desirous to conduct my research examining Black females historical and contemporary sporting experiences, share my perspective as a Black sportswoman writing on Black sportswomen, and earn tenure.

But, over the years I would, interaction by interaction, learn that my enthusiasm was not shared. I came to understand my scholarly endeavors "did not constitute credible research" as it was just not valued amongst my "White" peers. So, I began to feel pressure like Patricia Hill Collins describes in Black Feminist Thought: Knowledge, Consciousness and the Politics of Empowerment. I began to feel a need to compromise my approach toward my research and seek to "objectify" and quantify Black women rather than maintain them as the qualitative "subjects" of my research. From my understanding, a number of scholars that chose to examine marginalized people and groups faced this question during some point in their quest for tenure, and each responded differently. I pondered this question because I had bought into the myth that my value was based on my ability to publish a specific number of data-driven manuscripts and a "jury of my 'White peers'" would determine if my work and efforts were worthy of tenure and promotion. It would turn out that some of these peers would know and understand the fruits of my work and institutional service and support me. Others did not support me, as they either did not know who I was or thought they knew me . . . but merely as a graduate student and not a tenure-track professor. While the fullness of this experience alone bares much social (in)justice fruit, I will save its story for a later date. However, I must say that the role it played in my journey to "strengthening my core" is significant.

According to observations and similar experiences, by my elders and Black colleagues with whom I worked, I was an "outsider-within" and placed on the margins of the academy in the eyes of persons in power. This label and designation were due to the fact I chose not to compromise my approach toward research. I remained steadfast in my scholarly journey, but it came at a painful cost that equaled denied tenure, ostracization, feelings of failure, and living with functional depression. Years of living as an "outsider-within" would consume me and emerge as felt sadness and crying tears to the point that my daughter, not knowing the depths of my despair, would ask, "What's wrong, mommy, why are you always crying?" while simultaneously trying to console me with hugs. This caused me to question my decision to stay steadfast in my quest to illuminate the experiences and tell the stories of Black women; and would result as internalized mental battle causing me to doubt my value to academe and, as tough as it is to admit, my value on this good earth. This professional career experience and range of feelings would leave me to meditate on Audre Lorde's words, "Pain is important; how we evade it, how we succumb to it, how we deal with it, how we transcend it."

My feelings of failure and functional depression (supported by weekly visits with a therapist) was my greatest challenge to my core to date because, at this point in my career, I had become a wife and a mother of two children under the age of five years old. Thus, my academic life would encroach on my roles and duties as spouse and mommy, throwing any sense of work-life balance out the window. My center of gravity was off as the addition of marriage and children added another dimension to work-life balance that was unfamiliar. See, I thought I understood how life with a career and family was to be because I grew up in a dual income home with parents that had been married for over 45 years. My paternal grandparents were married for over 70 years. Even my godparents and our family friends maintained multiple decade-long marriages. So, when I got married, I had a pretty good idea of what marriage was to look like for working couples and what my role as a wife should be. Well, all would have held true, but I married a collegiate athletic coach.

As presented, I was an athlete through my undergraduate studies. I was quite familiar with the occupational time demands that college athletic coaches maintained to include the amount of travel required to the emotional investment necessary to foster the developmental potential of college athletes. However, what I viewed as an athlete and what I experienced as a wife were markedly different. So much so that I began to think, "they did not cover this is on Basketball Wives of Los Angeles, Miami, or New York. Nor did they cover this on WAGS." Being a coach's wife, or coach's husband for that matter requires independence, confidence, resilience, resourcefulness, patience, and trust. Often times, it requires a person to play their role and that of their partner with planning and decision making especially when away for recruiting and/or competition travel. And in my experience as a wife, it required altering career goals and relinquishing a part of the "self" for a coach, team, and athletic career stability. But, pursuing a career as an academic, as a Black woman, who was also a wife and mother was challenging. So, would I achieve the academic-life balance? How would I find center of gravity? I had to gain strength.

My core was strengthened through reconnecting with my faith, my family, and myself. This was necessary to overcome the judgment and depression to reaffirm my value. First, I knew I had to read the word, sit in fellowship, and just stand still to listen and allow God to speak to me and speak through my parents, my other mothers, my Sista Docs, my close friends, my supportive colleagues, and my husband and children. Second, I had to remember that I received strength from my parents and my family, especially my husband and children that spoke much truth like "if people are not treating you good, you need to leave. You don't need to stay there for me." And, "Mommy, I want to be like you." Their words let me know that they were not disappointed in me, but supported and celebrated me. And while I did not need their approval, I wanted their approval. I needed to know that they were proud of me and wanted to hold me in their arms. These two efforts allowed me to, third, find my center. I had to let go and let God take me on a journey to illuminate my gifts and passions, to wade me through waters of discomfort and pain to find healing, joy, and me. So, I am blessed to say ten years later, I continue my journey as a Black feminist sports scholar striving to give voice to the voiceless, promoting education, and encouraging and empowering young and old to be their best authentic selves.

CHAPTER 10

FROM F.M.C. TO PHD

The Journey of a Ride-or-Die Chick

Adrian Clifton

Key Challenges: teenage-parent; peer pressure; gang activity; colorism; curriculum violence; racial isolation at school

My name is Dr. Adrian Clifton. I am a wife and mother of four beautiful children. I graduated with honors from the University of Missouri-Columbia and became the first classroom teacher of color at the elementary school where I taught first grade for five years. Professionally, I serve as the community partnership liaison for the College of Education at the University of Missouri-Columbia. I am a community activist, serving also as co-founder and executive director of a local nonprofit known as Worley Street Roundtable. This grassroots organization connects the community's social capital and educational resources to marginalized students and families to make viable ways for children of color to succeed in and out of school. Worley Street Roundtable recently created a school to teacher pipeline aimed at training minority students to become teachers in their community. To see where I am now; it may be difficult for people to realize the journey behind my success. This chapter will provide a glimpse into my past, and take you, the

A Second Helping of Gumbo for the Soul: More Liberating Stories and Memories to Inspire Females of Color, pages 37–40.
Copyright © 2020 by Information Age Publishing
All rights of reproduction in any form reserved.

reader, to the root of this blooming flower...and since roots grow in dirt, there was plenty of it in my history.

My story begins in the small Midwest town of Hannibal, Missouri. Hannibal was also known as Mark Twain Country; where children read about Huck Finn and Nigger Jim in school. I was the youngest of four children, born in 1984 to a mother who worked as a social worker and as a praise and worship leader. My father worked at a cement company and served as co-pastor of our ministry. The last memory I have of my family together was a trip we took to Disney World when I was three years old. It was rare for a Black family in a small town like Hannibal to go to Disney World, but we took trips like that at least once a year. I remember riding on the teacup ride with my father, laughing and spinning to the song, *It's a Small World After All*. As a three-year-old, my world seemed warm and safe, and like nothing could be disrupted.

Upon returning home, the warmth of my world gradually became cold when my oldest sister wrote a letter to our mother describing the sexual abuse she endured at the hands of her step-father, my biological father; the co-pastor of the prominent Black church in our small community; the father that laughed with me in the little teacup and made me feel safe. My mother, a social worker, had to "hotline" herself. A Black woman in a small, racist town, where everybody knew your business—the weight my mother had to carry on her shoulders was unbearable. In what seemed like an instant, we left our lives in Hannibal and moved our shattered memories to Columbia, Missouri, where my mother relocated her social working position. Adjusting to a new "big city" was not easy for my siblings and I. Coupled with my confusion of what transpired, I saw school as the perfect place to distract me from my reality. It pacified my questions of, "Where is daddy and why can't he live with us anymore?" At five years old, I did not understand the substance of the storm we escaped.

Though school was an escape from my reality, I hated the fact that I was one of only a few Black kids in my school. Besides my sister and brother, I could count on one hand the number of Black kids that attended my elementary school. It was not easy being the rare brown face in a class full of White middle-class children. When Black History Month came around, I felt so isolated amongst my peers. When the teacher would raise questions about slavery or the civil rights movement, I felt like I was expected to speak for all Black people about the trials and struggles of that time. Yet, when Columbus Day rolled around, I was taught that Columbus was a hero and was expected to celebrate his contributions to discovering our land. I did not realize until later in life, the detrimental effects of the curriculum violence I endured. Not seeing myself in books or represented positively in the curriculum welled up resistance inside of me. It was a regular occurrence for me to be pulled off a White kid at school or in my neighborhood who called me "a nigger." My activism started early.

One can imagine my excitement when, in the fifth grade, my mom announced we were moving to an area of town where more Black people lived. This meant I would be attending a new school where most of the kids were Black! I was so excited, and I anticipated playing with other Black and Brown girls who looked like me. On the first day, I was shocked to see how many Black kids were in my class. Out of 23 kids, I counted one White boy. I was even greeted by a Black teacher. I felt like I finally arrived at home, that is until I opened my mouth to speak. "You talk White!" Kids giggled and pointed as if I was some type of disease. I can remember feeling so humiliated that I wanted to disappear. I spent the entire week rehearsing slang and dropping the r on words like car and here. At home, my sisters laughed and said I sounded silly.

Looking back, it was interesting how my siblings and I handled the move; my older brother began entertaining the street life. With our dad in and out of prison, the street life became a major source of influence for the both of us. Our oldest sister Niecy, who had become a teenage mother, entered the army. Shaila, the middle child, became a social butterfly, and although her peers would ridicule her for "acting White," it never seemed to bother her or sway her from being her authentic self. I, on the other hand, thirsted after my peers' acceptance, and was willing to do whatever it took to earn street credit. What I thought to be authentically Black was the ride-or-die chicks I saw in rap music videos; the ones with the small waist and big butts who spent their men's drug money on jewelry, clothes and getting their hair and nails done. That was the life, or so I thought. Boys in my neighborhood seemed to like that type of "loyal" girl, so that was what I emulated. Even my dad had ride-or-die chicks by his side willing to take a case for him if they had to.

I loved going back home to Hannibal to visit my dad. There, I had the freedom to do pretty much whatever I wanted. My dad was so heavy into the drug game; he introduced my brother to selling drugs before he became his main consumer, smoking up his supply. I can remember smoking joints with my dad as early as 12 years old. It was nothing to look up and see him at the same house party I was attending. His bad influence only flamed the lost identity of my brother and me. At one point, my dad and brother were cellmates, and you would have thought my brother graduated from college the way my dad gloated with pride about him. By the time I was in high school, I was the leader of my own gang, Female Mafia Clique (F.M.C.), and on trial for murder charges because of the role I played when my boyfriend at the time committed a murder. I stepped up as his ride or die chick to help him hide from the police, and I stole clothes for him and took him food every night.

Juggling two drastically different lifestyles was becoming stressful, but even as a gang leader, I still had hopes of one day becoming a teacher. As a senior in high school, I was in a work-release program where I attended school half a day and worked at an elementary school during the other half. One day, I was working in Mrs. Orca's 5th-grade class when someone knocked on her door. I jumped up to answer it so Mrs. Orca's lesson would not be interrupted. As I opened the door, I was surprised to be greeted by two police officers looking for Adrian Harris, a suspect in a murder trial. I reluctantly admitted I was she, while Mrs. Orca insisted they were making a mistake. The students, who adored me, witnessed their role model being handcuffed and taken away in a police car. While riding to the police station, my mind raced with excuses. I tried to get my story straight. I had been manipulating and fooling everyone up to this point—surely, I could talk my way out of this one. However, reality set in as soon as the cell door clanked behind me. The "ride-or-die chick" mentality flew out of me before the door slammed. I wanted my life back. I realized nothing was worth me losing my future over. I was ready to say 'yes' to being who I was created to be.

I was the daughter of a praying mother, and my lawyer was able to get all charges dropped against me. I was blessed with a second chance to be my authentic self. The transition was not easy, but I had the audacity to shift my mindset into believing in the God within me. With the faith of a mustard seed, I pressed forward to graduate high school and enter a teaching program at a local university. I am thankful for the alternate route I traveled before getting back on the main road. I have been able to use my journey as a roadmap to inspire other children of color hiding behind facades and afraid of living their truth. So often we look for approval in all the wrong places, not realizing that loving and accepting ourselves is the key to life. I want to dedicate this chapter to all the young girls out there who are lost and insecure, and who feel like they are not enough. Know that you are worthy, and in the words of the great Maxine Waters, "your time is worth reclaiming!"

CHAPTER 11

"YOU SOUND LIKE
A WHITE GIRL"

One Black Girl's Experience in
Accelerated Learner Spaces

Raven K. Cokley

Key Challenges: discrimination; peer pressure; low income; racial identity; colorism; racial isolation in school

Every morning before school, my grandmother prepared my breakfast and sent me directly to the bus stop on the street corner, with the rest of the kids from the neighboring housing projects. Once the bus arrived, I sat alone in the seat behind the bus driver. Upon exiting the school bus, the kids from my neighborhood and I were physically and metaphorically segregated from each other, as the remodeled International Baccalaureate (IB) wing was totally isolated from the rest of the buildings on campus; this meant that I did not see any Black students (other than my neighborhood friend, who was a Black male) again until the end of the day when it was time to get back on the bus to go home. On a typical school day, I ate lunch alone in the library, because I felt socially isolated and invisible among my peers. Despite the social, cultural, and racial isolation that I endured while being

*A Second Helping of Gumbo for the Soul: More Liberating Stories and Memories
to Inspire Females of Color,* pages 41–43.
Copyright © 2020 by Information Age Publishing

one of only two Black students in this space of academic privilege, I graduated with honors from my high school's IB program in 2009.

Like many academic environments, my high school was historically White due to the remnants of legal segregation within the district's public school system. As such, I was encapsulated by unchallenged constructs of whiteness and White supremacy on a daily basis. I remember sitting in classrooms, day after day, feeling that my being and expressions of self were inherently at odds with my academic environment. These feelings of isolation and invalidation were further compounded by the lack of Black educators at my historically White high school because I never saw myself in the classroom. My very existence in academically gifted and accelerated learner spaces was questioned and invalidated every time I entered the classroom.

Despite feeling isolated among my Black peers and White classmates, I still tried to prove that I could fit in with either group. On one hand, I wanted to prove my blackness to the kids that I shared a bus ride with to school every day; I wanted to prove that I was Black enough (whatever that meant) to be their friend. The challenging piece is that I am not quite sure how I would have proven my blackness to anyone. All I know is that I became frustrated with hearing, "You sound like a White girl," from my friends and family every time I opened my mouth to speak. What did that even mean? How can you sound like any race of people? What about me, or the way that I spoke, said that I wanted to be or felt more aligned with whiteness? Would I ever be able to just be...me?

On the other hand, my adolescent years were also marked by wanting to prove to my White teachers and counterparts that I was just as smart as they were and that I could be their friend, too. Every time I entered the IB wing or any accelerated learner environment, I was reminded of the sacrifices that my ancestors made in order for me to even enter that space of academic privilege. I have always been acutely aware of the value and importance of earning an equitable education for Black folks, particularly for Black folks from lower or working-class families. With this socio-historical awareness, I did my best to disprove any and all myths that my White educators may have held about Black students and our capabilities. I worked diligently and fervently to perform to the best of my (academic) abilities.

Further, in terms of fitting in with my White classmates, my family's socio-political history in the American south frequently reminded me that I would never be White enough to be accepted by my White counterparts. Despite this realization, and in a futile effort to access some form of integration among my high school peers and classmates, I accepted invitations to attend White Barbie doll-themed birthday parties on the other side of town (this basically meant that I was traveling to local White neighborhoods where, historically, Black folks did not live). My classmates did not look like me nor did they live where I lived. I found it challenging to make friends with folks who I felt did not truly understand or value me as a person. From my experience, classmates and I existed in two totally different worlds. In the classroom and in their homes, I felt the burden and pressure of being the only one. I felt simultaneously hyper-visible and invisible, which compounded my experiences of double consciousness (DuBois, 1994).

Experiences of racial and academic socialization served as buffers for me against societal myths and stereotypes that say that Black girls, specifically Black girls from lower-income families, cannot be both Black and gifted. Despite Ogbu's (2004) notion of the *Acting White* phenomenon, which indicated that a fear of being aligned with traditionally Eurocentric values (i.e., educational excellence, use of western English, etc.) causes gifted and talented Black students to underperform, my reality was that these accusations did not hinder my academic achievement. In fact, I achieved (with distinction), despite feeling that I did not fit in with my White classmates and Black peers.

To clarify, my experience of the Acting White phenomenon was not solely the result of neighborhood kids making fun of me for speaking a certain way. It was, however, a result of the more systematic issue related to Black students' access and recruitment into gifted education and accelerated learner courses. As such, I want to encourage educators (counselors, teachers, advisors), to think critically about the messages that we send to gifted and talented Black girls about their brilliance and capabilities, particularly if they are the only Black girl in gifted/accelerated learned spaces; this under-representation, in and of itself, is a national problem (Ford, 2013).

In conclusion, I want to share the following personal affirmations with other gifted Black girls who may feel misplaced, mislabeled and misunderstood: Stand in the fullness of your brilliance. Do not allow any teacher, counselor, advisor, principal, or anyone else to dim your light. Your giftedness is real and your voice matters. You have earned the right to be a gifted Black girl. You may be the only one and I know how lonely that can be; but do not be ashamed of who, how, or what you are. Proceed with confidence toward whatever your calling may be because the world desperately needs whatever is brewing inside of you. Do not allow anyone to silence your voice. You may be misunderstood; speak anyway. You may be misrepresented; speak anyway. You may even be mislabeled in our society, but speak anyway. It takes courage, bravery, and boldness to be a gifted Black girl. Please know that there are other gifted Black girls out there, just like you, who are fighting for the right to be acknowledged, affirmed, and validated, too. You are not alone!

REFERENCES

DuBois, W. E. B. (1994). *The souls of Black folk*. New York, NY: Dover Publications.

Ford, D. Y. (2013). *Recruiting and retaining culturally different students in gifted education*. Waco, TX: Prufrock Press.

Ogbu, J. U. (2004). Collective identity and the burden of "acting White" in Black history, community, and education. *The Urban Review, 36*(1), 1–35.

Like a steaming hot bowl of gumbo on a cold winter day, we hope that each story will fill your spirit and warm your soul.

—*Michelle Frazier Trotman Scott*

CHAPTER 12

THE LEGACY OF GREATNESS

Alexandria Connally

Key Challenges: parental loss; sexual abuse; physical abuse; foster care

A legacy is something of value that is handed down from one generation to the next. As an African American, the legacy of my ancestors was storytelling. A legacy can be seen as values, rituals, and celebrations that a parent passes down to their children. Greatness can be defined as a comparatively higher degree, power or intensity. So, the phrase "the legacy of greatness" can be characterized as the importance of the stories of our ancestors that live inside of each of us.

I have experienced trauma since the day I was born. During my mother's second trimester, the doctor encouraged her to have an abortion. He explained that if both of us lived through childbirth, I would have an I.Q. of about 70, would never grow past 4'7," or be able to walk. However, my mother had faith! She exclaimed, "This is my legacy, and she will be a legacy of greatness! My mother had Lupus, and my birth caused her to develop kidney failure, and during the course of my life, I witnessed her illness take her down a dark road.

I recall a cold winter day in March when I performed in a St. Patrick's Day Parade; the parade route went right past the hospital where my mom laid as a patient with a brain tumor. As we marched past the hospital, I felt a pit in my stomach. At the conclusion of the parade, I immediately I ran to the hospital. For the first

A Second Helping of Gumbo for the Soul: More Liberating Stories and Memories to Inspire Females of Color, pages 45–48.
Copyright © 2020 by Information Age Publishing
All rights of reproduction in any form reserved.

time in days, my mother was conscious and, although she was unable to speak, we always had a way of communicating. The next day, I received a message that she had passed. At that moment, an experience happened to the 12-year-old me. I have continued to ponder on her words of wisdom, even today.

There were three things that my mother instilled in me. The first was the notion of education, which leveled the playing field. She also shared the importance of being nice to everyone and the understanding of a phrase that would see people past who they were and view them as who they could be in society. She would say, "Everyone has value and purpose." Lastly, she encouraged me to have faith. For me, the concept of faith could eliminate barriers and tear down walls. The expressions of optimism shared by my mother encompassed one significant theme—the legacy of greatness. She would tell me. "You have greatness inside of you. You will be a great success, or you will be a great failure. Only you can decide your path." As a current doctoral student, an intern to the New York State Chancellor of the Board of Regents, and an assistant principal in a school that received a Gold Medal from "U.S. News and World Report," people often ask me how I made it from the poverty world to the scholarly world. I simply tell them that it is because I stand on the three principles that my mother instilled in me during the early developmental years of my life and I often fall back on those lessons that I learned from her!

At the age of 16, my mother was molested by her stepfather. Her mother (my grandmother) had to make a choice between her daughter and her husband, and she chose her husband. As a result, my mother was sent to a group home and did not have contact with her family until she was 32 years old. At the age of 25, she became a single parent when she had her first and only child—me. She worked full-time, went to dialysis three times a week, and went to school part-time. In my eyes, my mother was a superhero.

My mother wanted only the best education for her child, so she sent me to a Catholic school. On the weekends, we would go into Manhattan to visit museums, go to the theater, and dine at fine restaurants. But during the week, I had a strict schedule. When I came home from school, I changed out of my uniform and after I completed my homework, I had an hour to play. There was no shortage of items that I had at my disposal. For example, I was the first kid in my neighborhood to have a personal computer. Also, in honor of my love of Barbie, my room was decorated in pink and light blue. I had the Barbie house, dream boat, car and a number of dolls. At the conclusion of my play hour, we would review my homework, cook dinner together, eat and discuss our day. The day was ended with bath time and one hour of television. I was in bed by 8:00 pm.

Three months before my 13th birthday, my mother became increasingly ill. One weekend in March, she complained of leg pain, so I slept in her bed so that I could check on her every hour. When the alarm went off at 4:00 am. I turned to check on her and realized that she was no longer in the bed. When I got up to look for her, she was on the floor, having a seizure, covered in blood. I called 9–1–1, and she was taken to the hospital but, three days later, she died as a result of a brain tumor.

After my mother died, my life took a drastic turn. I entered the foster care system and went from a structured, stable environment to one of disarray. I went from a loving mother to a system of abuse. I was abused sexually, psychologically and physically. I was physically beaten for things that my mother would have turned into a learning opportunity, and my behavior began to reflect my situation. I was sent to public school and had to fend for myself. In essence, the character I portrayed did not reflect a legacy of greatness.

At 18, I exited the foster care system, and I found myself homeless. One evening, I dreamed about a time when my mother and I sat at the dining room table talking about the legacy of greatness that she often explained to me. I was reminded that I had greatness inside of me and I was forced to make a decision. I decided to be a great success, especially since I had already experienced great failure. My mother had clearly laid out the path for my success; all I had to do was follow the path.

I began seeking assistance for housing so that I could consider the possibility of employment. By age 18, I was working three jobs and going to school; I had begun the path of becoming my mother's legacy. Within the next nine years, I obtained four college degrees, two of which were Masters. After some time off, I entered an Ed.D. Program. I felt that obtaining a doctoral degree would be the ultimate goal of fulfilling my educational quest.

Every degree that I have earned has been dedicated to the legacy of my mother; because I am her legacy. Please understand that education is not only academic success and the collection of degrees; it is also learning how to manage emotions, live a healthier lifestyle, and have a spiritual connection. The word 'educate' derives from the Latin word 'educare,' which means to draw out, to nourish, and to bring up. Today, I have internalized the value of the quote by Horace Mann, "Education is a great equalizer."

The second piece of advice that my mother gave me was—be nice to everyone. Every person has human capital that improves society. How many times has a kind word, a smile or wave from a small child turned your day around? Recently, my pastor visited my school. As we left the school, she asked me, "Why does everyone love you so much?" I replied, "Because I am nice to everyone. I treat people with the same respect that I want to receive. It is important to build a community of love." As an assistant principal, I don't just have an open-door policy, I have a, "mi casa is su casa" policy. There are students in my office all the time. I express to my students that they are not just our students; they are also our clients. My job is to serve them and ensure they have the best educational experience possible.

The third word of wisdom I received from my mother had to do with faith. The notion of obstacles being stepping-stones dissolved the theory of glass ceilings. The Bible explains that faith is the things hoped for and evidence of things unseen. The phrase has built an ever-growing, self-reflecting resiliency in me. The movement from foster homes could not stop me from excelling. The negative words from the adults who were supposed to take care of me were a great obstacle, but it never stopped me from reaching my goals. Resiliency is more than the ability to bounce back. For me, resiliency became a lifestyle that is constantly used as an opportunity for learning.

In all leadership roles that are bestowed upon me, I try to share the values that my mother instilled in me. I often explain to my MBK (My Brother's Keeper) scholars that the success that I have acquired does not belong to me. My job is to climb to the top rung of the success ladder with the next generation on my back to propel them into their destiny. This is done through three key inspirational phrases of the legacy of greatness: (1) Education is the great equalizer; (2) Be nice to everyone because you never know who they will become; and (3) Have faith; there are no barriers that cannot be broken.

Today, I have become the woman that I am because I decided to be a legacy of greatness. I am thankful for my ancestors, the trailblazers, and my haters. I stand on the strength of my ancestors, the faith of the trailblazers, and the necks of my enemies. I use all energy to build academic capital, intellectual capital, and social capital. Allow the greatness inside of you to fill you up, until they overflow. Then, you can infect everyone around you in a positive way. Be the legacy of greatness!

CHAPTER 13

PERSEVERANCE

Gwenetta Curry

Key Challenges: divorce, single parent, racism, deficit thinking

I grew up in New Bern, North Carolina, in a close-knit neighborhood called Pembroke. Race was rarely discussed in my house during my childhood, but I was quickly educated on the matter via life experiences. When I was four years old, I was walking down the street with my aunt when a few White men riding in a pickup truck threw a beer can at us. The can hit my Aunt's leg, and she had to get 32 stitches. I often thought about how I could have been damaged for life if that can hit me instead of her. This early memory has been etched in my head for years; not only because I didn't understand, at the time, why someone would do such a thing, but also because no one was ever punished or held accountable for the assault. I remember how angry my great-grandmother was because we did not obey her. She told us not to walk along that street, but I also remember that something was missing. Where was the outrage at the person who threw the can? My family had always been the type who did not dwell on negative events too long but instead, looked at the positives. In this particular case, the positive was that at least my aunt was still alive, and she would go on living her life. Still, no one talked, or ever discussed what happened that day.

A Second Helping of Gumbo for the Soul: More Liberating Stories and Memories to Inspire Females of Color, pages 49–51.
Copyright © 2020 by Information Age Publishing
49

During my childhood, I was a part of a youth group named Youth Criteria for L.I.F.E. (L=Love, I=Integrity, F= Frugality, and E=Education). The leader was our neighbor/landlord, Mrs. Ernestine Moore. She was very strict, but always stressed the importance of education. Neither one of my parents went to college, but my siblings and I always knew college was going to be our next step after high school. I did not come from a wealthy or well-to-do family, but my parents always made sure we had everything we needed and some of the things we wanted. I lived a pretty "normal" life until my parents divorced when I was in the 7th grade.

After the divorce, things began to change quite a bit around the house; since my father no longer lived with us, I was made to grow up due to an increase in responsibilities. I had to babysit my little brother every day after school and do more of the cooking while my mother worked. I also had to help my little brother with his homework while managing my own homework assignments. My friends used to joke that I was like Cinderella because I had a list of chores I had to complete when I came home from school before I could rest and focus on schoolwork.

While I was in high school, I struggled with self-esteem issues because I was always seen as the smart girl—but never the cute girl. I was also teased because I developed keloids from having my ears pierced. I had them removed before I headed to college, and found a new level of confidence. Once in college, I joined Zeta Phi Beta Sorority, Incorporated. Membership in this organization provided me with a level of support and sisterhood that I had always longed for. Through my involvement with Zeta, I gained leadership skills and more confidence in my abilities and myself.

I was fortunate enough to begin working in a Food Science lab during my sophomore year at North Carolina A&T State University (NC A&T). While working in the lab, Mrs. Sarah, the lab technician, taught me how to conduct science experiments properly. One of the first tasks I was assigned was to inventory all of the chemicals in the lab. I recall one day while I was putting away the chloroform and a 4L bottle broke, the entire building had to be evacuated. I felt utterly terrible about the whole event, but after everything was properly cleaned, things went back to normal. During my time at NC A&T, I learned a lot about science, which garnered my passion for research. For example, during my studies, I was responsible for measuring and comparing the amount of omega-3 fatty acids inside of wild sea bass versus farmed sea bass. Thanks to the help of the lab technician, Mrs. Sarah, and my advisor, Dr. Seo, I was able to present my research at the North Carolina Capital and numerous other conferences.

Once I graduated from NC A&T State University, I was accepted into Southern Illinois University—Carbondale. So, I moved to work on my master's degree in Animal Science. I never saw myself as a farm girl or someone who would work closely with live animals, but there I was in the thick of it with 12 Holstein cows.

During my time at Southern Illinois at Carbondale, I did not have a car at the time, so I would ride my bike back and forth to the farm for my research and take the bus to the grocery store. One night, a male student who was working on his

Ph.D., saw that my roommate and I were taking the bus to Walmart, so he volunteered to drive us to the store because he did not feel it was safe. This was because there were many acts of racism against students of color at that institution. For example, one man riding in a red pick-up truck drove by and yelled the N-word at me as I walked the cows back to the pasture. So, his worry was valid. This man has since become my husband. I did finish my degree, and to my knowledge, I am the first Black person to receive a Master's Degree in the Animal Science Department.

This incident was just one example of the types of racist acts students of color faced while living in Carbondale. After graduation, I had to decide whether to continue to earn my doctorate, or enter the workforce. I decided to work and ended up accepting an associate food scientist position at ConAgra Foods in Omaha, Nebraska, where I would be responsible for rewriting all of the Manufacturing Standard Practice documentation for the plant. I was assigned to work on the Peter Pan Peanut Butter relaunch team, and I began traveling back and forth to Sylvester, GA. While working at ConAgra, I was often the only Black person on the projects. Nevertheless, I was able to excel while employed there and I played significant roles in some of the top projects within the company.

My husband was offered a job at a university in the south. I was still unsure if I wanted to pursue a doctorate, but I did decide to meet with a faculty member of the institution about possibly working in one of the laboratories in the university. Despite having a master's degree and years of corporate industry experience, the faculty member suggested that I should look into working at the WIC office. When I inquired about pursuing my doctorate, the same faculty member suggested that it would be better for me to look into the HBCU in one of the neighboring towns. I pressed on and started my Ph.D. in Sociology, focusing on issues of nutrition, race, and health disparities.

During my time as a doctoral student, I had two children who were never enrolled in daycare. I was not the only graduate student to have children. But while the department would say they were family friendly, I did not find everyone supportive of the idea of having children while working on a doctorate. When I became pregnant with my second child, I recall being asked "Don't you know about birth control?" Also, there were some projects that I missed out on because people assumed that I would not be available to participate.

There are three major lessons to take away from my story: First, even when you think you can't do something, try anyway. Being persistent and ignoring the naysayers helped me to achieve my goal of earning my doctorate. Secondly, do not let others dictate when you should start a family. There's never a perfect time to have children. Having my girls during graduate school was not an easy task, but I was able to spend time with my girls as they reached each milestone. Finally, it is important for young Black girls to see that their mother is striving for and achieving her goals. Never stop pushing forward!

CHAPTER 14

THE DEFINITION OF BLACKNESS

Shared History and Experience of Injustice

Rebecca OluwaToyin Doherty

Key Challenges: racial identity; racial division; acceptance

"...be confident in your heritage....
Be confident in your Blackness."
—*President Barack Obama, 44th President of the United States of America*

As a Black person, I have often pondered upon the discourse of internal division that Black people bring amongst ourselves. I wonder why the common origin that we share through our ancestral lineage, our history of oppression, and our present-day struggle to advance as a race, has not been enough to bring us together as one—as a simple guide to focus on self- and group-actualization and elevation; a resource to equip us in dealing with the oppression we face.

EXCERPTS OF DIVISION AND UNITY OF THE RACE

In my culture, when friendship lasts beyond one generation, and you have shared so much history, including giving birth and raising your children together, you automatically become family, and your children call each other cousins. Interestingly, this is not so on my father's side of the family; they are from the Yoruba tribe in Nigeria, but tend to be more of what others may see as Westernized in their practices. Another example, any elderly person that can be of age to be your aunt, mother, uncle, father, or grandparents are also automatically called "mummy, daddy, aunty, uncle, grandma," etc. Even cousins that were old enough to be your mom or aunt were called aunty or cousins, but as stated previously, this was not so on my father's side of the family. On his side of the family, cousins were not to be called by their first names if they were older. Instead, they were identified as "Cousin Renny" or "Cousin Thomas," for example. There were also more intercultural and interracial marriages on my father's side of the family.

On a warm sunny summer afternoon, I joined my cousin Yemi to celebrate her birthday with a group of her friends. Yemi is my cousin by traditional African, Nigerian, or more so Yoruba, standards. Yemi is actually a second-generation family friend, so my relationship with Yemi as a cousin was due to the aforementioned cultural practice. It was based on the friendship of our mothers and their siblings, which lasted throughout the years that brought us together from our childbirth into adulthood. As we walked through the historical sites in DC after attending a cultural event at the Smithsonian Museum of African Art, a conversation came up among me, Yemi, and two other Black women. One was from Haiti, born and raised in America, who preferred to self-identify as Haitian. Another was born and raised in Germany and her parents, who were originally from the Congo, migrated to the U.S. but chose to identify more with Berlin. Yemi was born and raised in the U.S., and her parents migrated from Nigeria, and I was born in Nigeria, and moved to the U.S. when I was 12. Prior to moving to the U.S., I had lived in London, Saudi Arabia, and Nigeria. When I moved to the U.S., I stayed in New Jersey with my aunt by marriage who was originally from New Orleans, so my experience growing up in the U.S. was different from the other three because I assimilated by default.

At one moment during our conversation, the topic and the experiences of first-generation Americans came up. Yemi said to me, "You're not first-generation American because you were not born and bred here." Immediately, I responded and said I would consider myself a hybrid because I came to the U.S. when I was young and actually grew up American, without any influences from my "tradition." Then I said, "More importantly, why do we as Black people have to define our blackness?" This question brought me back to President Barack Obama's speech at Howard University's 2016 Commencement when he said:

> First of all—and this should not be a problem for this group—be confident in your heritage. (Applause.) Be confident in your blackness. One of the great changes that occurred in our country since I was your age is the realization there's no one way to be Black. Take it from somebody who's seen both sides of the debate about whether I'm Black enough. (Laughter.)...There's no straitjacket; there are no constraints; there's no litmus test for authenticity.

Second, even as we each embrace our own beautiful, unique, and valid versions of our Blackness, remember the tie that does bind us as African Americans—and that is our particular awareness of injustice and unfairness and struggle. That means we cannot sleepwalk through life. We cannot be ignorant of history. (Applause.) We can't meet the world with a sense of entitlement... .We have cousins and uncles and brothers and sisters who we remember were just as smart and just as talented as we were, but somehow got ground down by structures that are unfair and unjust.

The representation, misrepresentation, education, miseducation and many other factors about Blacks and blackness has been debated and remains controversial—even among fellow Black people. Over the years and many generations, however, a few things have remained constant —the color of our skin, the source of our ancestors, and our soul. Today, this commonality has transcended to the history and current reality of our struggle for equality.

I have traveled far and wide and have seen the struggle of the Black race remain the same. The fact that we were displaced, not by choice, but by circumstance across the diaspora and were placed at the bottom, created dissatisfaction with where we are as a race and lent to our unrelenting zest to still rise (as inspired by Maya Angelou's Still I Rise).

So, I thought about Yemi's statement again as we walked through the historical sites of DC and wondered, can I or should I be more or less Black than any other person with the same color of my skin because of my experiences? And what are those experiences? In my experience interacting with Jews through work or life, I have not seen a Jew say another is more or less a Jew because she or he came from Australia, lived in Israel, because their great-grandparents went through the Holocaust, or because one person observes the Sabbath and the other one does not.

Why is it so common among Black people to find ways to divide ourselves within our group? My experience has placed me in different settings where some Africans would say they are better than African Americans or some African Americans would look down on Africans. Instead of creating division, we need to create a guide to focus on both our personal and group actualization along with elevation. To every Black brother and sister out there, let us put an end to the division we face in our community.

We should also develop a resource to equip us with dealing with the oppression we face. What I have come to realize is that our history and our common goal to advance as a race is enough to bring us together. Whether it is by slavery, colonization, post-modernization, or whatever, the simple fact remains...we are at the bottom of the race, we are actively being suppressed, and our ancestors are from the same source. That in and of itself is worthy enough to bring us together as ONE NATION.

CHAPTER 15

PUPPY LOVE

Latasha Drax

Key Challenges: sexual violation; unconventional marriage; domestic violence; dealing with trauma

MEETING MY CHILDHOOD SWEETHEART

I have always loved my husband. Or maybe I was just infatuated with the idea of us as a couple. And why not? Throughout his adolescence and teenage years, he was a ladies' man and a man's crush. Girls wanted to be with him, and boys wanted to be like him.

One day, as I looked from my 9th-floor window in the Brooklyn housing project where we both grew up, I caught a glimpse of him swaggering by. With little thought, I raced down the stairs in leaps and bounds, to reach the outdoors, right before he rounded the pathway which led to his neighboring building. Our dialogue went something like…

Him: "You walkin' your dogs?"
Me: "Yeah," (which was a little white lie).
Him: "I have puppies. Come to my house to see them," he invited casually.
Me: "Why can't you just bring them outside?" I countered.

Him: "They're too young," he replied.
Me: "Oh well, I will wait then."

He shrugged his shoulders in dismissal and sauntered on his way, while I went mine. In retrospect, it wasn't the canines that were too young; it was us. But it was this encounter that began our puppy love.

I married my husband on March 20, 2005, in a small ceremony upstate New York, despite his 25 to life prison sentence. At the time, I believed that I wasn't marrying a man but a destiny. We had remained friends and lovers, lovers and friends for over 10 years, and in 1993, he became a state-identified number. Yet, I remembered his name, his face, his style, and his company. It took bad choices, tumultuous relationships, a son and salvation to come to terms with my childhood love's incarceration. Although I roamed free, I was held captive by the lack of possibilities and opportunities that his prison sentence truncated.

On the day that I said, "I do," I was naïve in my belief that "love bears all." So idyllic were my thoughts that we had the biblical verse engraved in our matching wedding bands and vowed to be together 'til death do us part. The first couple of years were truly a honeymoon. The love letters from my beloved were plentiful, the anticipation of ensuing conjugal visits was climatic, and the idea of him and I as a couple was romantic. I was that young girl again chasing that guy, so innocent and unassuming.

However, it was during the remaining few hours on one of our "trailer" visits that I cried quietly in the bed while my husband lay still beside me. He didn't reach out to touch or comfort me. He was physically near but emotionally distant. Feeling foolish and neurotic, I asked myself "why are you crying?" and the response in my spirit was, "you are mourning innocence lost."

VIOLATED

As a naïve and unsuspecting virgin, I willingly accompanied him to his apartment. I was fearless in my journey with the cute, older, and most popular guy in our neighborhood, and delighted to have been invited into his home. Yet, the dream come true was nothing compared to the nightmare that later occurred. I did not realize that what I considered innocent petting was to him, foreplay, which lead to more involved physical contact. I had barely started junior high school, so, for me, sex was not on my to-do list. But, it was on his. I was not plied with drugs or alcohol; all it took was a fierce and sudden slap across the face to silence my protests and force me into submission.

Shaken, ashamed, and sorry I ever went to his house, I walked home after he callously dismissed me. Only my dearest and best friend at the time was aware of the incident. She did her best to comfort me, as I sobbed deep pangs of uncontrollable regret. But being young and inexperienced, we did not know what to do. I suppose our thoughts were what could we do? It was over.

Shortly after the incident, I avoided my perpetrator at all costs. I hid my face if he walked past my apartment window. I strategically planned where not to go in the neighborhood to reduce the chance of meeting him face to face. But as time went on, I realized that what happened was not my fault. It was then that I made a conscious decision to no longer give him the power to control me as he did that dreadful day. Instead, I began to taunt and heckle him when I saw him in passing. He said nothing. He too had decided to keep our secret.

MOTHERLY COURAGE

At 21, I give birth to my man-child. His father was—I believed—the love of my life. A tall, charismatic older gentleman with a bad boy swag and an intoxicating Jamaican lilt. I was fearless in my journey to spend the rest of my life with him. But time would reveal his controlling, possessive and womanizing nature. Although he was my one and only, I was not his. Eventually, I mustered the courage to leave him and raise my son—alone and afraid. Then, one day, during a visit to see his son, I saw Satan in his eyes. He had come to seek revenge. He came after me, his height overwhelming, his charisma contorted into rage and his tone no longer intoxicating. I managed to escape averting the crystal ashtray he aimed at my head. The following day, he called and said, "Next time, I will be OJ, and you will be Nicole." I left NYC shortly after that.

MARITAL BLISS?

I raised my son without incident, without a male companion, and without a father figure. It was when he was about 9 or 10,that I married my childhood sweetheart. My marriage was safe. He couldn't harm me from behind the wall, and I wouldn't have to fully commit to him either. From 30-minute monitored phone calls and weekend conjugal romps, I became the aggressor, the dominant one—the controlling force in our relationship. I deserve better. I should expect more. But my first sexual encounter with a man conditioned me to be fearful, distrustful and undeserving of a healthy, happy relationship.

My husband was not aware of that awful period of my life or the insecurities I clung to. I became overwhelmed with self-doubt and began to question our union. Could the rape have caused me to fear rejection, be distrustful towards men, become more dominant and aggressive in relationships, fear intimacy and be non-committal? What was our relationship really based upon? Did I really know this man that I had known practically all my life? As I began to meditate heavily on these questions, I had to answer them honestly. For years, I have been in denial. With closer examination of my life, I realize that all the questions raised were in fact—the ugly truth.

Once we approached our 4th anniversary, I contemplated divorce and mailed what I termed a letter of release. We had not been on the same page for some time, or maybe we were not taking the time to read the writing on each other's wall. We argued, fussed and fought over petty things easily forgotten. The letters became fewer and farther apart, and the trailer visits stagnant. I was angry, hurt, and confused. As was he. How could something that seemed so right suddenly seem so utterly and completely wrong? I wanted to cut ties with him and convinced myself that our marriage and relationship was emotionally draining.

DEALING WITH THE PAST, HOPE FOR THE FUTURE

I am older, but still have more wisdom to gain. However, I am wise enough to know that I need to be healed of emotional hurt. The silent trauma of sexual abuse manifests itself subtly in my actions, words, and deeds. Somewhere deep within me, I hope to fully forgive the man who stripped me of my virginity and dignity at such an early age. In retrospect, I wish that I didn't wait to address the pain caused by that sexual assault. Maybe then I would not have become involved in relationships that continued to leave me vulnerable and wanting. Each day, I am grappling with self-identity, self-expression, and societal pressures that dictate what and how a woman should dress, speak and behave. I am learning that my recovery is in my response because (even though, at times, I feel naked and ashamed) it is only in that moment that I will regain my power and strength.

My marriage has been between a rock and a hard place, but individually a position of personal growth and maturity for us both. Can we let go of our puppy love to pursue, with dogged determination, the mature love we need as adults? In retrospect, neither of us had fully changed—me being emotionally detached, and him being physically distant. Even in our youth, my husband was distant. Whether it was physical or emotional, there was always a cloud of mystery that encompassed him. I suppose it was his enigmaticism that intrigued me and maybe it was my cool air of interest that wooed him. Yet, regardless of time, distance and challenging circumstances, the spiritual connection we always shared supersedes all. When I see myself gray-haired sitting in a rocking chair on my front porch, it is he that rocks beside me. As controversial as it seems, our marital relationship is no different than any typical married couple dealing with the issues of life and the storms that come. It is only our circumstances that make us unique.

Shortly, after we announced our marriage, we extended blessings and hope to our friends and family and encouraged them to pursue their purpose and God's plan for their lives. Then, in the interim, we failed to stay true to our guiding words that "love bears all." Despite our maturation in age, at the time, we were too young and still not ready to take on the challenge of a "new kind of normal" marriage. Over 10 bittersweet years later, we finally understood that, for 'us' to survive, we must not only deal with the ghosts of our past, but also continually revive, refresh and reconcile our relationship with the unconquerable love that connected us with bulldog tenacity. In less than two years, my husband will be eligible for parole, and I am willing to wait for destiny to be fulfilled. I have always loved my husband, and the idea of him and I as a couple still romances me.

CHAPTER 16

PREGNANT AT 17 TO PH.D. PROGRAM

This Race is Not Given to the Swift nor to the Strong

Donna M. Druery

Key Challenges: teenage pregnancy; educational resilience; parental relationship strain

Well, son, I'll tell you: Life for me ain't been no crystal stair.
—Mother to Son *(Hughes, 1994)*

Let's keep it real. Life happens. Stuff happens, and sometimes we try to clean up the pieces from a life made with choices on the way up the proverbial yellow brick road. When I got the news that I was pregnant, I was a junior in high school. My boyfriend took me to the clinic during school hours. The nurse conducted the test. She asked me if I wanted to keep it. I was in a state of shock, but I wasn't crazy. My Baptist church upbringing taught me that a sin is a sin, but do not compound sin with another sin. I was taught that abortion is murder and, since we cannot give life, we should not consider taking a life. I mumbled that I needed to think about it and would return if I changed my mind. My mother did not find out until I was past three months pregnant, when we went to shop for prom dresses in May. She noted that nothing I tried on would fit my slender frame. After trying on a dress, she said "That dress makes you look pregnant." I was fighting back tears. I do not remember what happened next, but I bought the dress, and finally located my mother in the car. Thankfully, she did not make me walk home—or put me out of the house, which is what I feared would happen. That summer, my boyfriend went away to technical college. We only saw each other on some weekends, but he was able to call once a week and charge the call to his parent's number (pre-cell phone days). I was in this thing alone.

I think my mother did not talk to me for the remaining six months, except to yell at me about something I did or did not do according to her unspoken wishes. I guess I was supposed to read her mind on what she wanted. I tried to make myself invisible. I spoke only when necessary and became very depressed and quite introverted. The one time my boyfriend came home from school, and I stayed out too late because we went to eat pizza, when I returned home, I got beat with an extension cord, at five months pregnant. After that, I hardly left home, except to go to school and to go to church. The only saving grace was my boyfriend's mother, Mary, who would try to cheer me up and would call to check on me every few days. Mary and her best friend, Gladys, also gave me a baby shower and invited some of my friends from school. That was how I finally had a few things for the baby.

WELCOMING BABY

When school began in September, I was seven months pregnant. I began having contractions on a Monday in November, while home alone. I called Mary and said, "I'm hurting." She rushed over and took me to the hospital. They kept me overnight, and I had the baby the next day. It was November 1979. My boyfriend was at school 80 miles away when I went into labor, and he could not leave school until Friday. I was in the hospital for a week, and our son was three days old before his dad saw him for the first time. When my son was almost two weeks old, I was home and began passing red blood clots. They were getting larger until they were grapefruit size. With much trepidation, I finally asked my mother, who was a licensed vocational nurse, if she could look at the clots now filling the toilet bowl and see if what was happening was normal. She said little to me, except to yell at me as to how long this had been going on. I mumbled, "All morning." I went to lie down because I was feeling weak. When I woke up, the ambulance was there, and they were putting smelling salts under my nose to revive me. We discovered that the doctor had not removed the afterbirth and I had to have a D&C. I stayed in the hospital a couple more days, while my sister (I think) cared for my son. I had been resurrected.

SCHOOL DAZE

I was on Homebound (a program where they come to your home at least twice per week, brought assignments, and then picked up your completed work) for six weeks. I did not know what I was going to do after these six weeks was over. It was my senior year, and I really wanted to finish school. I did not have a car, and there was no public transportation. I wasn't born with a silver spoon in my mouth—heck, I didn't even own a spoon! I also did not have a babysitter or funds to pay for one. I did not know what I was going to do.

My mom and my dad divorced when I was two; my dad lived in another city 30 minutes away. When I saw him, I mustered up the courage to ask him to help me. By this time, Mary was taking me to school and keeping the baby—her first grandson. There was a car for sale for $600.00. I felt that if I had a car, I could make some opportunities happen. I could get a part-time job after school to buy pampers and other baby items. But my father said that he could not help me, and from that day until the day he left this world, I never asked him for another thing. (Sidebar, I still have a problem asking anybody to do anything for me. My motto is "Just move out of my way; I'll do it myself.") Once again, Mary and my boyfriend's dad stepped in and bought me the car. I also got a part-time job after school, working in a gift shop. I dropped my son off to his grandmother Mary, went to school during the day, worked until 6 p.m., picked my baby up, went home and did my homework. I kept this routine until I graduated from high school.

THE GREAT ESCAPE

My relationship with my mother continued to deteriorate. It escalated one night when it was very cold, and my baby was laying on the sofa crying. We had one space heater in the room, and no central air or heat. My mother would not allow me to pick up my son, even though he was crying. She said he was just spoiled, and crying was good for his lungs to open fully! I truly believed she would have attacked me if I had picked him up, so I adhered to her instructions. When I finally picked him up, I said out loud. "His hands are freezing!" With tears in my eyes, I promised my son that things would get better. My boyfriend later returned home from the technical college he was attending, and we got married the year I graduated from high school. I was 19, and he was 20 years old. We are still married today.

COLLEGE YEARS

Since taking a field trip to an HBCU when I was in middle school, I knew I wanted to go to college. It was the first time I saw some students who looked like me. However, having a baby delayed my plans. After I got married, I enrolled in the local community college. I was newly married, working a full-time job, and had a toddler. It was more on my plate than I could handle. After I finished the fall semester, it would be a full 10 years before I returned to college.

My impetus for returning to college was due to training other salespeople on my job, only to see them become my boss. These were college students who had not yet earned their degrees. When I asked the manager why I could not get promoted, he said it was because I did not have enough college experience. When our last daughter was two, I returned to college full time. It was fall, 1991. I began at a two-year college, but I got a copy of the four-year college transfer plan. I took classes under the four-year plan and made the Dean's List, and received awards, accolades, and honors along the way. I also revived the Student Government Association. For two years, I attended classes during the day and graduated with an Associate's Degree in Business Administration. I applied to a four-year university and was accepted with almost 70 transfer hours. Two years later, I graduated from a Tier I university with a Bachelor's Degree in English and double minors in Business Administration and Speech Communication.

BECOMING A TEACHER AND BEYOND

Several years after graduation, the local college offered a Post-Baccalaureate program for those with degrees who wanted to be teachers. I applied and was accepted into the program. I interviewed for a position as an English teacher and was hired on the spot as a ninth-grade English teacher. The next year, I was asked to be the lead teacher. I was not certified and had never taught school before, but I absolutely loved it! I worked with an HBCU on a certification plan and finally passed the exam. I taught three years and was tapped for the 'Grow Your Own Leadership Program' where I worked on my Master's Degree in Administration to become a principal. I was hired after my fourth year of teaching as an Assistant Principal, took the certification test right before the school year began, and passed.

CONCLUSION

I spent 15 years in education. In year 13, I decided to return to school to get my doctoral degree. After two years of working on my Ed.D. and going to school on Saturdays, I resigned from my position as an assistant principal, went to school full-time, and later switched from an Ed.D. to a Ph.D. program. I plan to graduate next year and become a professor. I encourage young mothers to write their vision and make it plain. It may be difficult, but it is not impossible. Do not accept the current situation as your lifetime situation. Continue to work toward your goals. God has appointed someone to help you. Find your advocate, mentor, and muse. Most importantly, keep the faith. I am still climbing!

REFERENCE

Hughes, L. (1994). *The collected poems of Langston Hughes*. New York, NY: Knopf.

CHAPTER 17

DANCING TO THE BEAT OF GOD'S HEART

Leslie Duroseau

Key Challenges: faith ministry; purpose; abuse; teen pregnancy

I am a dancer; I was born to dance, and one of the best gifts I received is the ability to dance. Growing up, my mom placed me in dancing school at the tender age of 7 years old. Back then, I did not realize the profound effect dance would have on my life, and the role it would play in the shaping of my destiny.

I have always loved to dance. As a child from elementary school up until high school, I was active in professional dance school, was the captain of the high school dance team, and as I got older, I continued to dance, in the social arenas of clubs and night bars of New York City and abroad. I was a pretty good dancer but, more than that, I loved the way I felt when I danced. I felt free, I was happy, and I loved the interaction with others in dance as a professional and on the social scene.

Dancing was often an escape for me; I would go into another world, almost oblivious to all that was around me. Long after dance school and the clubs, I would find myself dancing in my everyday activities. One time, while working, it was brought to my attention that I was always dancing around (I did not realize it). I learned about another type of dancing, known as dirty dancing, and I found myself pregnant at the tender age of 15. It was then that my dreams of becoming a dancer, and pretty much anything else I dreamt of becoming, began to fade. I suffered from low self-esteem, isolated myself from family and friends, and fed into the stereotypes that I would always be a welfare mother, and nothing else. So, by the age of 18, I was pregnant with my second child, and my relationship with my significant other was abusive. By this time, I had been hit, had to jump out of cars, hid in my neighbor's yard, had a gun pulled out on me, and walked a mile or more in my bare feet in the cold to try and get away.

Although I had no relationship with the Lord, I began to question God. During this time, I remember telling God "I don't believe you created me or allowed me to be born to be beaten by some man and to die. I just don't believe that." The response was, "My daughter, I didn't create you for this. I created you for more." I held on to those words and believed them with every fiber of my being.

I then began to engage the dance of survival. What I would learn early on is that dance must be done in partnership with God. It was then that I would learn that dance was a gift given to me by God. I did not fully stumble upon this realization until I came to church and met the Lord of the Dance, Jesus. This actualization happened relatively quickly as I became a member of the church and was appointed as the director of the dance ministry.

From my first steps in the church, I became engaged in dance. However, this dance differed greatly from the other dancing I was accustomed to. This dance would lead me to the beat of God's heart. This dance led me to love and to live life more abundantly.

The more I engaged God in the dance, the more I became an empty vessel. This dance led by God, the "Master Choreographer," tore deep into my soul. No longer was I the same. It is here, in the sacred dance, that the Spirit of God would reveal itself to me through purging and refining. Sacred dance is about becoming more holy, and being stripped down, naked before our God. It is here that transformation occurs. The more I engaged God in the dance, the more equipped I was to engage others.

This is what the journey is all about—an intimate relationship with God and intimate relationships with others. As I dance with God, I am better able to dance with others and to look beyond faults, to forgive and to help supply needs. For this is what the Lord has done and is continuing to do for me.

I cannot think of a more creative way to view my relationship with God and with others than as a sacred and holy dance. God leads and I follow and often enough, He allows me to leap out on my own and ever so compassionately, He leads me back in and wraps his arms around me. As I turn and kick my way out of situations and circumstances, God is right beside me, gliding along with me, and every so often, He lifts me up and carries me away, allowing me to make a grand exit out of a mess.

The sacred dance is a dance for all; it is no respecter of person; the professional and the novice are welcome. Although I was a professional dancer, as the director of the dance ministry and as a sacred arts minister, most people I engage to enter into the sacred/holy dance do not have a professional dance background.

They often come believing they will learn dance steps and choreography only, which is not far from the truth. But they also end up gaining more because the true leader of the dance is God. So, often the technique and choreography become challenging, because it is about God leading them out of their brokenness and pain, and discovering who they truly are; whom God has ordained and created them to become. Dance is an awesome way to engage God and to engage others. It is through the art of dance that I believe the lives of all can be transformed.

In my understanding of God as relational and as a God who covenants with His children, I view "God as creativity, emergence, and God as dance and movement." As a dancer, I totally identify with this concept, and so for me, dance is not only about steps, it is also about the heart and spirit of a person. Before I can choreograph steps to a dance, the dance is already within me. Dance is an art, a discipline that creates a mind, body, soul, and spirit connection. It is about the formation, bringing everything together in order to operate fully in one's purpose. This is what God is about, bringing us into His formation so that we become agents of change here on the Earth.

The importance of formation and relationship is demonstrative in the Trinity. The understanding of God as a Triune God, Father, Son, and Holy Spirit help

John Damascus describes the trinity in his *Doctrine of Perichoresis 1* of the relationship as a "cleaving together." He states in the Godhead that "the Father and the Son not only embrace each other, but they also enter into each other, permeate each other and dwell in each other." This is how the art of dance functions. The movement of one's body is totally intertwined with the soul and spirit of the person. When the mind, body, soul, and spirit connection is operating fully and together, one is able to fully experience freedom.

As a sacred dancer, I truly embraced the concepts stated above. My preparation as a dancer is to enter into the presence of God and line up with the Spirit of God in bringing forth the movement. This, in turns, connects my audience, not to me the dancer, but to the Spirit of God. Once this connection is established, the power and Spirit of God is able to heal, deliver, and bring forth salvation and the captives are then set free. This can be liberating, and again, one can experience freedom.

In the United Methodist Church Hymnal, Hymn number 261, is the song the "Lord of the Dance." A verse of the hymn states:

"I danced in the morning when the world was begun, and I danced in the moon and the stars and the sun, and I came down from heaven, and I danced on the earth. At Bethlehem, I had my birth." The chorus states, "dance, then, wherever you may be; I am the Lord of the Dance, said He. And I'll lead you all wherever you may be, and I'll lead you all in the dance, said he."

"In the procession of the Spirit from the Father, the Father gives himself to the Son; in the procession of the Spirit from the Son to the Father, the Son gives himself to the Father, for the procession of the Spirit, like the begetting of the Son is the going forth of the being of the Father to the Son and the going forth of the being of the Son to the Father as Holy Spirit." (p. 261)

In my understanding of the Holy Spirit as the creation of new life, I understand that in this new life, I dance to the beat of a different drummer. God, through His Son Jesus and by His Holy Spirit, consumes my soul and permeates my spirit and a new dance emerges from the depth of my being. This dance allows me to "taste and see that the Lord is good." (Psalm 34:8, The New King James Version). This dance invites me into a relationship and to become a part of His family.

REFERENCES

Http://perichoeresis//
Ibid
Carter, S. (1963). Lord of the dance. In *The United Methodist hymnal: Book of United Methodist worship.* Nashville, TN :`United Methodist Pub.

CHAPTER 18

BLACK JELLY BEAN

Overcoming Insecurities and Perceptions by Finally Embracing and Living in My Truth

Stashia L. Emanuel

Key Challenges: imposter phenomenon, insecurity, self-worth, self-esteem, perception, love, confidence

I absolutely love jellybeans. Red ones, blue ones, green ones and all the gourmet styles, but the black ones really never appealed to me. They looked like they just did not belong, and they tasted different...bitter if you will. When I reflect on the mere thought of the black jellybean, my mouth turns bitter. Growing up, it was clear that, I was not the only person who felt that way because as I would frequent the candy jar, the only jellybeans that remained were the black ones; the darker ones, the ones that looked like they were just... nasty. I immediately thought of how every person who wanted something sweet, something enjoyable, and something tasty completely overlooked the black jellybeans. For me, the jellybean jar reflected the experiences that I endured during my adolescent years and even into my adulthood.

When I was younger, the jar of dark jellybeans caused an overwhelming emotion of rejection, hurt and loneliness to come over me. I compared the black jellybeans to myself and the many curvy "plus" size women and teens who were

A Second Helping of Gumbo for the Soul: More Liberating Stories and Memories to Inspire Females of Color, pages 69–73.

69

treated just like those black jellybeans. I was overlooked, frowned upon, and in last place when it came to mainstream beauty. Department stores did not accommodate my size, and when they did, the clothes would look like tents and most times, were located at the back of the store in a corner. I would literally have to pass all of the "pretty" clothes, which often had beautiful displays so consumers could get the "full effect" of the outfit, to get to the clothes that fit me. Walking to the back of the store brought about a sense of shame, disgrace, and disgust. It made me feel as though the people who wore these clothes or needed this size had no business being in the front of the store or being seen. It was as if this size was not appreciated by the mainstream, so it was given the name plus or husky. Walking to the back of the store was like walking the green mile; you knew what was back there, but you had no idea what it looked like or if it was a part of the stylish trend; but there was one thing that I knew for sure: the clothing was OVERPRICED AND UGLY!!!

PERCEPTION SHIFTS

Since I was raised by a single mother, I had to learn to be creative and appreciative of whatever she could afford, because she was raising two "fluffy" kids. On Saturdays, when we would go to the mall, I would walk past the many upscale clothing stores of that time, such as Macy's, John Wanamaker's, and Strawbridge & Clothier, but I knew that their clothes were really expensive. Honestly, it felt good to walk through such a department store and gleam at the fact that the bigger clothes were chic and stylish. While at the mall, my mother would always stop by the candy counter and allow us to select a quarter—pound of our favorite candy. I would always pick the chocolate covered peanuts clusters. One particular Saturday, my eyes wandered to the jellybean section and noticed it was filled to capacity with nothing but black jellybeans—several bins to be exact. Not only were there bins of black jellybeans, but also there were specialized arrangements with nothing but black jellybeans as the confection of choice. I thought to myself, what happened and why was the black jellybean so popular? I even asked the cashier about the new phenomenon. She mentioned that the store manager could not keep the black jellybeans in stock. My mind immediately recalled a time when the black jellybean was frowned upon, even called disgusting if you will. What changed, I thought? It was still the same candy, the same taste, the same shape, and the same form. So, what happened? I had to think long and hard about this, and quite frankly, it bothered to me a bit. But then, like a ton of bricks, it finally hit me. PERCEPTION!!!! See, it only takes ONE person to challenge a thing and cause mindsets to change and to follow in that direction.

Growing up, the perception of a little chubby girl was that of one who couldn't run, so she was to be picked last as a team member during gym class; she wasn't pretty so the boys never asked her out or asked her to dance during the slow songs. She had plenty of friends, but none of them ever turned out to be boyfriends. That was me, and I was the black jellybean. I was always overlooked when it came to dating and being admired. Many had always liked me. I had a lot of friends, and was an excellent student, but was never asked to be the girlfriend. The boys would laugh with me and dance with me during fast songs. They also enjoyed my company, as they were quite impressed with my level of sports knowledge. But I knew firsthand what it felt like to be the black jellybean…left out.

I did not feel as isolated by the females at my school, except by those who thought they were super cute and had a body to die for. My true girlfriends always accepted me for me and never tried to change me. I was always included in every activity, but when I noticed that I still was not getting the same type and of attention they were getting, I immediately tried to change my dress, my makeup, my way of thinking and overall character, just so that I could be accepted; asked to slow dance and receive the late-night forbidden phone calls from the males in my high school and surrounding neighborhoods. What young girl doesn't want to be accepted by varsity football and basketball players, or admired by the cutest boys in the school? To prove that a big girl could do just as much as the skinny girls, I tried out and made the cheerleading squad. I was the senior statistician of the varsity basketball team, but that was only because a really cute guy that I absolutely adored, was the captain. Despite my efforts, nothing changed. I did all of these things, and I still did not receive any phone calls, invitations to slow dance, or asked to be in a relationship. Absolutely nothing happened, but that all changed in the matter of one summer.

THE SUMMER OF 1988

Working during the summer break was the norm for many high school students. As for me, it was my senior year, and I needed to help contribute to the many assessments and fees that were to come. Right before the end of the summer break, my best friend and I took a trip to visit her family in New Haven, CT. It was an exciting time as we were "grown." We took the train to the city and were ready to have a ball before we returned for our last year of high school. Upon our arrival, her family greeted us. But what happened next was something that I was not used to, and it shocked me to the core—so much so that the person I was when I arrived in Connecticut was not the same person I was when I left.

As we got settled in for the week, my best friend's cousin welcomed one of her friends over so that we could all get acquainted. He was a dear friend of the family and would have most likely been around during our visit, so she figured she would invite him over. We all greeted each other, and I just knew that he would automatically favor the "less weighted" visitor since that is what usually happened. But to my surprise, things took a unique turn. As the introductions went forth, he looked and my best friend and was very cordial. He engaged in conversation and was the perfect gentleman. But then, he looked my way and said, "She is cute, but you? You're beautiful!" Now be mindful that we he was older, in his mid-twenties, and because I was not used to getting such compliments from total strangers, it took me back a bit. He repeated those sentiments several times and in various ways throughout the day. He hung around a bit, shared in some conversation and then he left to take care of some business. So much happened to me in that one moment and in the moments to come, but the one thing that ignited within me was that I was just not the cute girl with the fat face, but cute just for being me. His perception was different from any male that I had ever encountered in the past. I could even feel the sincerity in his voice. He didn't want anything from me, but he looked at me, the inner me; the me that I didn't even see or realize was there. From that point on, I was new. I became alive. I finally felt worthy of a compliment from a male outside of my family, and I didn't owe him anything for it. His actions and words towards me will be with me until the end of time. The summer of 1989 came to a close, and I entered and completed my senior year feeling more confident than ever, and this confidence transcended into my freshman year of college.

FALL SEMESTER 1989

Here we go! New school, new experiences on deck, and a new confidence that surpassed all things fearful, intimidating, and insignificant as it related to my frame and the insecurities it brought. September 1989, the semester began. I mentally claimed and maintained my peace and acknowledged that I was at this institution of higher learning to better myself by obtaining my degree while enjoying all that life had to offer during this time. College was the best. Words cannot describe my experience and the relationships that were created. These relationships turned into family and some, in particular, turned into memories that will be forever etched in my heart and mind. I met wonderful people, some of whom continued to push my confidence onward and upward. Friends looked out for me with encouragement during this transition period. I was energetic and carefree but focused on my academics. As I reflect back on this time, I realize that it was important for the transformation during the previous summer to take place as it could have truly affected my studies and the path I took, which could have caused me not to be where I am today.

Time continued to pass, and the year kept getting better and better. I was introduced to so many people that noticed that I was a beaming individual and genuinely interested in my ideas, my thoughts, and my personality, and it made me feel good! No longer did I hide behind the stigma that I had been associated with for so long and most importantly, I found something. Something that I needed more than I even realized; I found love.

The love I found was essential to my soul as it was feeding me and allowed me to reciprocate it in a way that only I could appreciate. I had to first fall in love with myself before I could even begin to experience the affection of another. In my past, I was so worried about receiving external affection that I never realized that the love I thought I was not getting was actually the love I should have been giving to myself. I found love and love found me. It tiptoed in ever so gently and took my breath away. It was tender, kind, caring, charismatic, fresh, subliminal and engaging. Everything that I dreamed could not even compare to my reality. My reality was as crystal clear as a fresh stream flowing into the river on a spring morning. In totality, I was experiencing the best time of my life, and every fiber of my being was satisfied with me.

The journey was one that had to be. There was no getting around, under, or over it. It was distasteful and unappealing just like the black jellybeans were perceived and I, most of the time, was my own enemy and my worst critic. I did not see myself as curvy, voluptuous, and vivaciously attractive; but then my perception changed. I no longer wanted to fit in. Instead, I dared to stand out!! Out of the shadows of basic and ordinary; and out of the shadows of bitterness and shame; I became a confident young woman. Without really realizing it, there was a movement on the horizon. A movement of women who refused to continue to sit down and be quiet and unnoticed. Unbeknownst to ourselves, we became united. During this time, we became women who demanded that designers take notice and when they still refused, we became entrepreneurs and designed our own clothing lines, comfortably fitting and hugging every curve our body owned. A market was discovered that was thirsting for more. Out of the creative minds of Lane Bryant, Ashley Stewart, Torrid, Avenue, IGIG, Eloquii, PinUp Girl, Monif C., Kiyonna, Karen Scott and many others, they purposefully set out to build a curvy brand and change the attitude of mainstream America. What these designers did was way more than textiles and textures. These designers birthed a movement while giving confidence, meaning, desirability and sensualism to all curvy women.

Today, I am more confident than ever!! I know who I am and more importantly, whose I am. I realize my self-worth. I am absolutely amazing!!! I am fearfully and wonderfully made!! Nothing and no one can tear me down with their stares, their laughs or even the size of clothing they don't carry. I have found my inner strength, and it gives me vivacity when life tries to bring me down. My smile now has meaning. My curves fuel me to carry myself in a way that allows my presence to command respect in any setting. My weight does not define who I am by any means as I have learned what it means to appreciate the totality of an individual rather than isolate them by one irrelevant characteristic that is naught as it relates to thoughtfulness, substance, and possessing a good heart. I hold my head up high and do not look down on anyone. I realize that I am no better than the next person and they are certainly no better than me. In no way am I conceited, but I am 100% persuaded that I am at the top of my game and there is no turning back.

REFERENCES

Clance, P. R. (1985). *The impostor phenomenon: When success makes you feel like a fake.* Toronto, Canada: Bantam Books.

Cokley, K., Mcclain, S., Enciso, A., & Martinez, M. (2013). An examination of the impact of minority status stress and impostor feelings on the mental health of diverse ethnic minority college students. *Journal of Multicultural Counseling & Development, 41*(2), 82–95. doi:10.1002/j.2161-1912.2013.00029.x

CHAPTER 19

THE LOSS: GOING WITHOUT CAN PROPEL YOU FORWARD

On Dealing with Loss and Rejection

Shandis English

Key Challenges: parental loss, rejection

On Wednesday, March 8, 2006, at 1:32 pm, my grandfather passed away due to complications related to congestive heart failure. Words cannot express the loss, but we all knew he lived a fulfilled, meaningful, and blessed life. For me, in my twenties, his death left a crack in our pot of gumbo, and everyone was searching for bowls to catch the excess. For me, this was the beginning of a lesson of learning how to go without and finding out exactly what kind of young Black woman I would become.

I was born in Columbus, Georgia on July 12, 1983, at 1:12 am. From the moment that I can remember, my home was filled with countless parental figures. See, my grandfather was the patriarch of the family, and he provided a huge house to accommodate everyone. In the household were my grandmother, grandfather, my mother, two aunts, and five uncles. This created a large pot of flavorful gumbo that could be stirred by the youngest soul and member of the house.

A Second Helping of Gumbo for the Soul: More Liberating Stories and Memories to Inspire Females of Color, pages 75–78.

Around the age of three, the pot began to bubble over, and my mother decided she wanted her independence. At the time, she left me to go prepare a home and ready herself to care for me as a single parent in the South Suburbs of Chicago. Despite her quest for independence, my mother moved into what we now call our family building. She moved to a city where my brilliant grandfather owned several businesses and properties at the time, and over the years, everyone eventually relocated to Illinois to create yet another pot of spicy, flavorful gumbo to nourish our souls.

While growing up in Illinois, I always had my grandfather and some of my uncles around to guide and protect me. They were also the men in my life who I knew and looked up to as father figures. At the time, a lot of love was put into my sheer existence because I was the first and only grandchild. I can still hear my aunts and uncles telling stories of jealousy, due to me being spoiled beyond measure. As members of my family got older, many went off to the military to serve our country; some started their own families, while others sought to forge their own paths in life. As the years continued to roll by, my mother eventually had two more children, and one of my aunts moved right next door to us. My grandparents divorced as well, but I still had a solid bond with everyone and had all the closeness of a loving father personified in my grandfather.

Around the time of my grandfather's passing, I realized some very harsh realities. I did not know my biological father; neither did I question, or even care about his existence and lack thereof in my life. But then, I wondered—was this the truth or something I was just telling myself? Around the age of 22, I began to search and dig for answers to my questions. There was a flicker of curiosity, especially because the light had gone out on the main father figure in my life. My curiosity was fed in the form of some old court documents that I found in my mother's room. It was a court order my mother and father had in place for the past twenty-plus years. The documents indicated my mother was supposed to be given a hundred dollars per month to support me, along with other legalities they had agreed upon. However, what stood out to me was the fact I had never even known his name. "Ok, this is a start," I told myself. The next step was to question my mother for more information, which led to her actually giving me a phone number. Being the strong Black woman that I was, there was no hesitation; I wanted to know more about this person.

THE REJECTION

I can remember, like yesterday our first conversation, out of maybe three in total. I finally called my biological father, and as I expected, he sounded very surprised to hear from me. He vaguely questioned me about my life and simply said for me to contact him if I ever came in town to visit, but the impression I got was that he was trying to cut the conversation short. I then let him know that I would definitely be interested in coming to meet him and I expressed the importance of meeting other members of that side of the family as well. I asked him to let those members of whom I have never met (like my two brothers, of whom I was made aware, or the cousins I had imagined meeting), know that I was coming. I also gave him the month that I was planned to travel south, which was scheduled for July. The plans were already in place because my mother was living in Alabama, and I knew I was going to visit her that summer.

The second phone call was a major shock to me. To this very day, I don't quite know how I feel, but I believe that my older brother answered the phone. He asked no questions—it was almost as if he already knew who I was and who I was calling for, but he did not want to be involved. I had never been the type of person to push myself on anyone, so I kindly asked to speak to my father, but he responded that he was not there, and that was the end of that.

A few weeks later, I had finally arrived in Tuskegee with hopes of a warm welcome and meeting some new relatives from my father's side. After a few days of visiting with my maternal family members and getting settled, I decided it was time to meet my paternal side. I had a few things to do in Columbus, Georgia on this particular day (which is where he lives), so I handled my business and gave my father a call as promised. When I called, he answered almost immediately. I thought to myself, "Well, that's a good sign since he answered the telephone." I let him know I was in the area and asked if I could take him to lunch. This was my way of showing I had no hard feelings and that I wasn't coming around because I wanted something in return. But I received a response that I would have never imagined. He did not accept the invitation and told me that he was taking care of his mother (who technically was my grandmother). In turn, I offered to come any other day of his choosing during my stay, and he simply said "No."

As I prepared to go back to Tuskegee, I was disappointed, hurt, and truly felt rejected. This was a wasted trip I thought, and if he knew he wanted nothing to do with me, he could have spared me the embarrassment of going out of my way. I spent the next few days of that trip down and out. I wondered how my flesh and blood could treat me this way. But all of the answers came to me while making the long journey back to Chicago. All the words of wisdom spoken to me throughout my life from my family who truly loved me swirled in my head. Up until that point, he had never reached out to me, but that was fine with me. When I got home, I threw his number away and never looked back. But, that experience was needed and I knew deep down in my heart that I had done the right thing. Although he was the father, I, the child, did what the parent should have done—reach out. That experience taught me a life lesson that I would not change for anything. It also shaped me into the successful, determined, educated, and wise person that I have become today. I had grown and learned from this experience.

PROLOGUE

Words of wisdom—in life, no one owes you anything, and you don't owe anyone either. I have lived by these words, and they have given me the strength and determination to do everything I have set out to do in life.

Casting all your care upon him; for he cares for you (1 Peter 5:7).

During the days that I was dealing with rejection, this Bible verse showed me that I do have a father and He truly cares for me more than any man ever will or can. Knowing this to be true, I have never had to search again and no longer feel the restraints of rejection.

I have also learned that it is best to deal with the issues that come up in life. Doing so will provide you with the possibility of resolve, to live honestly, and most importantly, it will bring peace. Your outcome may not always be positive, but it doesn't hurt to try. When you face issues as they come up, you will gain the strength to overcome anything.

CHAPTER 20

LIVING WITHOUT REGRET

Chiara D. Fuller

Key Challenges: self-doubt, multicultural education, world travel

Feel your dreams flow through your veins, occupy your thoughts and dance to the rhythm of your heartbeat. Life is precious. Now is the time to dream big! At the age of twenty-five, I made a promise to myself to live without regret. My purpose is to live with courage, faith, love, and kindness. Over the past 13 years, adventures revealed themselves in my dreams and my heart spoke to curiosity as my passion to grow in the world led me to step into my destiny.

The passion that I hold for my professional work, academic pursuits and personal growth have immensely shaped the path along the global journey that I have been blessed to live. My calling to work in the field of International Educational Development began when I completed courses in African politics, history, culture, and the Twi language during a junior year study abroad program at the University of Ghana Legon in Ghana, West Africa. My spirit fell in love when my feet danced to the beats of Ghanaian drums. I humbled myself at the door of "no return" in Elmina, a former slave Castle. Gaining rich knowledge about Ghanaian history and culture through the kindness of the life-long friendships that were formed in Ghana inspired me to find a way to pay what I gained forward.

A Second Helping of Gumbo for the Soul: More Liberating Stories and Memories to Inspire Females of Color, pages 79–82.

After successfully graduating from Mount Holyoke College with a major in International Relations, I began my two-year service as a Community Development and Education Peace Corps Volunteer in Barranco Village, a small Garifuna community in Southern Belize. The 150-member village is in the most southern community of Belize. My Peace Corps Country Assistant Director told me that if the world were to end, Barranco would be the last to find out. The community that I would call my home for two years had just received electricity; the local bus traveled into town on market day four days a week, and chickens walked around as they pleased.

I grew to love the community. The trust and mutual respect through my relationships with the Barranco Community laid the foundation for diverse community projects. I taught sixth grade, coached elementary students who won the top medals in the Belize National Track and Field Championships, and led a community cross-country field trip to the National Zoo. Health and literacy issues were addressed through the organization of community STD, HIV, and AIDS prevention education workshops, and by opening a library in my home for the young adults in the community. Upon completing my Peace Corps service, the teaching and coaching experiences in Barranco led to studying at Cambridge College and receiving a Master's degree in Education. As an educator, it was paramount to be well equipped with the knowledge, techniques, methodology, and skills needed to make effective change in my classrooms.

Over the next five years, the Japan Exchange and Teaching Program (JET) in Yamagata Prefecture hired me to work as an Assistant Language Teacher (ALT) for two years and a JET Prefectural Supervisor for three years. I co-taught dynamic English language classes to over five hundred Japanese students, along with twelve other Japanese English language teachers. Work presented opportunities to run three engaging English clubs, assist in classrooms with students who were visually impaired and blind, and tutor high school students who were the city, district, and nationally ranked English speech contest finalists. In addition to teaching, leading a multinational team who organized Prefectural professional development conferences and training sessions brought together hundreds of Japanese English teachers and sixty-one international Assistant Language Teachers over a two-year period.

Learning conversational Japanese and adapting to new cultural norms was rewarding. Teaching myself to become independent and literate in a culture that was different from my own was challenging. My most humbling experience happened when volunteering in solidarity with Japanese volunteers to clean desecrated neighborhoods and collect personal items to return to the owners who had survived the 2011 tsunami and earthquake that had claimed over ten thousand lives.

Immediately after completing the Japan Exchange and Teaching Program, I joined the World Teach Organization as an English Language Instructor and moved to Esmeraldas, a coastal African Ecuadorian community in Northern Ecuador. I taught English classes and Linguistics classes at the Pontificia Universidad Católica del Ecuador Sede Esmeraldas (PUCESE). Two years later, PUCESE hired me as Language Department Coordinator, and that entailed working with twenty-four Ecuadorian and American English language University Professors, nine schools and more than one thousand Ecuadorian students to improve the English language curriculum. Over the four-year period, I worked closely with the university community to organize the first English Speech Contests, an English Spelling Bee, two English Language Camps and one "Super English Conference" for teachers.

My international experiences have taught me the significance of inclusiveness, health, and nutrition, community involvement, racial and linguistic equity, and student-centered pedagogy in multicultural classrooms. I have transferred these invaluable lessons into my class dialogues, group work, individual research projects, and social interactions at Teachers College, Columbia University. My love for curriculum design emerged when I worked on group projects that developed English language curricula for Syrian refugee children in Lebanon and immigrant adolescents who recently migrated from Latin America to Los Angeles, California.

Today, I study in the field of Curriculum Design and Teacher Training. I work closely with a team of education specialists in the Hands in Outreach (HIO) and Nepal Education Support Trust (NEST) organizations. Together, we develop English and Nepali language curricula, design online materials, and give teacher training literacy workshops for students and mothers in marginalized communities around Kathmandu, Nepal.

My dream to live, learn and grow in the world has come true. Over the past 13 years, diligent work has helped to strengthen the quality of educational resources, teacher training, curricula and pedagogical practices in Belize, Ecuador, Japan, Nepal, and the United States. Waiting for the perfect travel companion wouldn't deter me from seeing the world. Traveling alone to the majority of the destinations on my bucket list was empowering. Pursing my destiny was a reward for the hard work that was accomplished in the field of international education. My hands have touched the Pyramids of Egypt. I have experienced a boat ride down the Nile River. I have explored the Cuyabeno Amazon, Galapagos Islands, Coastal communities and the Sierra in Ecuador. My feet have toured the Taj Mahal in India, watched the sunrise at Angkor Wat in Cambodia, marveled at the Iguazu waterfalls in Argentina, and stood above the clouds on top of Mountain Fuji in Japan. I rode on elephants in Thailand, taken a mountain flight around Mount Everest, and hiked through the Himalaya Mountains in Nepal. My eyes have seen the slave castles in Ghana, danced Punta in Belize, and journeyed through the caves in Hanoi, Vietnam. I have loved walking around Machu Picchu in Peru. I have danced Salsa and Bachata in Columbia and sunbathed in Jamaica.

The unconditional love and prayers of my parents and friends have supported me along this amazing life journey. Immersing into cultures and languages of 22 nations, living in six countries and stepping on four continents influences the way I think, how I see, and how I speak. My eyes see the world through different cultural lenses, and my ears hear the world through different languages. I have experienced loneliness, helplessness, sadness, and doubt, but I have also chosen to live with hope, faith, joy, and courage. The teachable moments have taught me that the greatest forms of communication come in true patience, kindness, humbleness, respect, love, and acceptance.

Some people have asked me what inspires me to live this life; I call it destiny. Fear has no place in my steps. Faith is my guide. I work hard to make my dreams reality. The words "no" or "you can't," inspire me not to settle. I strive to be the best I can be, despite the obstacles ahead. I stand on the bold, secure, devoted and magnificent shoulders of my ancestors, mentors, and family. Lessons of love and trust were taught by being my best friend, and when I leave my comfort zone, I leap, I run, and I fly. When I look back, it is only to remember that I have come a long way and this journey is not yet done.

CHAPTER 21

THE STORY OF A CHAMPION

Pain Always Has a Purpose

Renee L. Garraway

Key Challenges: domestic violence, foster care, forgiveness, extended family, emotional healing, perseverance

"Healing begins where the wound was made."

—Alice Walker

I come from a family of strong Black women who have overcome major obstacles—not all caused by an unjust society, but from the folks within their own homes. My great-grandmother, grandmother, mother, and aunts were very secretive about the pain they endured at the hands of the men who were supposed to love and protect them. Although these women didn't talk about their struggles, I witnessed their strength and observed them develop plans of action to escape the emotional and sometimes physical abuse they endured. They are survivors—my champions! I too am a strong, successful, Black woman and in spite of obstacles, I realize that my pain had a purpose...

I woke up facing a powder blue colored wall and realized that I had not been dreaming, but in fact, had spent the night in an unfamiliar place. The previous night my mother, younger sister, and I walked down the hall of a shelter carrying our blankets and a few other items from our trunk in hopes of finding a safe place to sleep. We had planned our "get-away" for several weeks, and I remember collecting and hiding my most precious treasures in the car trunk in anticipation of our escape. The night of our escape, I remember sitting anxiously in the parking lot of Pizza Hut for hours as my mother tried to figure out our next move. I can still hear my 3-year-old sister crying and begging my mother to go back home while I tried to reason with her why we should leave our dad for good.

Warm tears rolled down my face as I stared at the blue wall and imagined what lies ahead of us. After two days in the shelter, my mother decided that it was time for us to go back home. I felt we had been defeated and my dreams of freedom and starting a new life were crushed! After several years of broken promises from my mother to protect us, I ran away from home. In the middle of a family argument, I snuck out of the house with nothing, but the clothes that were on my back. I was taken into custody by the Department of Social Services and became a ward of the state at the age of 15. While living in several foster homes, I experienced depression, anxiety, and exhibited defiant behaviors. School was no longer a priority, and all I could think about was surviving. I could not focus due to severe anxiety and failed my freshman year of high school. The feelings of low self-esteem that I experienced were exacerbated by my academic failure.

The Department of Social Services worked diligently to find me a permanent family placement, and at the age of 16, I relocated to another state to live with my aunt and uncle to finish high school. My uncle, a retired veteran and adjunct professor, helped to get me back on track academically. My aunt, who majored in psychology, often used her counseling skills to get me to open up about my past and helped me to feel more self-confident. Both my aunt and uncle held me accountable and demanded academic excellence and sophisticated social skills. Although I failed my freshman year of high school, my aunt and uncle required that I go to summer school and night school to gain the credits necessary to graduate on time. I was required to empty my locker of all my books each Friday and study even if the teachers had not assigned homework. I felt like a nerd, had no social life, and hated the new demands that were placed on me. I remember telling my aunt and uncle that I was going to ask the social worker for a new placement, and they replied, "You ain't' going nowhere!" We are your family and are here to help you!"

After two years living with my very strict, but loving aunt and uncle, I was able to graduate from high school on time and with honors. I had no idea what I wanted to major in when I got to college—I was just happy to be accepted! I decided on an undergraduate major in psychology and later received a scholarship to pursue a master's degree in social work at one of the nation's top social work schools. It wasn't until I began my masters' degree in social work that I realized that my past was haunting me. Although I made excellent grades in college, it was difficult for me to concentrate in class because I was still grieving inside-longing to feel free and worth something. I didn't realize that the years of suffering without a healthy outlet would cause me to sink deeper into depression and low self-esteem. During my final semester of graduate school, I received a job offer to move to an urban city on the East coast as a social worker for the Department of Human Services. Little did I know, my work as a foster care worker would open up opportunities to touch many lives by sharing my journey and encouraging Black youth to view their painful circumstances as steppingstones to greatness. I mentored Black girls in my assigned foster homes that had little interaction with their families so that they could experience meaningful educational and social activities. My heart yearned to help them see that they too could be successful and that neither their family nor their circumstances determined their destiny.

As a young professional, I learned quickly that college degrees, job opportunities, new cars, and romantic relationships would not take away the pain from my past that continuously haunted me. It was through the support of the pastoral counseling staff at my church that I started to heal. I remember my first day of therapy telling the social worker at the church that I was there to discuss my college sweetheart who broke my heart. After a few sessions, the social worker encouraged me to deal with the deeper issues that caused my pain—healing from my childhood so that I could develop a healthy sense of self. The therapist coached me until I believed that I was valuable, loveable, and a champion. While I was working on healing, my parents were also healing and getting their lives in order. My parents received counseling and recommitted their lives to one another. Years ago, I would not have imagined that my family would be reunited and that we would experience healing and renewed relationships.

After leaving my position with the Department of Human Services, I became a school social worker in a predominately Black suburban school district and fell in love with the idea of educating children who looked like me. I received a full scholarship to obtain a second master's degree in special education with an emphasis on emotional disturbance. While employed at a special education school, I was able to work closely with my administrators who mentored me and suggested that I complete requirements to also become an administrator. I was nervous at the thought of becoming an administrator because I didn't feel confident or worthy of such a position. But, years later, I obtained administration I and II certifications and vowed that any child I encountered in my school would have access to rigorous, engaging, and relevant learning opportunities regardless of race, socioeconomic status, or exceptional ability.

As an educational leader and mentor, I want to be known for positively impacting the lives of students and to ensure that they have the academic and social-emotional skills needed to lead productive lives. I have committed my life to mentoring children of color, and I want them to have hope and confidence that they can have a successful future. Every day I strive to have a positive impact on those I encounter and to help them realize that regardless of obstacles, they can become champions. A champion overcomes obstacles and is able to defeat the challenges that stand in their way. I am appreciative of the Black women champions in my family that taught me to persevere and to always have hope regardless of challenges. All of my experiences have led me to a place of freedom, victory, and a renewed sense of self. Throughout my life, my family and mentors have taught me to believe that all things are possible with discipline and faith. Life experiences—both challenges and celebrations, have fueled my purpose and enable me to appreciate my journey. I am a champion, and regardless of your obstacles, you have what it takes to become one too!

CHAMPION

- Challenge the urge to blame others. Challenges can make us strong if perceived as learning opportunities.
- Hope for the best even if the situation looks bleak.
- Anticipate roadblocks and have a plan if things don't work out the way you planned.
- Make time to care for yourself.
- Persevere once a goal is set. The goal may not be easy, but it will be worth it in the end.
- Ignore thoughts of self-defeat. Feed your mind with positive thoughts. Get rid of negative thinking and negative people that bring you down.
- Offer support to someone else in need. Your story may help them make it through a tough time.
- Never let anyone make you doubt your self-worth, gifts, and purpose.

Author, Renee L. Garraway

We hope this book stirs your soul, warms your spirit, and provides a soothing reminder that you are not alone in overcoming whatever trials or triumphs life throws your way. The authors poured themselves into this book as a way to share how we as women of color are brilliant, bold, intelligent, and resilient. Read and be comforted!

—*Nicole McZeal Walters, Ed.D.*

CHAPTER 22

ONCE UPON A READER

Oh, The Places You'll Go!

Rhoda Myra Garces-Bacsal

Key Challenges: immigration, giftedness, poverty

For all those who have to fight for the respect that everyone else is given without question.

—N. K. Jemisin's dedication in "The Fifth Season"

It was 2008 when I moved to Singapore. That move marked my first trip outside of my home country, the Philippines. My passport was brand new (so was my husband's and daughter's), with nary a stamp in it. I was in my early 30s and just earned my Ph.D. in clinical psychology; my dissertation topic was a qualitative study of 22 gifted children from public and private schools. Fast forward to nine years later, at the time of the publishing of this book, I have been to over twenty-five countries and more than fifty cities. This is a Brown girl's story of facing odds with aplomb, rising up to the occasion when the opportunity presents itself, and being at the right place at the right time, with a book in hand.

I was born in the southernmost part of the Philippines, but moved to Manila when I was a toddler. We initially stayed with relatives in a squatters' area in Pasay. My father was a seaman. As a young child, I would only see him two months a year. While he came from a wealthy family of Spanish ancestry (my paternal grandmother was reputed to speak only in Spanish), he was considered to be one of the least attractive in a family that took immense pride in being beautiful. He also married my mother: a wandering, restless, beautiful soul who worked in a canteen, who was considered to be far below his station. It is not surprising that my father was essentially left to fend for himself when he started his family.

My mother told me that I started reading at age two. I enjoyed reading the Tagalog comics that were being sold by my auntie in her ramshackle sari-sari store. My father would bring home boxes of books with him as a present for me from his overseas travels. I grew up on Dr. Seuss' *Green Eggs and Ham*, P. D. Eastman's *Are You My Mother?* and *Ladybird* books. I was also deeply fascinated with stories of duwende, kapre, and diwata in Lola Basyang's stories (tales of dwarves and fairies from what I call our Filipino Grandmother Grimm).

My mother, despite being only a high school graduate, drummed in me the importance of learning and reading. In her distinct Visayan accent, she would speak to me in English, notwithstanding errors in pronunciation. She had a panache about her that defied grammatical lapses and considered proper diction as superfluous. She refused to speak to me if I didn't end up at the top of my class every academic year and expected me to be the best in everything that I did. I was admitted to first grade when I was six and was perceived as the wonder child in school—primarily because I could read very fast, with emotions, and with (surprisingly) proper diction. I went to an all-girls Catholic school that had been in existence since the 1800s in Manila. I was a big fish in a small pond, with teachers who had very little training (i.e., zero knowledge about gifted education). There were only 40 students in one class with only one section per grade level—so my classmates and I grew up like sisters. I remember being asked by teachers to demonstrate my reading skills to older students—they would ask me to stand on top of a stool so that those seated at the back could see me—while I read aloud from their selected, difficult text. After I finish reading, they would ask me what made me read so well, and I had a response that earned approbation, notwithstanding its falsity: I eat a lot of vegetables. I know that my teachers meant well, and for a time, I felt special. That is until the older students would come to me during lunch hour, demanding that I read aloud to them, like some freak show in a circus. Naturally, I refused—and was subsequently transformed from being a wonder child to an obnoxious brat.

We were wealthy at one point—we had two cars, drivers, and helpers. My mother sent many of my female cousins to college, and most ended up earning a bachelor's degree. My parents were one day millionaire kind of people. My mother, in particular, being a devout Catholic, believed that the more you give, the more you shall receive in return. She had a theatrical, expansive spirit that lived for the moment. There were a lot of get-togethers with dancing and loud Visayan music and a fiesta of food every weekend. My father was as good a provider as he was profligate and laughably arrogant. He lived big and proud—determined to show off what little he had, buying things he could not afford, promising things to people he wasn't able to deliver that would often get our family into trouble.

On top of that, he was a womanizer, a gambler, and a sometimes-dangerous and insecure drunk who would have angry and violent fits. Both my parents spent more than my father earned, leaving us in debt. Oftentimes, I wondered which was worse: to grow up in poverty throughout one's life, or to live large and wealthy one moment, and dirt-poor the next.

The lack of stability in our home could be seen in our frequent moves from one residence to the next since my parents could barely afford to pay rent. It became bad during my senior year in high school. One of our landladies who had a military officer for a husband, had his subordinates park themselves outside of my school gate, demanding to speak to my parents or me. My boyfriend, six years my senior (with the collusion of classmates, school teachers and administrators who turned a blind and supportive eye on the drama that was my life), would sneak me out of the back gate of the school, unbeknownst to the thugs, and take me home on his motorcycle which was on loan to him from the company where he worked as a credit collector. The irony of my motorcycle escape was not lost; I ended up marrying him as an adult.

I remember a time when we were locked out of our home. We had to force our way through poorly locked windows to sleep in our beds, with the electricity cut off. We did this for months. "Burning the midnight oil" was a reality for me, except that I used candlelight. I vowed during that time, that although I wasn't the valedictorian in high school, I would finish Cum Laude when I graduate from the top university in the country, which I did. Reading was my lifeline to sanity. While my entire world was falling apart around me, I read like a young girl drowning: from *Sweet Valley High* to classics; to thick encyclopedias and trashy romance novels—anything that would take me far and away from my all-too-colorful life, and the fact that our daily meals consisted of instant pancit canton and boiled egg.

My mother brought me to school during my first few months in college, but we never had enough money to buy the bus ticket. Once we spied the bus inspector coming, we would sneak quietly into the closest exit and get off on the next stop and take our chance on the next bus. My boyfriend and I would sit on benches with our packed sandwiches because we could not afford to buy the very cheap meals that would earn us a rightful seat and table in the often too-crowded university canteen. I did not make too many friends when I was in college; I regarded everyone as my competition. My university shocked my Catholic girl sensibilities as it freed my mind, making me realize my self-imposed limitations. I transformed my resentment and pain into a frenzied energy that fueled my studies. I questioned, critiqued, and argued with classmates and teachers—always with that hunger to make meaning of the world, to seek greater illumination for things that were bigger than myself.

I eventually ended up teaching three years at my university while I was enrolled in graduate school. I then taught at another private college that was patterned after and founded by the former president of my university, where I had the privilege of being the head of the very small Psychology Department. I encountered many brilliant, but spoiled, highly creative and misunderstood young adults who cared very little about education, but who eventually graduated under my tutelage and supervision. I worked tirelessly, doing psychological assessments and counseling in two clinics, teaching full time, finishing my graduate studies while raising my toddler and being a part-time wife. When I finally earned my Ph.D., I remember telling my daughter in earnest that I would show her the world. I hope I am able to continue to do that, as she accompanies me on many of my overseas travels.

A job offer in Singapore came at the perfect time when the university was still progressively looking towards equal opportunity employment for promising young academics coming from different parts of the world. It was a fortuitous moment that perhaps would not have happened if not for the right set of circumstances and the people who were big-hearted enough to see beyond my home country and give me the chance that I needed to prove myself.

As I look back and taste the bittersweet memories that shaped the woman that I am, I realize how important it is to always welcome challenges and opportunities with an open spirit. For the young and bright ladies who feel limited by who they are: rise to the occasion, and never fail to deliver with grace, good, and professionalism. Read to lose yourself and to free your mind: find poetry and beauty; revel in it. Own your weakness; wear it like a second skin until it becomes your strength. Acknowledge that life isn't fair, that the world won't do you any and that ultimately, you experience your pain alone. Value kindness above all. It isn't just your smarts that will take you places; it's how you treat the people around you. Go forward in life with a sense of purpose and meaning—out of a shared sense of community and commitment to better not just yourself but the world. You will only travel as far as the limits you impose on yourself, and once freed, "Oh, the places you'll go."

CHAPTER 23

MORE THAN A STATISTIC

The Journey from Teenage
Parenthood to the Ivy League

Judith Gil

Key Challenges: teenage pregnancy, teenage parenting, resilience, challenges/obstacles, educational attainment, positive trajectories

Driving up the I–95 highway on a beautiful and sunny afternoon, my eyes became filled with tears. Tears filled with raw, positive emotion; happiness, elation, fulfillment, reward-just to name a few. I was on my way to conduct an interview with a participant for my doctoral research study. I had already conducted two interviews prior and set out to conduct my third one. The first two meetings were back to back, and I did not have time to process all that I had heard from my first two amazing participants. The feeling was so intense that it led me to pull over and REALLY process because I could not keep driving until I had a moment to myself.

My dissertation research study focuses on educational attainment in the form of college degrees for former teenage mothers. More specifically, Black and Latina teenage mothers. Of teenage pregnancies, Black and Hispanic teen birth rates are more than two times higher than the rate for White teens. Young teen mothers who have children before age 18, are even less likely to graduate from high school. Of these young mothers, only 38 percent will graduate from high school, and only two percent will go on to attain an undergraduate college degree. Several studies have found that women who enter parenthood earlier have much lower levels of postsecondary educational investment over the eight years following high school (Stange, 2011; Rich & Kim, 2009). Black and Latina teenagers hold the highest rates for teen pregnancy. My research focuses primarily on these two racial groups because of the high prevalence of teen birth rates among the two. The study seeks to understand the shared experiences of women who were once teen mothers, yet were able to overcome their circumstances and pursue higher levels of education.

Now, back to that afternoon on the I–95 highway. I pulled over, took my pen and pad out of my bag, and began to attempt to formulate a sentence. But before I could begin to write one single word, the tears began to roll down my cheeks. I recalled the experiences of my two participants, and they mirrored so much of my own. Part of the reason I am interested in this population and topic, in general, is that I once was also a teenage mother. I was 16 when I became pregnant, and that event changed my life in ways that I never imagined.

At 16 years of age, when most teenagers were facing the decision of who to ask to prom, or what dress to wear, or which college to attend, I was faced with making a decision that would impact the rest of my life. There was never a question for me or a doubt as it related to the life that was growing inside of me. I knew this baby would come into the world, and I would do my best to provide him with all that I could, despite the many obstacles I knew I would face.

I am a first-generation born, Latina woman. My parents came to the United States from the Dominican Republic with a bag full of dreams and aspirations for themselves and the family they would create. Shattering that dream for them was something I was afraid to do and one of the scariest moments of my life up until then. I was the oldest of four children. I was expected to be the example, the role model for my two younger sisters and brother. I was always an excellent student with high educational aspirations for myself. I had dreams of attending college out of state and experience living away from home. However, those aspirations came to a halt once I learned of my early pregnancy. In the Latino culture, having a child out of wedlock, let alone becoming sexually involved at a young age, is something that is not easily forgiven. One is supposed to follow the norms of the culture, which include waiting until you are married to have sex for the very first time and then have your children. Conversations related to sexuality, safe sex practices or anything pertaining to the "S" word (sexo) was not allowed and was a complete taboo, never to be addressed.

Since I was afraid to tell my parents, I ran away from home, leaving a note with my then 14-year-old sister. Looking back on that experience, I cannot imagine what my younger sister felt. What a burden and responsibility to put on her young and innocent shoulders. The evening I ran away was an emotionally and intense evening. I remember pulling away from the parking lot in my boyfriend's car and seeing my mother in the front of the apartment building with tears in her eyes. 25 years later, that image remains vivid. The following nine months were filled with emotional turmoil and sadness. I was alienated from my family. I was not allowed to visit my parents nor was I allowed to see my sister. Going through this transition was one of the loneliest experiences I had to endure. It was during this time that I decided I would not allow this experience to deter me from continuing to pursue my academic goals. But even in that decision, I was faced with obstacles and roadblocks.

I attended a Catholic high school, and a teenage pregnancy was viewed as unacceptable. In no way were administrators going to allow such a negative example remain in the school. I was fortunate to have the help of my school counselor, Mr. O'Donnell. My mother, although upset and disappointed, put those feelings aside because she understood the importance of education, especially with becoming a young mother. She worked collaboratively with Mr. O'Donnell, and they were able to come to an agreement with school administrators. The agreement involved me being able to remain in the school only if my pregnancy was not visible. If I began showing before the school year was over, I would have to leave the school. Fortunately, the stars were aligned in my favor. By the end of the school year, I was five months pregnant, but I carried my pregnancy really small. Although I was able to remain in the school, that did not come without consequence. I recall the sly remarks from some of the teachers and being made to feel embarrassed and ashamed. Looking back at that experience, I truly appreciate the help of my school counselor. If he were alive today, I would thank him for going against the rules and school norms to help a student. Not many people were willing to do that for me.

The pregnancy was difficult for me. I experienced symptoms the entire pregnancy, and my emotional state was in shambles. I had no one to offer emotional support or guidance. My son's family treated me poorly, like an outsider who came to ruin their son's life. Towards the end of the pregnancy, my mother began to allow me to visit home and when she became aware of how ill I had been, she decided not to allow her daughter to continue to live that way. She was with me at my son's birth and coached me the entire 23 hours of labor, and although I was never an emotional person, it was the first time I felt emotionally connected to her. That is yet another memory I will never forget, and I remain forever thankful for all of her efforts.

After the baby was born, I had to make yet another difficult decision. My parents were willing to allow me back home, but with one condition, I would have to end the relationship with my child's father. While this was a decision that would be difficult, I thought about my future and what the advantages of going back home would be. So, at the age of 17, I made the decision to go back to my family's home where I was met with the support of my younger sisters who truly embraced their role of aunts to their baby nephew. My mother also graciously paid for child-care so that I could continue going to school.

Exactly one week after my son was born, the fall semester of my senior year of high school began. The determination to finish high school and not become yet another statistic was what helped me through this difficult time. In addition, I had a life to care for, and it was no longer about me. I graduated from high school and immediately enrolled in a four-year public college. While I was not able to fulfill the dream of being able to go away to college, that was an opportunity that was awarded to my son later on in his life.

The years went by, and I continued to learn and grow from this experience. I learned about my personal strength, my resilience and my ability to meet obstacles head-on. My family continued to be supportive, and with their help, I was able to pursue graduate studies. I graduated from Fordham University in 2007 with a master's degree in social work and began my career in mental health. Working with vulnerable teenagers and young adults was my professional focus and being able to be a change agent in people's lives has been rewarding and fulfilling.

As my son grew into a young man, he would engage in conversations with me regarding the positive trajectories of our lives and the outcomes for the two of us. He would always inquire if I had any information on the frequency with which teenage mothers become successful in their careers, as well as their offspring hav-ing success in their own personal lives. I promised him that if I ever pursued a doctorate, that would be the area of research for me.

In 2014, I was accepted into the University of Pennsylvania School of Social Policy and Practice Doctor of Social Work program. I will never forget the feel-ing when I received the call informing me that I, a former teenage mother and a Latina, was accepted into an Ivy League university. My wildest dreams had really come true. And today, I am fulfilling the promise to my son and turning what was supposed to have been a negative, life-altering experience, into a dissertation research study.

Life happens at the blink of an eye. How we manage these changes makes a significant difference. Find and cultivate your inner strength, seek mental health services to alleviate the stress and changes associated with life-changing process-es, connect to resources, accept the help being offered and have the belief that anything is possible!

CHAPTER 24

IT IS ALL GOOD IN THE NEIGHBORHOOD

An Academic Journey of Learning to Embrace and Shine Through Adversities

Tyra Good

Key Challenges: neighborhood crime; alcohol and drugs; low income; testing issues; poor quality education

I Am From

I am from a place where love was so strong that it kills. A place where love was so deep that it caused one's mind to believe that their hidden addictions were suddenly revealed. I am from a place where to be a man meant to hide your flaws and die in addictions' jaws. A place where greatness resonates in the home, and spills out into our communities, giving birth to entrepreneurs alone.

I am from a place where making money was the norm, using our God-given gifts, to share love, and shed light, on our community's perfect storms. A place where creating positive vibes, and love was the only way anyone could survive.

A Second Helping of Gumbo for the Soul: More Liberating Stories and Memories to Inspire Females of Color, pages 97–101.

A place where you were taught how to balance life's ropes, reaching back, while moving forward, in hopes of ending a place where street corners are filled with dealers prescribing cocaine and dope.

I am from a place where dreams were shattered by generational fears, a place where dreams were never obtained because of how you saw yourself in the mirror.

A place where you are defined by your flaws. A place where society sums you and writes you off. A place where your family's character has been assassinated and, in time, you defeat the odds, break down barriers in every shape, form, and fashion.

I am from a place where mom did it all. A place where her prayers saved us all.

I am from a place that produced strength to persevere, a place where you believed you could now stand up with GOOD courage and face all that you've feared.

I am from a place that planted seeds of courage, a place where your purpose was nourished. A place where your life was a legacy of service.

I am from this place, a community place, a village place, a place where Harriett Tubmans were raised up to break cycles of poverty, through forging brighter paths.

I am from this place. A GOOD Place. (Good & Dark, 2016).

In this chapter, I focus on my academic journey of surviving and thriving not despite of, but because of, my family and community upbringing that reluctantly propelled me into my professional calling. That is, once I learned to accept and embrace who I was created to be and whom I was created for. My love for the field of education is more than just a profession, but also a form of activism rooted in self-acceptance, passion and a call to ministry. Defining my work as a ministry (Dantley, 2010) is articulated in the social and historical context of many African American educators.

I grew up in a household with my mother, two younger brothers and my father who, although loved us unconditionally, struggled with alcohol and drug addiction. Even though my parents were not legally married, they were considered married through common law, so I never professed that I grew up in a single-parent household. My mother completed her Associate's degree at a local community college but struggled to find stable employment. My father worked as an independent carpenter, but the inconsistent contracts, lack of education beyond high school, drug abuse, and mental illness prohibited him from being a consistent provider for our family. My parents' low paying wages and inconsistent work resulted in our family being on government assistance to make ends meet. The financial challenges and drug abuse lead to many arguments between my parents. Despite this fact, my parents never ceased to love, encourage and support my brothers and me.

My mother was a praying woman and did not want her children to be entrapped in a cycle of poverty. She relied on community-based afterschool and summer programs to provide us with homework assistance, a hot meal and snack, and a positive alternative to hanging out in the streets. These programs provided a safe environment until she was able to pick us up after her long, laborious day of carrying mail for the U.S. Postal Service. The neighborhood that we grew up in was prone to gang violence and other illegal activities, so the afterschool programs were a must. My cousin and his friend were brutally murdered in the early 90s due to turf rivalry. I was 16 at the time and struggled to make sense of their horrific untimely deaths. This traumatic experience planted a seed of fear in me. I became depressed and obsessed with getting "out the hood" and recalled my parents saying that education was the bridge to transformational power that would get me "out the hood" and on a path to success. The hood represented pain and misery for me, so I immersed myself even more into my academics in hopes of being free—making it to college and getting a good paying job that would allow me to move away and never return to my city.

I was intelligent according to the school system's grading standard. I always received good grades in my scholar classes and participated in academic clubs. However, despite taking two preparatory courses for the Scholastic Assessment Test (SAT) and taking the test three times, I could not obtain a score over 800. I thought there was no way I should have made high honor every reporting period and fail to score above 1000 on the SAT. I was puzzled, hurt and embarrassed. I began to wonder was I going to become a negative statistic that was portrayed on our TV screens and scornfully blamed by society as what is wrong with Black youth? What factors contributed to my low standardized test scores? Were there other factors affecting the academic success of my African American peers as well? I did exceptionally well in school and was told that I was smart. Something was wrong and didn't add up. Nonetheless, I graduated in the 5% of my high school graduating class and went on to pursue my undergraduate studies.

I quickly discovered there was a massive gap in the level of rigorous academic work I received in my K–12 urban public school system and the level of work I was expected to be prepared to do in college. I had to take a remedial reading and writing course before taking English 101. I was starting college already behind. Again, I asked myself, how could this be? Instead of embracing the new city, I was in and attending the Historically Black College and University (HBCU) of my dreams, I felt lost in the crowd, surrounded by the "real" intelligent people. I began to doubt myself and feel inadequate. I became ANGRY at my teachers for passing me and at the school system for failing to educate me! I felt cheated, disrespected, and dehumanized! And what about the students in the mainstream classes? They were even more left behind.

Nonetheless, the aforementioned experience instilled in me a passion for education, particularly in educating African American youth from underserved communities. When examining the state of Black education, we must look deeper than what is on the surface (i.e., poor attendance; low grades; low standardized test scores; and unsatisfactory behavior). To address and conquer the problem, the factors contributing to these issues should be examined along with the cultural disconnection between schools and culturally and linguistically diverse student body populations.

African Americans are the majority of students enrolled in the urban public school system that I graduated from, but the majority of high school diplomas were awarded to Whites. My parents were correct in what they said that education was the bridge to transformational power to get "out the hood." My HBCU education bridged a paradigm shift to propel me into my calling. It exposed the deficit view of my get "out the hood" mindset. No longer was I going to run from myself or be embarrassed about who I was or of my academic struggles. I decided to return to my city and my hood.

I began working with African American youth who participated in an after-school program located in my community. The organization's mission was to provide prevention services to youth, ages 12–18, from economically disadvantaged communities through academic enrichment, recreation, cultural art, mentoring and career development programs. Since my Bachelor's degree is in Business Management, I was hired as a consultant to teach the youth business, entrepreneurial and developmental life-skills. As I worked with the students, I noticed that most of them were struggling academically in various content areas. Their struggles made me reflect on my experience of being educated in the same public school system that failed to challenge and academically prepare me for college. This was a turning point and clarion call for me to become an educational advocate for youth in my community and from similar backgrounds to receive an equitable education.

While pursuing a Master's of Arts in Teaching degree and a Doctorate in Educational Leadership, I noticed a disconnect between the African American students and their White teachers in establishing relevant relational and academic connections. Culturally responsive teachers work to soften the disconnection that many culturally different students feel between their home and school. Educating from within and outside the traditional school walls have shaped my lens as a practitioner and researcher. My personal narrative inspired me to cultivate a culturally responsive school, family and community partnerships that intentionally focus on eradicating systemic racial barriers to the academic success of African American youth from marginalized communities. Today, I am a university professor in an education department, a certified classroom teacher, and have worked for over 13 years with community-based organizations focused on serving African American youth through mentorship and academics.

This is H.O.O.D work, and we must unapologetically advocate to *Heal Our Offspring Daily*. Our goal should not be to make it "out the hood," but to liberate our mindsets so we can define our freedom of success. We must boldly share our stories of struggle, triumphs, and perseverance so our youth can levitate to their greatness. They must hear and see evidence of how we embraced, found strength and learned how to shine through life's adversities. They must know that the ingredients of life—the good, the bad, and the ugly—make *us*, uniquely *us*, and blossoms into our purpose. They must know that when the ingredients are all mixed together, it is GOOD for our soul.

REFERENCES

Dantley, M. E. (2010). Successful leadership in urban schools. Principals and critical spiri-
    tuality, A new approach to reform. *Journal of Negro Education, 79*(3). 214–219.
Good, T., & Dark, S. (2016). *I am from.* Unpublished Poem. Pittsburgh, PA.

CHAPTER 25

A SOB STORY

Chasitie Sharron Goodman

Key Challenges: primary education, extended family, perseverance, faith, minority

Pull up a chair, sit a spell; I've got a sob story to share. No really, it's a sob story; got your chair? Okay then, I will start at the beginning. I am a proud member of the Goodman family in this life. My childhood was Sunday dinners, cool food on SNICK Saturday's, home-cooked holidays, and summer evenings spent with lightning bugs. My family, my imagination, and me; that's all I needed. T'was paradise.

My grandmother and my mother were my first teachers. I learned to count standing under the prettiest trees you could ever imagine in this lifetime. One was a golden orange with a blush of red. It looked like the sunset fell asleep on its leaves. It was audacious; spreading its branches out wide to show off its beauty and standing tall over the house next door as if to lend itself to my grandmother and me. The tree beside it was fire engine cherry and merlot red, all at the same time. This tree, standing merrily above the brick houses burst up in the sky for my merriment. My grandmother, a retired school teacher, would go into the house and pull out a seemingly endless supply of old envelopes and lay out her challenge. "Let's see who can count the most cars? I bet you I can...who won last time?" I'd smile all giddy, and take her up on that offer every single time. If it were summer,

A Second Helping of Gumbo for the Soul: More Liberating Stories and Memories to Inspire Females of Color, pages 103–106.

we would sit on the porch and smell barbecue wafting in the breeze around us. We would wait greedily for the fall, and the arrival of "our trees." She'd take out those old envelopes, and we would count, sometimes using the American number system, while other times using Roman numerals, the number of cars that would pass on one of the streets close by. She would count the cars going up the street; I would count the cars coming down, and vice versa. We would take turns like that. I did not know then, in my preschool days, that she was teaching me number fluency, but she was.

We would sit out there, for, lawd, what must have been hours, counting cars and talking life. Grandma told me stories about her childhood, her teenage years as a basketball star, her Uncle Doc with the good hair, and the first time she met my grandfather. He was a businessman, well off, proud, and all the women wanted him, she would reminisce. Then she would look over at the trees and marvel, and recite a poem that sounded like the cool nectar of sweet ripe fruit. "I think that I shall never see, a poem as lovely as a tree. Poems are made by fools like me, but only God can make a tree." Later I found that the poet, Joyce Kilmer, wrote the piece. Grandma would also tell me about time. "To everything, there is a time and a season," she would recite, "a time to be born and a time to die, a time to be a child, and a time to put away childish things." Ecclesiastes. All things are done according to their time. That's a lesson that I have held deep in the core of my soul...I revisit it often.

I learned style, grace, and presence from my mom; she owned her own preschool. She put together the coolest outfits, and fix her hair and makeup so nicely. I was so proud of her whenever she would come around my school, even when my classmates laughed at her. Blood red tights, combat boots, short skirt, and a black blazer with all kinds of colors dancing on the fabric. She was walking art to me! I got my style and boldness from her. She and my grandmother would not even go to the mailbox if they weren't all done up. My mom would take me to the library, and she would insist that one of the books in the dozen that spilled out of my arms, be a book about myself. She was sometimes subtle, but she was fire; warm and soothing, but powerful. Side-by-side with her, I learned how to handle business.

Well, the time came for me to leave the house, and for my first teachers to go to school. I went to a predominately White school. I remember my dad telling me, almost ad nauseum. "You go to school to get a good education. These people you will be around don't look like you, but that doesn't mean they better than you. Don't ever think they better than you." He would take this message and wrap it around history and sociology and speak with the vehemence of a Baptist preacher.

I entered school happy and complete. A Goodman, a good girl. But, my first elementary school was hell. The only chocolate chip—more often than not—stuck in sugar cookie dough; I began to understand what it meant to be "othered." My first fight, well not necessarily physical, was in kindergarten. It was started by my best friend because my Reeboks were black and not white. It ended with her snatching my necklace made of multicolored ice cream cones to a swift, sad death on the concrete. Perhaps my ice cream necklace was too colorful, too. My parents were told that I was unruly, but it was determined that my former best friend had a "bad day." Hmmm. I walked away having lost a best friend and a necklace that day. What did she lose?

The next school I went to was all Black. The hell was much hotter there. I talked funny. I walked funny. I ate funny. I dressed funny. I thought I was smart. I thought I was cute. And I thought my hair was cute, but in my eyes, it was nothing but a greasy mess. Lawd, them children made fun of me! Taunts pushed me inward and, my escape was the pen. I would write poetry to drown out the sound of their comments.

My parents moved me to a private school where hell had an admission ticket. I spent my adolescent years trying to fit into the crowd or avoid the crowd altogether. My middle school teacher even confirmed in front of everyone, that all Black people were the cursed people of Ham and that the curse was our pigment. Middle school was so bad that my grandmother began to write bible verses for me on little slips of paper so that God, and in a small way, she, could walk with me in the hallways.

Ultimately this meant I had to do something large with my life. Something where everyone, and I mean every one of them who threw a taunt, started a rumor, or made a joke about me, or even laughed, including teachers, would have to see and marvel at the phenomena that was Chasitie S. Goodman, Esquire. That is how I signed everyone's yearbooks. I just knew that I was going to be the female Johnnie Cochran. I had been planning it since I was five years-old, even though my grandmother swore I was a chip off the old block. I had no interest in being a teacher, though.

Yet, two degrees down, the calling came. I was like a junkie needing a fix. All I wanted was my one year in the classroom. Then I would go off to prove the defendant, and my myriad of bullies, wrong without objection. A teacher was not big enough for me. I had to do something grand! I had to make the bystanders "oooohhhh" and "aaaahhhh." A teacher could never do that. Besides, I got pretty good grades in school, but the hell was too hot to bear.

With degrees in hand, and needing a job, I sought my year in the classroom. I sought my year for a whole year. I read the requirements, over, and over. I met them, or so I thought. That year was unfruitful. Eventually, law school ruled itself out, and I became relentless in my search of a classroom. I passed the tests, sent the emails, and lined up the interviews. But I got no, after no, after resounding no. This went on for four years. Four years... a presidency, the beginning, and ending of high school, or college matriculation, four years!

I kept pounding the pavement, going on interviews. "You were a great candidate, but...." "Thank you so much for your interest but...." "Thank you for taking the time to come out and interview today. There were many talented candidates...."

In those four years, I went inward again. I had to search. Years of bullying and rejection sent me inward. I went back to my mom's fire, my dad's sermons, my grandma and our trees. I searched for God in myself, and I loved her fiercely. Finally, on my grandmother's birthday, I decided to try one final time. I found a school with an opening and sent an email, and I got a response. Suddenly, I knew exactly how to respond. I followed the steps and was asked to come in for an interview.

My mom rode with me that day. She sat in the summer sun and prayed while I interviewed for job number 337. I was dressed in a nice black suit; pumps that hurt my feet; and my hair and makeup were perfect. I was doing great, answering questions, walking around, and hearing about the school's vision. I sat down for the one-on-one interview. The principal asked me what I would like to do in the classroom. Something inside me let go. I broke down in that man's office and cried. I mean, gut cried, I sobbed, shaky and snotty. And I couldn't stop! "I *sniff*, I *sniff*, I just, *sniff*, I just want to teach..." With a wad of tissues, I sobbed and told the truth. My spirit surrendered. I answered the call, and became like Grandma said I would, "a chip off the old block." I got the job.

336 times I fell. 336 times I rose. Learning every time. No weapon formed could prosper once I understood my lesson. I am perfectly me; I do not need to compete with anyone. I have nothing to prove. 336 times I fell. 336 times I rose, and in due time, just like grandma said, I walked through the hell of those classrooms to the peace of my own. A chip off the ole' block indeed. I stand in the footprint of my first teachers, my mother and grandmother, how could that not be big enough? You still got your tissues? If you must, let go, surrender, cry your truth, and go get your happy.

CHAPTER 26

BLOOD IS NOT THICKER THAN WATER

Pamela Grayson

Key Challenges: familial relationship; maternal relationship; parenting; self-esteem; colorism; adoption

They lifted her out of the bed, onto the gurney, and into the body bag. I was the last person to touch her. I kissed her warm forehead and removed the one pearl earring that was left, as even on her deathbed she still displayed class and etiquette. As they zipped the bag, I thought, "How will she breathe? She will suffocate. She will be scared." I came to my senses as they rolled her out of the house. They rolled her into the van that belonged to the only funeral home in town, which, in my mind, was never supposed to come to this house for anyone that lived here.

My mother was this beautiful powerhouse of a woman who was strong-willed, an impeccable dresser and had the reputation for giving what was needed any time anyone asked, even to a fault. Yet, she could not seem to give me, her own daughter, what was needed, which was simply tender maternal love.

A Second Helping of Gumbo for the Soul: More Liberating Stories and Memories to Inspire Females of Color, pages 107–111.
Copyright © 2020 by Information Age Publishing
All rights of reproduction in any form reserved.

THE HISTORY

I have often wondered why my mother behaved towards me the way she did. In reviewing the history, my maternal grandmother was half Native American and had two sets of children by two different husbands. The first set was what was considered light skinned; the second set was considered dark skinned. Historically within the African American culture, there was a sort of distinction between light-skinned and dark-skinned individuals and that distinction permeated the relationship between these sets of siblings. The lighter skinned children looked down upon and insulted the dark skinned children. My mother was part of the second set.

Additionally, I do not believe my mother ever graduated from high school. After two years of marriage, my parents adopted me as they thought they could not have children of their own, and their marriage was strained, to say the least. Therefore, you had a perfect storm of skin color and other personal insecurities, dealing with the inability to give birth to a natural child, and a stressful, abusive marriage. And within all of this, my mother was handed a substitute child that was light skinned, academically strong, independent, and strong willed.

UNLOVED

I remember different instances of abuse over the years that I did not understand. My mother would discipline to the point of abuse. I would get yelled at or struck with a belt or switch for minor or accidental infractions. I remember when I was four, my parents told me to go to bed when I did not want to. They asked me for a goodnight kiss, and I said "No, I don't give kisses when I'm mad." I was a child that did not know any better. Because of that one statement from a toddler, my mother never gave me a goodnight kiss again for the rest of her life. It grew to the point where my mother and I touched each other three times a year. We hugged on each other's birthday and at Christmas, and the lack of affection went on until I was in high school.

Many instances worsened over the years. When I was seven, my parents were able to conceive and give birth to their own biological child. Based on my mother's harsher behavior, I perceived that this eliminated the need for me completely. When I was nine years old, my parents sat me down and told me I was adopted. From that point on, they blamed every bad thing they felt I did on that exchange. Truthfully, I did not really understand the reality of what they were saying regarding my adoption, and it really did not mean that much to me. But I do agree that me being adopted did cause issues, but not based all on me. I recall how my younger sister could go in the kitchen and reach in the refrigerator and get a glass of Kool-Aid, but I had to ask permission. I recall a time when I asked my mom for a glass and out of the blue she turned and looked at me and stated, "You are a bitch." Another time my mother became frustrated with my sister and me over our Barbie dolls and confiscated all of our dolls and doll clothes. I had amassed a larger collection of items than my sister and knew my mother would give her my stuff and say it was hers. I began to document which items were mine. My dad asked me what I was writing. When I explained, he giggled, and my mom didn't say a word. Later, she angrily gave me my items back. There were also times when my sister would wrongfully take items from me or damage my items, and my mom would justify her behavior.

These events seem petty, yet the lasting impact these types of exchanges displayed as to the lack of value I had as a daughter scarred me for life. There is an article in *Psychology Today* that speaks of the unloving parent and gas lighting (Streep, 2016), something at which my mother was good. I recall a time where she handed me a fashion model recruitment card from JCPenney, saying I should apply. I was shocked. I thought that my mother did see something in me. A few days later, I was standing in front of a mirror in a cute fitted skirt and blouse and she looked at me and said, "You think you're cute, don't you?" And then came the cut down, "with those ol' black knees."

THE SUCCESS DESPITE THE OBSTACLES

Over the years, I have been the daughter that took care of her own children with minimal help from my parents. I earned my bachelor's and master's degrees and have recently completed my doctoral degree. Even as a primary school child, I brought home report cards with straight A's, and it was handed back to me nonchalantly with a half-hearted compliment. I have served in various leadership roles in high school, college, and in corporate America. I have obtained positions that were at the high-end executive level, and I was the first African American woman to fulfill an extensive leadership position for a major food provider in the US. I participated in a premier megachurch nationwide women's enhancement program where I competed against 350 other women locally, and hundreds more online that involved the completion of three projects and was a finalist in two of the three categories, and won one. One of my mother's longtime friends looked at me and stated that she did not understand why my mother treated me the way she did when I was a daughter that a mother would want to have. I worked hard and usually obtained success, but this still was not enough to make my mother love me.

THE GRAND FINALE

In 2013, my parents and I had the ultimate falling out that resulted in us not speaking to one another for three years. In 2016, after much debating with God, I finally returned home to find my mother with one month to live due to stage-four breast cancer that metastasized. When I discovered what was going on, within weeks, I left my good life and home in Texas and came back to Illinois to stay until my mother transitioned. I took care of my mother—everything from cooking, bathing, and toileting assistance, but she still said hateful things to me, even on her deathbed. When she died, I was then made aware of all the awful things she told others about me which included the myth that the fallout between us was all my fault. Our fallout actually occurred over the bad behavior of my oldest son whom I had to remove from my home. He would constantly disrespect me, and my mother justified his bad behavior and gave him the indication that his behavior was ok. To this day, the level of disrespect that my son has toward me has not been resolved. I also found out that she told people that I had unnatural affections for my father because she did not like the close relationship my father and I had; there are key lessons that I have learned in life from this catastrophe of a maternal relationship:

1.   Blood is not thicker than water. Proverbs 18:24 states "and there is a friend that sticketh closer than a brother." I have learned that this so true. I can trust most people, as long as they do not have my last name. Within Christianity, we are taught that everyone is our brother and sister. This has been proven to me time and time again, as I can trust my friends more than I ever could most in my family. There were times when my friends had to defend me from my own mother. Friends stood in the gap for me when I needed the love, support, and guidance of a mother and further supported me through the chaos she left me after her death.

2.   Blood is not thicker than water. It is okay to exercise the gift of good-bye, even with family. The three-year hiatus I took from my mother and the rest of my family were some of the best years of my life. When people constantly hurt you, it is okay to remove them from your life, regardless of who they are.

3.   Blood is not thicker than water. There is power in apology. "Apology is not just a social nicety. It is an important ritual, a way of showing respect and empathy for the wronged person" (Engel, 2002, p. 1). African American parents tend to engage the authoritarian parenting style. This is not what is always needed. Have the ability to have a level of mutual respect for your children and acknowledge when you, as a parent, have fallen short.

4.   Blood is not thicker than water. Sometimes in life, you will have to accept the apology that you never received. The day after my mother passed, I awoke and was lying in bed, still in shock. I heard an audible voice say, "I'm sorry." I jumped out of bed thinking it was my Dad telling me that he was leaving as well. No one was there. I thought maybe this was my mother's last message to me. It did not do much good, as it was not done in earnest, personally. I have had to work to move on, address the messes she left me, and work to forgive her anyway. The lack of forgiveness was only hurting me at this point.

In essence, the greatest lesson that I have learned throughout my life ordeal is that blood is not thicker than water.

REFERENCES

Engel, B. (2002, July 01). *The power of apology.* Retrieved from https://www.psychologytoday.com/articles/200207/the-power-apology.

Streep, P. (2016, July 07). *Why it's so hard to see this form of childhood abuse.* Retrieved from https://www.psychologytoday.com/blog/tech-support/201607/why-its-so-hard-see-form-childhood-abuse.

CHAPTER 27

APRIL SHOWERS
TO MAY FLOWERS

Jasmine M. Hamilton

Key Challenges: domestic violence; self-acceptance, perseverance

April…May…June. It was a night that I would never forget, forged with the details that I wish I could. On a typical Louisiana humid June summer night, my daughter and I had just come in from a late movie. I put her to sleep in my bed and grabbed my Bible to read for comfort and clarity in the living room. My mind was racing from reflecting on the symbolism in the movie and what (if anything) I could learn from it. Needless to say, the movie wasn't the intended escape from my reality and the new normal of my life. In a month's time, I had gone from the euphoria of a newlywed (April) to contemplating divorce (May). And now another 30 days later (June), I was struggling; struggling to find answers and trying to hang on to the sliver of faith that I felt I had left.

As I was sitting quietly, flipping through the pages of my Bible, I heard a rattling at the front door. It was more than the rustling of the wind as if someone was trying to open the door. Terrified, I immediately jumped up, grabbed a knife and cautiously tiptoed my way downstairs. For a moment, the thought of the "dumb" girl going towards the danger popped into my mind, in which everyone yells "No girl, don't do it!" at the screen. But then, Mama Bear kicked in; I had to protect

A Second Helping of Gumbo for the Soul: More Liberating Stories and Memories to Inspire Females of Color, pages 113–116.

my daughter. We lived in one of those new luxury townhome apartments with the personal attached garage underneath; once through the front, a set of stairs opened to a two-bedroom flat.

The noise at the front door stopped; no one was there. I returned upstairs to sit with my knife resting on my thigh, heart racing, and body still jittery from the adrenaline. Just as I began to calm down, I heard the same noise. But now, it was at my patio door, which was above my garage, a flat surface, not easy for someone to climb without a ladder. Then, to my horror, I heard my bedroom window open where my daughter was sleeping. I frantically rushed to the window and jabbed at the curtain and air determined not to let whatever it was come in. Then, I heard a familiar voice say, "Baby, it's me! Baby, it's me!" The sound of his voice struck a sharp pang of fear and anxiety to the depths of my soul. You see, in May, he had packed up and moved to another city two hours away. This was after the police were called to our home because he assaulted me. He had thrown wine in my face (which I learned from the responding officers was assault) because I wanted to go to the library. On another occasion, he slapped my glasses off of my face. I can still vividly recall the expression on the officer's face when he learned that we were only married a few weeks. Eerily, his words of caution became my reality only a few weeks later: "Ma'am, things like this only get worse." And on that summer night, they did.

Stunned by recognizing the intruder, I took a break from frantically stabbing the curtain and tried to close the window to deny his entry, but he was stronger. After crawling through the window, he began to engage in endeared greetings and pleasantries as if any of the past seven minutes was normal. I played along because I quickly deduced it was the best strategy to deal with the craziness of the moment. I returned to my attempted space of solace on the oversized living room chair and opened my Bible, hoping that visual would be enough of protection from what was to come. Doing my best to blend into the chair and not engage with him in conversation, the words on the pages seemed to melt into a blur of black and gray splotches. I was nervous. If I called someone, including the police, I knew he would flip the story to make me out to be the villain.

So, I commenced to do what was ingrained in my DNA; I was going to handle and diffuse this situation myself. He sat on the opposite end of the sofa staring at me. I was too afraid to release my gaze from the black and gray splotches, but continued to force myself to think in a crazy manner and fix this situation. But since crazy thinking didn't come naturally, and I couldn't relate to crazy, my strategic contrived crazy responses were no match for his expert level of crazy. The abuse that ensued lasted until the morning and culminated with him demonstrating his affection with his fists, while I was trying to protect my daughter from seeing the horrors that were unfolding.

Because these events occurred so soon after saying 'I do,' I was often asked one of the most dreaded questions: "Well, you didn't know he was like that?" You see, after what I called my Detox Phase, I realized that I had been groomed into accepting the abuse. It was disguised as constructive criticism and evolved into name-calling, invasion of privacy, and isolation from friends. How did it happen? Low self-esteem? Lack of confidence? Feelings of not being loved? No, none of these were my issues. He posed himself to be a man of God and used my religion against me. Don't get me wrong; he had some great qualities that initially attracted me to him. I was a single mother, and he accepted my daughter as his own. He was also the first person to actually put action to his words and propose to me. During the Detox, I had to unlearn all of the behaviors and lies that I had accepted. But first, I had to acknowledge their existence. It was extremely easy to play the victim, but what was there to gain from staying in that space? The labels and names we accept greatly affect our thoughts, words, and actions. It takes a deliberately conscious effort to accept the positive and learn from the negative.

So many questions and thoughts derived from that night: How did I end up here? I'm smarter than this, right? What are people gonna think? How do I protect my daughter and myself? One thing was for sure—I was determined to finish my Doctorate and not let the mishap detour me. When I met "him," I was two years into my doctoral program at a prestigious R1 (Research One) institution. That June, two years later, I was at the beginning stages of working on my dissertation and teaching as a graduate assistant. The incident happened on a Friday evening and I was back at school, teaching, that following Tuesday. I was determined not to outwardly look like the disaster that was on the inside. But because I did not show up to teach my class on Monday with no explanation, I was forced to explain the circumstances of my absence with my advisor. Here I was, the only 'fly in the buttermilk' in my program at a predominantly White institution going through this negative experience.

Furthermore, it couldn't be hidden. I remember seeing the color slowly disappear from my advisor's face as I matter-of-factly explained the events of my weekend, in the oh-so-typical fashion that we (Black women) so often display. We dust ourselves off and keep moving, and do not allow ourselves any time to decompress.

Supportive friends and family would tell me to 'Let go and let God'—but HOW? No one suggested how! I struggled with this because "God" put me in this position. The foundation of my faith had been uprooted. I discovered the 'how' was in making a concerted effort to move forward. Ironically, as I embarked on dual journeys of personal and professional growth, my art was an imitation of my life: the paths were intertwined, even when I fought to keep them separate. Social Identity Theory was the framework used to guide my research explorations of physical activity behaviors of African American women. The mechanisms in how we choose to identify ourselves are outward reflections of our personal beliefs. I had tapped into such a clarifying logic and understanding (spiritual, conceptual, et,) that in turn reflected an unrealized strength, a revelation that occurred after a conversation with my mother.

In the months following that night, I studied and researched my way through the Detox. I wanted to understand the whys and hows of myself. That situation left me feeling broken, defeated, damaged, and not good enough—my love wasn't good enough for my husband. These feelings fueled my fortitude to control what I could—my future career. I learned to objectively look at others and subsequently myself. I had also buried myself in my studies and did not converse much with anyone, especially not about that night. The shame would not allow me to do so. One day, my mother brought it up; she was naturally worried about her baby. Once she finished speaking, I explained what I understood about him, my role in the situation, and what I wanted for my daughter. When I finally finished and focused on my mother's face, it was a look I had never seen before—a mixture of shock and amazement. With a calm voice, she said: "You are the strongest person I know." Huh? Cue the record scratching sound. Here was a woman who was a high-ranking Navy officer, raised three kids, one of whom had autism—my hero, telling me I was stronger than her!

Through this all, I felt like my circumstances were not anything special. I had done what any "grown" person would do, right? Since then, I have come to comprehend that "grown" is relative and not commensurate with chronological age. Likewise, self-acceptance is also a journey that is not paralleled to maturity. At this point in my journey, I continually work to accept my greatness and know that I am good enough. Some days are better than others and that is OK. The April showers will come, just as the flowers in May. But "how" I navigate those showers will determine the quality of flowers I enjoy. April…May…June.

CHAPTER 28

WHEN LIFE GIVES YOU LEMONS, GIVE LIFE BLACK GIRL MAGIC

A Story of a Memphis Girl Overcoming Homelessness and Educational Inequity

Jamesha Hayes

Key Challenges: homelessness, bullying, educational inequity, poverty, classism, systemic oppression, educational debt

The chapter below follows a proverbial phrase "When Life Give You Lemons," you make the best lemonade ever tasted. The lemons in the recipe represent life's adversity, the water in the recipe represents the essence of people of color, and the sugar represents the blessings that come in life. This chapter uses my life experiences to model the method other young women can use to overcome life's adversity.

In the early hours of a fall morning, my parents fighting jarred me from my sleep. I got out of my bed, walked from my side of the house, passed the living room, and through the kitchen to my parents' bedroom. I looked through the door

A Second Helping of Gumbo for the Soul: More Liberating Stories and Memories to Inspire Females of Color, pages 117–120.

with the gaping hole in it—the hole that had come about when my father tried to beat the door down when my mom locked herself in the bedroom. I knocked on the door. When my father opened the door, I saw my mother crouched in a corner. My father barked at me that I should mind my business and go back to bed. As the door slammed in my face, my mother's words, "the choices you make today, Jamesha, will affect your tomorrow" rang out in my head. That day, at the age of eleven, I decided that instead of being a bystander to my father's abuse of my mother, I would fight back.

I ran to my side of the house, picked my sister out of her crib, and began shaking her to make her cry. Once she started crying, I ran back to the other side of house, knocked on my parents' door again, and held my sister up as a sacrifice. My father allowed my mother to come out of the room and as the three of us sat in the living room, I decided to move forward with my plan. As blood rolled down my mom's face, I told her that we needed to leave my father at that moment. My mother, my sister, and I fled the house in our pajamas and bare feet to countless neighbors' doors, asking for a sanctuary. Finally, a couple opened the door and let us in their home to call the police. When they arrived, the police stated that my mother had 30 minutes to pack her car and leave the premise. As I helped my mother pack, I began to ponder about the effects my choice would have on my future. What was going to happen to me, my sister, my mother? Would we have to leave our suburban home in the county and go back to the inner city? Would the near future be brighter and better?

Unfortunately, the future did not get brighter; darkness fell upon me like fire falls upon a lit match in a gasoline drenched room. On the night that we left my father, my mother took my sister and me to a homeless shelter. Shortly after that, she informed me that we would be changing schools. She told me that she had stood in line for hours to get me in the best school in the inner city with the best honors program. I got excited because the one place that was always safe and comforting to me was the classroom. I clung to education the way that cheese clings to macaroni noodles in a mac and cheese dish. Sadly, though, my first day in that inner city middle school ripped my safety blanket of school and education from me.

As I entered the 6th-grade hallway, I ran into some old friends I knew when I was attending a low-performing inner city elementary school before moving to the county school as a 5th grader. Instead of embracing me, they taunted me by saying, "Oh what happened to your rich, White school, Jamesha? I thought you were too good to go to our ghetto school. See you're just like us…ghetto, Black, and poor." As the girls laughed and mocked me, I did not know what to say back to them. I wanted to scream that I had spent the last couple of weeks sleeping on people's floors and in the homeless shelter. I wanted to scream that I was hurting because we had left my father and my world was shattered. But instead, I said nothing and walked away with the hope that the classroom would be the refuge that it had always been.

As the White teacher began the lesson in my honors class, my heart was broken into a million pieces. My face became hot, my throat was itchy, and my eyes welled with tears because the lesson that the honors 6th-grade teacher was teaching was information I had learned in the 5th grade when I attended a predominantly White, suburban county school.

At that point, I lost all hope and sobbed on my desk. As I wept, I let out all of the pain of my life with every tear. My classmates began to notice and wanted to comfort me. My teacher yelled at them and said, "Sit down! Whatever she has going on is her problem. I am here to teach and y'all are here to learn. When she is ready to learn, she will act correctly in the class." The class obeyed our teacher, and eventually, I stopped crying because I remembered what my mom told me on the first night at the homeless shelter, "When life gives you lemons, Jamesha, you have to make lemonade."

From that point forward, I decided that I had to turn life's lemons into lemonade. For me, the lemons in life are the adversarial situations that are often sour and shock us when we experience them. I began to take the lemons that I experienced like homelessness, educational inequity, classism, racism, and sexism and squeezed the juice out of them. The juice is the lessons that can be taken from those adversarial situations. As my grandma said, "You can learn somethin' from everybody, Jamesha, even a fool because from a fool, you learn how not to be a fool."

As I matriculated through middle and high school in the inner city, I realized that life would keep presenting me with lemons. At first, it was disheartening to know that, because I was a Black female living in poverty, I would continue to face systemic injustices in my school and community. However, I realized that, with each battle that I endured, I was victorious and fortified with the strength to fight another battle. Moreover, with that realization, I was able to identify the next ingredient in my lemonade.

The next ingredient in my lemonade is water, which represents the God-given essence of people of color. Throughout my life, I have had to identify the God-given gifts that form my essence, so I could use those gifts to persevere through challenges. God-given gifts like strength, wisdom, faith, determination, and leadership are key molecules in the water used in my recipe. I was able to identify those molecules by watching my mother persevere through the aftermath of leaving my father. After leaving my father, my mother worked tirelessly to provide for my sister and me by working at a non-profit organization, at a factory, and as a housekeeper. But, the toll of multiple years on multiple jobs affected my mom, and she was losing the ability to walk, but she couldn't afford to go on disability due to her not having a retirement fund or not receiving a pay raise for ten years. Seeing her working while disabled made me ask her how she keeps fighting every day. She told me, "I was born with everything I needed to succeed. It is destined for me to win. I just have to keep putting one foot in front of the other." That conversation and so many more exposed me to the God-given gifts that we all possess as women of color. Once I realized that I had been born into a race of people full of so much greatness and strength, I began to see the manifestation of the final ingredient in my lemonade.

The last ingredient in my lemonade is sugar. Sugar is sweet and represents the sweet spots in life. It is important to keep a hawk-like eye out for the sugar in life because often times it is easy to focus on the lemons. For example, after that disheartening day in the 6th grade, I vowed that as an adult, I would help to eliminate poverty and ensure every child had access to opportunities to turn their dreams into realities. This called for me to be a leader and to seek opportunities that would prepare me with the skills necessary to dismantle the social injustices in our world. I began to join clubs, became captain of sports teams, participated and led various organizations in the community for teens, and participated in national leadership development programs. Because of my efforts, I received one of life's cubes of sugar when a prominent local magazine featured me as an emerging leader.

I received another cube of sugar, when I earned a full scholarship to a prominent four-year institution. But, I did not stop looking for sugar once I got in college, nor did I stop mixing it in with the other ingredients of my lemonade. In fact, I perfected my recipe and ended up with some amazing opportunities. I was president of various organizations and honor societies in college. I was also one of the first Black people to attend a study abroad program in 2009 that allowed me to attend at a prestigious university in Oxford, England for a semester. I received an international scholarship, and was selected to be a member in a highly competitive national teacher preparation program. All those sweet experiences mixed in with the lemons and water of life to create *Jamesha's Black Girl Magic Lemonade*.

Currently, I use my Black Girl Magic Lemonade in my director role in a national teacher preparation program to ensure that teachers are prepared to holistically support children in the classroom and that they are teaching students how to make their own lemonade. Additionally, as a doctoral student in an educational leadership program, I use my Black Girl Magic Lemonade to create an educational curriculum that will dismantle the oppressive curriculum that is currently in place in our schools. Now that I have shared my recipe for turning lemons into the best lemonade anyone has ever tasted, I hope that you will be inspired to create your own recipe!

CHAPTER 29

WHY TRY TO FIT IN WHEN YOU WERE BORN TO STAND OUT

Navigating College as a Low- Income First Generation Student

Tiffany Hollis

Key Challenges: first-generation college, resilience

I have had to battle and fight to beat the odds multiple times during my educational journey; however, the most intense and significant battle was fought as I proved my worth and my value as a female, first-generation college student of color at a predominantly White institution during my undergraduate years. In fact, my undergraduate years were equally the most enlightening and challenging years of my life and served as a crucial turning point during my trajectory of life. I was faced with numerous situations that helped shape me and mold me into the person that I am today. As a Black female from a low socioeconomic status background, I often faced microaggressions and other forms of subtle racism. Despite the quality liberal arts education that I received at Davidson College, the most important thing that I learned was something that was not taught by the professor. I learned that there was no need for me to be ashamed of who I was and where I came from.

A Second Helping of Gumbo for the Soul: More Liberating Stories and Memories to Inspire Females of Color, pages 121–125.

As time progressed, I learned that I could use my negative experiences and leverage them into positive experiences that could be used to educate others who had a distorted view of what it meant to be from a low-income background. I used my background and my interpersonal skills to initiate discussions about diversity, more specifically, the socioeconomic diversity that appeared on Davidson's campus. These conversations helped change the face of Davidson College. I came in with the attitude that I was not going to let another obstacle hinder me from moving closer to my dreams. I began to advocate for other first-generation low-income students at Davidson, and as a result, to address the systemic and historic inequalities that were present, Davidson intentionally sought out more students who had the dream of attending college and getting a top-notch education, but lacked the money or social capital to make it a reality.

Throughout my four years of enrollment at Davidson, I worked to change the mindsets and ingrained hate that I saw in students, faculty, and in some cases, within entire departments. This leads me to share the following story about the worst part of my undergraduate experience.

While a student at Davidson College, I received a letter from the institution that stated that I had not signed up for the college insurance. The letter went on to say that I had to opt-in and pay the insurance premium or opt-out by showing proof of insurance. If I did not provide proof of insurance or pay the premium, I would not be able to register for classes and would eventually be dropped from classes and not allowed to attend school. The thing was, I had health insurance, but it was Medicaid, an insurance 'company' the institution had never encountered at.

I knew that I could not call my mother and ask her for the money as she was struggling herself, and I cried because I knew that this would be yet another barrier in my path. I also did not call my mentor because I felt I had already asked her for too much, and unfortunately for me, my refund from financial aid was not scheduled to come for a few weeks so I did not know what I was going to do.

I sought advice from my hall counselor who had no clue of the seriousness of my dilemma, so I found my way to the Dean of Students who suggested I speak to the University President, President Bobby Vagt. By the time I met with President Vagt, he had already heard about my financial situation and made the decision to either pay or waive the fee for me (I am not sure what he did), but as a result, I was able to continue as a Davidson College student and able to enroll in the school health insurance plan for the duration of my time at the institution. Despite this victory, I had grown weary and was lost in despair during this time because no matter how hard I tried, something always seemed to get in my way. However, I shared this story to display one of the many stories of how the faculty and staff at Davidson took a vested interest and strongly believed in me when I did not believe in myself, at least not enough to keep fighting. Thus, there were members of the Davidson faculty and staff who were supportive along my journey, which at times, was difficult to navigate.

In the next few pages, I will highlight several incidences that demonstrate my educational journey and the importance of the roots and wings I possessed as I entered new territory and worked tirelessly to fight against institutionalized forms of inequality, injustices, and even micro-aggressions.

It was during interactions with others, as well as in times of isolation and in-trapersonal reflection, that I was able to initially articulate and make meaning of my identity. I had to define and examine, for myself, how I wanted to describe my identity as an African-American woman. It was challenging as I found myself often having more questions than answers. It was as if hearing my mentor's voice and being reminded of the wisdom that she planted in me helped me to recognize the importance of having roots to help me overcome obstacles and succeed in spite of the doubt and other obstacles that were placed in my path. I kept hearing my mentor's voice, something that she would always remind me: 'Trust in the Lord and lean not unto your own understanding.' I tried so many times to show strength so others would not think I was weak. I also found myself in daily battles with the external boundaries. Society challenged me as an African-American woman from my circumstances to stay and fit within this echelon of students whose culture I had now involuntarily become immersed in. I was angry, indecisive, but most of all, tired. I was angry because I found myself in isolation (almost invisible at times), often feeling as if I was the only one experiencing the journey of having to prove my worth and value as a woman of color in academia.

Consequently, finding a refuge among other people who understood my jour-ney became important as I experienced many emotions and even became de-pressed to the point where I wanted to give up. I began to question who I was and if I was truly where I needed to be. I was torn between being "too Black," "too hood," or "too ghetto" for the students of color, but not being white enough for the Whites. It was a draining process—living in two worlds and not fitting in either. I was tired of explaining myself to my family, peers, professors, etc.; tired of being perceived as the angry black woman; tired of being the only one to speak up in class and show up and mobilize others when there was a racist situation on campus. But most of all, I was tired of other people not understanding my experi-ence, including members of my immediate family.

My mentor who consistently provided me with the support that I needed to overcome my bouts with depression and doubt, always reminded me to remember who I am and whose I was. I came into college believing the environment was supposed to be a place where my mind would be challenged, where I would be nourished, my identity and purpose created, and where my interactions with oth-ers would lead to growth and development. I was longing for the "home" away from home and the nurturing environment that I so desperately needed to experi-ence.

I remember coming to Davidson College with a sheet, a pillow, a few pictures, some beat down binders, lead pencils, one suitcase of clothes, one used bar of soap, and a dream. As a young lady from my background, I could only hope that this new adventure in my life would be the turning point for me and allow me to pursue an advanced degree and have a chance at eventually getting out and securing a better paying job or opportunity. I admit that I did not know how to operate in this new environment, but one thing that I did know was how to use my resources to get what I needed. I knew how to survive. I knew that I could not afford to give up or give in. I knew I did not want to live paycheck to paycheck. I had to persist and succeed, despite any obstacles in my path. My roommate gave me a comforter, and several of my hallmates helped me out as my hall counselors realized my financial constraints and raised some money for me to buy items until my mom could get something else. It was a hard transition for me as I was around all of these people who had money or whose parents had money; here I was, sending care packages and money back home with the little money that I got back from financial aid refunds to help my mom out with my younger siblings. I often had to send home packages of nonperishable food items and money so that my family could make ends meet. While my classmates were having care packages sent to them, I was sending care packages home to help out as much as I could. My mother worked so hard to make sure that we had what we needed, but often we still went without so that we could have our basic needs met. In a way, I felt obligated to help out back home, but I also felt a little resentment.

I learned a lot considering the K–12 education that I received was mediocre compared to that of most of my peers with whom I was in class. Academically, I learned how to improve my writing and become a better student all around. One of the most disheartening experiences for me was when I wrote a paper my freshman year in my English class, and I was accused of plagiarizing by my professor and had to go before the Honor Council as a result. His grounds were that I spoke one way and that I did not write how I talked. It hurt me that this professor was so culturally insensitive. He did not try to sit down with me and ask me to write a sample for him, but instead automatically assumed that because I spoke "Ebonics" or used slang, that I was incapable of producing a product of that caliber. I remember telling him how much of a racist he was, and I vowed that I would not let that happen to others. So, I spent the next few years serving on the SGA (Student Government Association), creating and implementing various diversity initiatives on campus and on the west side of the town, using my platform in whatever organization I was a part of to create a community where people, young and old, embraced the differences of others. I let my voice be heard.

I remember being called into President Vagt's office. I thought that I was in some BIG trouble. After all, who gets a formal invitation to the president's office in the middle of the day? I remember walking in and being told that he had heard about how much I was rocking the boat on campus and in the community. I gulped and put my head down as my eyes began to tear up. I thought that he was going to tell me that I was facing suspension. He looked at me and immediately said, "I appreciate your courage to stand for what is right and your passion for promoting change. Please let me know if there is anything that I can do for you to help you with your endeavors. This is what this campus needs. I hope that you will continue to let the fire spark, but be careful that you do not let your emotions cause that fire to be so enraged that it consumes the cause that you are fighting for, and there is nothing but ashes left." I never believed that I could and would impact so much change on campus and in the community. I developed myself as a leader and a social change agent whose anger was transformed into action through passion and perseverance.

It was during these positive interactions that I received my wings, and hope was restored. I was given more motivation to continue my fight. I received some advice from Ruth Pittard, the Dean of Community Service at the time, who reminded me that I needed to seek to understand to be understood. I began to humble myself and turn my anger into action to serve others, and be transformed by my interactions. This transformative encounter was yet another incident in which I received another pair of "wings" and was able to soar as a leader on campus and use my experience and my identity to help educate others and promote social change on campus. I worked for several years in public service positions where I could make a difference and help others attain a sense of achievement and personal satisfaction in a society where the odds were stacked against them.

Be sure to give back and pay it forward in return for those people who have been integral in helping you nurture your potential. Remember who you are and whose you are when you start to doubt why you are where you are. Remember that you stand on the shoulders of giants who have come before you and who sacrificed so much to pave the way for future generations. Most importantly, remember where you came from, remember your purpose, and remember why you have been given a certain mountain to move. Never forget that you earned a seat at the table, so pull up a chair and get ready to eat!

CHAPTER 30

LIVING UP TO THE SILVER SPOON EXPECTATION

Keena D. Howell

Key Challenges: low teacher expectations, racism, low self-esteem

No, I am not a statistic that is portrayed by Hollywood or the traditional educational research on the teenage mother, high school dropout, or victim of poverty-stricken circumstances. I am an experienced educator pursuing my doctoral degree in educational leadership, married to an educated Black male, and mother of two children. My grandfather was a doctor, and both my father and older brother followed in his footsteps. In addition, my mother held a teaching degree, and I followed in her footsteps.

I am the second oldest of four children and the oldest girl of three daughters. Our traditional family was defined by society as middle-class suburbians. Our friends and extended family members referred to us as the Huxtables from the 1980s television show that portrayed an African American family which consisted of a father who was a physician and a mother, an attorney. This couple had four children who lived in a middle-class neighborhood.

I was raised in a home that held very high academic, intellectual, and professional expectations, and my parents strongly influenced and encouraged me to uphold the family legacy of excellence. At the age of four, my parents relocated our

A Second Helping of Gumbo for the Soul: More Liberating Stories and Memories to Inspire Females of Color, pages 127–130.

family from the inner city of Washington, D.C. to a suburb in Maryland, where they are still the only family of color who reside on that street after 45 years. My parents decided to live in this particular neighborhood to access the school district that would afford me the opportunity to gain more rigor than the schools located in the inner city.

As a young student of color, I learned early that I was different from my peers. It was me and two other girls who were the only students of color in the class out of thirty. Recess, lunch, and pairing up for group work were always uncomfortable, not to mention, my kindergarten teacher insisted on home visits to ensure that my family lived in the school attendance area. The more friends I made and the more frequent the play dates that I had at the homes of my peers and close friends, I began to realize how successful my parents were, in comparison. Unlike many of my friends, I did not receive free or reduced meals; I still lived with both parents and was held accountable if I broke any school rules.

My parents were very engaged in the educational process that I found to be essential during my senior year in high school. The transition to high school was eye-opening, and the racial makeup of teachers and the student demographic did not work well for several students, including myself. Regardless of the middle-class neighborhood where we lived, I believe many of my teachers held low expectations for students of color regarding our readiness for college. My counselor did her best to derail me from following my goal to be accepted into a college or university, which was not what my parents encouraged and expected. But, despite the behavior of my counselor's behavior, I was motivated to be successful (and continue to encourage other minority students and colleagues today).

As I continued to inquire about my career goals and interests as a senior in high school, it became apparent to me that my counselor did not have my best interest at heart. I remember scheduling a visit to the counseling office to request recommendations for college admissions as instructed by my parents, and when called to the office by my counselor, she suggested that I pursue transitioning into the military or a community college. These options, she suggested, may be appropriate for students that may not be ready academically or financially for a four-year school. However, my parents and I had other expectations for my life. My counselor never asked me anything about what I wanted to do or about my goals. I felt that she judged me by the color of my skin. She did not get to know my family, or me, and had she done so, she would have known that my father had three private offices and worked full-time as a senior physician at a local hospital. My parents always shared the importance of having a solid education to be able to support yourself and your surrounding community. My older brother was already a sophomore in college, and I was expected to have the same transition. Considering my foundation and roots, I did not have any other option after high school except to go on to college!

I still remember every word of the conversation with this counselor 25 years later! I was totally devastated and torn on how I would go home and tell my parents that I was not going to college. I cried when I got home because I was nervous, anxious, embarrassed and ashamed that I was no longer going to be able to meet my parents' expectations to go to college. Needless to say, when my father returned home late from work, I shared the news with him that I couldn't go to college because my counselor would not complete my recommendations. He immediately said, "I am taking you to school tomorrow, and we are meeting with your counselor." The next morning, we arrived in the counseling office to meet with her. My counselor reluctantly accommodated my dad's request to complete the recommendations for college. My counselor stated that she thought it would be a stretch for me to get accepted. I felt so proud and relieved to hear my dad say, "thank you and we will worry about the rest."

My father explained to me later after the meeting that things were the same when he came through school in the 1950s, and receiving an equal education was even more difficult. He shared that his father had the exact conversations with school staff members to ensure that he was being treated fairly. I believe it frustrated my dad more than me because he was also a victim of discrimination. The main reason for relocating our family to the suburbs was to avoid any difficulty or challenges with me and my siblings doing well in school.

Despite my negative high school experience, I completed my Bachelor's in Science and Master of Education from Howard University. I must say one of my best experiences was attending a Historically Black College which allowed me to interact with and be surrounded and supported by staff, peers, and a community that looks like me. Attending an HBCU was strongly encouraged by my father, not only because my grandfather and both parents attended Howard University, because it would also allow me to grow from the experiences that I encountered during my school-aged years in the suburbs.

My education has allowed me to serve in several roles as an educator over the past twenty years including classroom teacher, school counselor, college admissions officer, school administrator, central office specialist, and most importantly, my current role as a pupil personnel worker. All of these roles combined have allowed me to do what my parents did for me on a much larger scale for all students. I am an advocate for families, and I serve as a liaison between the community and the school district. I am also a consultant to school staff in reference to school law, procedures and policies as it relates to academic programming and decision making for students.

In one of my roles as a college admissions counselor, I was asked by the school district where I graduated to serve on a college panel for a parent workshop. As a participating member, I noticed that the individual that was leading the discussion panel was my former high school counselor! I could not believe this person was still in the position to work with children. After the panel discussion, I made a point to introduce myself to her as a former student. I informed her of the impact she left on my life and recalled the conversation in 1991 when she told me that I was not going to make it through a four-year college. She denied the conversation and stated that she would never express that to a student. I let her know that indeed she did, and I would never forget her words and then thanked her for giving me the motivation to be the educator that I am today. It was amazing to me how all of the weight that I carried throughout my educational and work career from her doubt was lifted from me after I let her know that I had made it through school and held the same credentials as her!

In 2009, I suffered a stroke. It was then that I realized that I tried to compensate for poor self-esteem and confidence both at work and home, which seemed to be common for most working moms, single or married. My body was letting me know that I needed to slow down. I believe trying to prove to society that I would not be a statistic, stemmed from my experience from my high school counselor, but God gave me another chance to stay on my path, this time, with a different perspective, doing what was important to me. I continue to work with organizations such as my sorority, my church and local and national education associations to provide parents, students and leaders information that will directly impact minority youth and their families.

Professionally, I am at the end phase of completing my doctoral degree in educational leadership in my quest to continue to be a more informed voice for students and parents. I hope to offer my services to families who do not have an advocate to assist them in navigating through school procedures. In addition, I plan to be a major game player when it comes to creating and changing policies that impact decisions on school discipline as it relates specifically to students of color in grades kindergarten through 12.

Message: My family instilled in me to work hard at everything. I carry on this philosophy with my kids and students I serve. Not everyone you encounter will have your best interest at heart including home, work or community organizations. Also, besides working hard, make sure that you have a healthy balance of faith, family, friends, and finances!

CHAPTER 31

FINDING PURPOSE

Javetta Jones Roberson

Key Challenges: gifted and talented, student loss, resilience

I come from a family of "firsts." My parents were the first to receive both Bachelor and Master's Degrees in our family. My dad was the first Black head football coach and athletic director for a high school in Dallas, Texas. My mom became the first Black teacher and cheerleading sponsor for a predominantly White middle school in Lancaster, Texas. This occurred in the early 1970s during a time in the south where racial disparities and injustices were heightened. For two Black kids who grew up in poverty, I'd say they didn't do too badly for themselves. And with me…well, I've followed in their footsteps—just a little. In 2016, I became the first Black Dean of Instruction at a high school in the Dallas Fort Worth Metroplex area. Yes, Black people are still making "firsts" in the 21st century. We've come a long way, but have so much more to go.

You could say that learning was always in my blood. Growing up with parents who were teachers and leaders in the community caused me to not only value education, but also be a spotlight for education within the community. As a coach, Daddy brought kids home all the time, and Mama mentored students on a regular basis. But they always had time and made time for my two older brothers and me. I can remember every summer going on a vacation and every holiday is a big deal.

A Second Helping of Gumbo for the Soul: More Liberating Stories and Memories to Inspire Females of Color, pages 131–135.

Family, friends, and students of my parents would celebrate birthdays and special occasions with us for as long as I can remember. I loved growing up in a house that had a sense of community. A sense of togetherness. A sense of Black Pride. My parents magnified the blessing of being Black in the South and America in general. They always wanted us to be proud of who we were. They did not want us to change who we were for anyone. In other words, they wanted us to be authentic in every sense of the word by serving those in need but humbling ourselves in a way to identify with the struggle. They wanted us to realize that every breath was a blessing, not a right. However, I realized the blessing of life the most after my Dad died. The life lessons my father taught were priceless. But, some life lessons, including the blessing of life, was a lesson that I had to learn on my own.

Upon graduating from college, I began teaching in a high poverty-stricken area. I knew my purpose was to teach in neighborhoods such as this because I felt the students needed me and that I could offer them what they would get if we were in an affluent area. I made it my life's mission to only serve students who were educated within these areas, and I loved it. The children and the community became "my kids" and "my parents" and my fellow colleagues became my family because somehow, working in a high need environment for a high purpose, caused us to ban together.

During my first year of teaching, I began working on my Master's Degree and started conducting Gifted Education professional development opportunities at the district level. Within my first two years of teaching, things began to blossom. I did encounter obstacles, including almost not being able to graduate due to the principal in my building, not believing that I was "ready to be a principal or assistant principal." She prohibited me from doing my internship on campus, which was a requirement for me to graduate! You can only imagine how I felt being told by my institution that I was ready for a practicum, only to be told by my "boss" that "You're too young right now…you need to wait ten years like me in order to be in leadership." Honestly, I believe she wanted me to grow as a leader, but she was not equipped with any other words or actions to use at that time. Luckily, I had made enough connections within the school district to complete my internship at a school 3 minutes away from my teaching campus, and I graduated during my second year of teaching. The ambition was in my blood. During that time, I wanted to transition into a leadership capacity and advocate for diverse populations on a state and national level, and I knew that earning the degree would increase those odds.

I continued to teach on that campus and eventually become the On-Campus Gifted and Talented (GT) Coordinator. I am a firm believer that every child has untapped potential, and it is the educator's job to foster and hone their abilities to bring it to the forefront so that students can shine effortlessly. I worked in a neighborhood where parents hadn't graduated from high school; students would turn in homework on the back of food stamp applications; parents and family members were in and out of jail; the only meals students would eat would be from school, irate parents on drugs who were manipulated by students who told them, "the teacher doesn't like me... go cuss her out!"; there were major community and parent involvement issues within the school; child abuse and abandonment... the list goes on. With these circumstances, many people would not believe that smart, bright, or "Gifted" kids attended this school. However, I knew better, my colleagues knew better, and even my new principal knew better. Therefore, I continued to serve in this capacity, working with a dynamic and diverse group of kids, identifying them as Gifted and Talented all while still teaching classes.

During the summer of my last year of teaching, however, drastically changed my life. It did something to me, my career, and my purpose for the better and worst. During this time, I was still a GT Coordinator and teaching 4th grade. This particular year, I looped up with my kids, which meant that I went from one grade to the next grade with the same kids. As you can guess, I drew extremely attached to these kids. This was especially prevalent for a young 10-year-old named Eddie. Eddie was mild-mannered, funny and liked by many kids. I previously taught his sister, who had a demeanor that was not as positive, so it was refreshing to learn about another member of the family. Eddie loved science. He loved experiments and learning about the solar system and volcanoes. He was always excited when it was time to do project-based learning in science. Eddie had wonderful penmanship, and his writings kept the reader engaged. Within his writing, the imagery in his stories was impeccable. But math...that was another story. Math was a struggle for Eddie. Even though I did not teach math, the team teacher kept me informed of the status of all the kids.

Eddie's writing and high interest in science caused me to nominate him for Gifted and Talented testing. In Texas, you must have parental permission to complete the nomination process for gifted testing. I only met Eddie's mother towards the end of the previous year due to her being incarcerated; therefore, I only had contact with the Aunt, Sister, or Grandmother. Eddie's mother was a Black woman who had a muscular medium build and tattoos on her neck. When I first met her, she had on Jordan Sneakers and sweatpants. I never judge a book by its cover... but to me, this woman was intimidating. She came to the school during the first week of classes and said to me with no smile and a straight face, "Ms. Jones, I'm Eddie's Mama. What does Eddie need and what do you need for the classroom?" I was shocked! It was rare for parents to offer to help with things in the classroom as I purchased school supplies, Kleenex, etc. It was so refreshing to have her help me out. When she brought the supplies the next day, she said, "Let me know if you need anything else. I'll be staying on Eddie about his homework and schoolwork." I replied "Thank you so much for helping. I appreciate you for this and you know I'll keep in touch about Eddie." The weeks went on, and the assessment window for Gifted was coming to a close. I realized, as I was gathering documents I did not have Eddie's paperwork. So, I called his mama. She expressed to me she had never gone to college and didn't know anything about Gifted nor what it meant. I told her to come to the school, and I'd explain everything to her. She was apprehensive at first, thinking if Eddie was identified as Gifted, he'd have more work to do. But still, she came to meet with me, and I appreciated her transparent spirit. She talked about her struggles in life and with school, and how she didn't want that for Eddie stating "That's why I stay on him. Stop playing in class, listen to your teacher and do your work. I do it with him sometimes." Once I explained the value in him possibly being identified especially as a Black male, she signed without hesitation, and I was able to continue with the process. Sometimes you have to learn the background of a situation before you jump to conclusions. She needed to understand the process, and I needed to understand her apprehension. From there, we continued to stay in contact.

Eddie was tested, and according to our district's matrix, his scores fell in the "Talent Pool" area. This meant that his scores were high in Verbal but low in Quantitative (Math). I informed his mom that he could test next year to see if he qualified for Gifted and she obliged with no hesitation. She thanked me for helping Eddie and for everything in general. Throughout the year, Eddie's mom and sister would pick him up from tutoring, participate in our literacy nights, and remain active in our school community.

I always held a class party at the end of the school year. During this time, kids were allowed to bring food and goodies to share, and I would do the same. As always, Eddie's mother brought something for the class as well, and we had a great time. We decided that it was best for Eddie to attend summer school for math, but he was still filled with excitement for the coming of summer. I taught summer school that year, so I was able to continue to interact with Eddie, and when summer school ended, Eddie waved and yelled out "Bye Mrs. Jones." I replied "Bye baby. Have a good summer." But little did I know, that would be the last time I saw Eddie.

My team and I received a telephone call in June of 2014 while we were in Washington, D.C. at a school conference. The purpose of this conference was to prepare all teachers and administrators for the upcoming school year. The call came from a parent of a child I taught the previous year. She stated that Eddie had been shot and killed by his sister's boyfriend. The boyfriend also killed Eddie's mother and Eddie's sister, who was eight-months pregnant. I was hysterical. I was in shock. And I couldn't stop screaming. How could this happen? How could you kill a family? How could you kill your unborn child? And why my Eddie? Why a mama whose only mission straight from jail was to help her children succeed in school and in life? I just didn't understand. I called my Mama after I had somewhat calmed down. I said, "Mama...how did you and Daddy do this? How did y'all deal with the death of a student? You both taught for 30 years...this wasn't hard?" My mama replied, "Baby, losing a student is a pain indescribable. You never forget your first student you lose." She went on to tell me the story of her first student and my Dad's and how they coped with it. "You just have to know your purpose. Be a blessing to these kids and these families, because you never know." From that point on, nothing made sense anymore. Depression became deeply embedded in my everyday life. I felt helpless. I felt broken. And I didn't want to teach or lead anymore. I figured that if I left teaching, I wouldn't have to experience this pain ever again. When I got home, I had the chance to speak to my mother again, and she mentioned the word "purpose." I started to read scriptures and words of encouragement for women and teachers. I then began to realize that purpose is a hell of a thing in any profession. You have to understand and recognize your purpose in life. My purpose was to help kids, help teachers, help families, and advocate for diverse populations. Purpose is embedded into your character and what makes you who you are. I knew my purpose from that point on in life and in my career. I knew I needed to continue to work with students and families from all backgrounds. I knew I needed to teach educators how to work with diverse students and families. I knew I needed to lead. I knew I needed to advocate on a large platform for these populations, and I knew I needed to live through this tragedy to help others be triumphant in their roles. Purpose.

Always understand you were created for a divine destiny. A destiny others may not understand. A destiny you may not understand. But in time, you will know. You will grow. And from that, you will live a purposeful life deemed strictly for you. Eddie, his mom, and his sister, led me to my purpose and now, the only time I look back is to reflect. Education is evolving. I am evolving, and I must continue to advocate when no one else will. Especially for my Eddie.

CHAPTER 32

THERE'S A BULLY IN
MY PH.D. PROGRAM

Defusing Imposter Syndrome
Perpetuated by Others and Self

Tammy Lane

Key Challenges: imposter syndrome; academic bullying; discrimination, competition

The pinnacle of my educational aspirations was acceptance into a doctoral program. I entered full of energy and enthusiasm, with a million ideas that soon turned to self-doubt, feeling stressed and unwelcomed. In spite of my high achievement and notable accomplishments, I found myself being confronted by bullies who perpetuated Imposter Syndrome within me. A phenomenon coined in the 1970s by psychologists Suzanne Imes and Pauline Rose Clance, Imposter Syndrome is commonly experienced by high achievers who are rendered the inability to internalize and accept their successes as valid. Imposter Syndrome causes individuals not to appreciate their accomplishments, and to see their successes as luck and not talent. They fear being exposed or unmasked as a charlatan. In society or situations where there is immense pressure to succeed, no one is excluded from

A Second Helping of Gumbo for the Soul: More Liberating Stories and Memories to Inspire Females of Color, pages 137–141.
Copyright © 2020 by Information Age Publishing
137

developing this extreme case of self-doubt, especially folks of color. In their 2013 study, Cokley, Mcclain, Enciso, and Martinez found that people of color were notably vulnerable to Imposter Syndrome.

Furthermore, although once thought to be experienced more by women, both women and men fall victim to the imposter phenomenon. Imposter Syndrome is often self-inflicted; however, other factors can compound these fraudulent feelings and is exactly what I experienced in my Ph.D. program. It was inconceivable to me that bullies existed in graduate school; furthermore, I had no idea one of my bullies would come in the form of a professor.

For the sake of privacy, I will refer to the professor as Dr. Lee. Specifically, Dr. Lee's research denounced educators who failed to recognize the potential in Black students. She publicly called out educators who showed evidence of a lack of cultural proficiency and a deficit mentality. In contrast to Dr. Lee's rants on cultural responsiveness, she was guilty of weeding out Ph.D. students who did not "fit the bill." Her expectations reflected that of racial biases because, as far as she was concerned, Black scholars needed to prove they had the juice to compete with White scholars. Through her observation during one of two classes, I was scrutinized and labeled a not-so-worthy student. There was no doubt that my scholastic abilities were impeccable, my undergraduate and graduate grade point averages were near perfect, so I asked why? She indicated that to be deemed 'worthy' meant performing well to impromptu presentations, otherwise my inclusion in such an exclusive club of scholars was questionable. On another occasion, she was flustered when I asked her to clarify a statement she made about qualitative methodology, which contradicted what had just been taught to me and my other cohort members in the previous semester by a different professor. Dr. Lee became defensive and informed me of her 20 plus years of experience in which I knew at that point my presence agitated her tremendously. Dr. Lee shamed me in class for not being a spontaneous presenter, and that day was just one embarrassment of many, that is, until I took control of my destiny. I realized I was fighting a losing battle trying to reason with Dr. Lee, and that it would serve me well to stay encouraged, change my thinking, recognize my expertise, rely on my mentors' support, and continue to excel.

Next, my second bully, which I will refer to as Gina, was more of a surprise because I believed that students at the graduate level were more interested in academic collaboration, and at the least that they were mature. Gina and I shared a few commonalities. We were members of the same cohort in my doctoral program, and we both demonstrated equal eagerness and passion for education, leadership, and marginalized students. Surreptitiously we seem to bond; however, I realized my bully's appreciation for me was disingenuous. In spite of my cohort member's disdain for me, early on I somehow felt she deserved forgiveness because none of us were perfect.

POWER, ENVY, AND INTIMIDATION

Overall, I found my Ph.D. program's cohort model to be beneficial because there was a camaraderie shared like no other between twenty plus individuals with similar goals supporting each other while learning and confronting challenges along an arduous journey. I had no idea competition and jealousy was brewing and would raise its ugly head in the form of childish antics. I was hungry absorbing all the advice I could from professors who encouraged me to do more than just come to class. I believed my professors when they advised us doctoral students to seek opportunities in conjunction with the program's requirements. As time went on, 99.9% of my professors and colleagues praised my work, and the more I took advantage of research, publishing, presentations, conferences, and various networking opportunities, "hatorade" began to flow my way.

At one point, Gina doubled down with the antagonism. I was being heckled during my participation in class discussions and presentations. Gina gossiped about my clothes, my hair, my accent, my pronunciation of words, and my obvious trepidation. She even tried to recruit cronies, who would eventually fall victim to her pompousness. Whereas I entered the program full of confidence, I did not enjoy class anymore. I began to ponder whether I was good enough to be in the program. I wondered if I was a fraud. I found myself sparsely participating in class, fearing that my responses or contributions would be seen as irrelevant or subjected snickering. I stopped sharing about projects that I was involved in out of fear of being labeled a showoff.

Neither of my perpetrators had any idea of my personal struggles or resilience, which will be revealed in the future, and had the audacity to ostracize me! I was at a tipping point, so I sought the advice of two peers with whom I developed a sincere relationship and who had been observers of the intimidation. With sureness, both would be honest and give a fair assessment of behaviors from both bullies in addition to my inadequacies. It was obvious to those on the outside looking in that the lack of leadership, the abuse of power, social awkwardness, as well as this phenomenon of Imposter Syndrome were the main factors at the root of my experiences with two seemly well-rounded scholars. As for my shortcomings, well let's just say, I was not alone. I gained a multitude of insight about my bullies from this horrific experience.

WHAT I DISCOVERED ABOUT THE BULLIES

I discovered several things about my bullies. I would later learn that Dr. Lee delighted in creating an environment of intimidation and hazing of doctoral students. She did not subscribe to the notion similar to other academics who were marginalized in pursuit of the professoriate and who vowed to mentor and support those seeking the same path. Dr. Lee believed in supporting only those who she deemed worthy of acceptance in a select club, those who demonstrated the ability to measure up to standards set by Whites elites. In other words, although she spoke against White supremacy, she exuded tendencies of a "Negropean" a term used frequently by educational scholar Dr. Donna Y. Ford. It turns out that I was just another prey in her battle of confusion about her own identity. Dr. Lee perpetuated in me her own conflict with Imposter Syndrome.

Similar to Dr. Lee, Gina enjoyed a sense of control and power over others. In her career, she was once in a position of authority, and was often recognized for her competitive nature. Her competitive nature and envious spirit transposed to our Ph.D. program. It was challenging for her to see me applauded and admired. In fact, bullying me gave her that charge and rush of being in power. She yearned for attention and validation and relished attention even if it was negative. She also presented herself in ways, which I will not mention, to gain attention from a certain persuasion, and such behavior pointed to someone deeply confused about her own self-worth. Furthermore, countless conflicts between Gina and others in and outside of the classroom suggested she had faced in her life nothing short of pandemonium. I am positive that she felt as much of an imposter as I felt about myself.

UNDERSTANDING MY BULLIES AND FIXING ME

Bullies will never vanish. They are always lurking, waiting to inject others with their uncertainties whether it be in the classroom, workplace, etc. What is important is how to combat situations that threaten our endeavors. One must be accountable for their actions and feelings. Finally, I recognized that no one had the power to stand in my way except for me; in other words, I had to get the bullies and their frolics "out of my head." I took back the power that I had given my bullies. I had to embrace my feelings of Imposter Syndrome to understand my value to education, leadership, my doctoral program, my colleagues, as well as my bullies. I had to define what I was feeling in order to teach myself how to cope with the situation as well as future feelings of inadequacy. I reminded myself of all that I had accomplished and the hard work put forth to achieve my goals. I reminded myself of the loss of family, friends, sleep, leisure, and other sacrifices made in order to embark on a journey that was so near and dear to me. I dared not to allow myself to cop-out because I couldn't cope with criticism or erroneous feelings of fraud. I refused to sabotage myself. Consequently, had I not taken control of my downward spiral, the negativity would have resulted in me not reaching my maximum potential and not to mention a win for my naysayers. Instead of succumbing to a negative cycle perpetuated by self or others, I chose to embrace my good, bad and ugly, and to share my experiences in hope of helping someone who might find himself or herself in a similar place.

A FEW SIGNIFICANT WORDS OF WISDOM

As I came to terms with my case of Imposter Syndrome, understanding the constant agitation of my bullies, and the need to fix me, I acquired wisdom and understanding to share with those who find themselves in similar situations. I realized that antagonism is a saboteur of focus. We should never be consumed with the aggressions of others because doing so assures the loss of focus. It is vital to one's success to confront and seek a resolution to distractions in order to remain focused or to regain focus. Always concentrate on your purpose and revisit your goals to make sure your actions align with them. Next, it's imperative to recognize self-limiting talk and thoughts and to seek help from mentors, friends, family, and professional counsel if necessary. Lastly, love who you are and never give power to an oppressor. Be the best at who you were born to be, always having compassion and be willing to make a difference and help improve the lives of others. Most of all—live to educate and create an even playing field for underserved students.

Let me do a quick stir, girl.

I don't want it to burn it 'cause if it do, it will be a waste of time, and it smells so divine.

Let me do a quick stir and let me get a quick taste.

Ooo, it's so good...I don't even care if it goes to my waist.

So, let me do a quick stir.

—*Michelle Frazier Trotman Scott*

CHAPTER 33

IT WAS NECESSARY

Positioning or Punishing

Tiffany Y. Lane

Key Challenges: loss and grief, self-doubt; perseverance

The lyrics "Every trial you've been through happened for a reason, it was to build you" from Dennis Reed & Gap's (2014) song entitled *Necessary* clearly describes my experiences leading up to the loss of my mother and earning my doctorate. This song is a true testament of my journey to purpose and position...my journey toward earning a doctoral degree began in the fall of 2009.

I was accepted into an amazing program and was ready to embrace the experience. With the exception of my boyfriend at the time, my friends and family were supportive. Despite being aware of my acceptance into the Ph.D. program, on the first day of class, my boyfriend casually said, "You are doing too much." He said that because he felt that I should be satisfied with my Master's degree. At that moment, I reflected back to when we first met. I told him that I wanted to pursue a Doctorate in Social Work. He would even greet me as Dr. Lane from time to time, and so you can imagine how his unsupportive statement blew my mind. I was bamboozled. My nonverbal reply to his statement was a complex look, yet inside it ignited doubt—could I start over? How would this work considering the

A Second Helping of Gumbo for the Soul: More Liberating Stories and Memories to Inspire Females of Color, pages 143–147.

fact that I paid $1000 to break the lease on my apartment to move into his home? Where would I go? I quit my full-time job because he and I agreed that I would be responsible for the household groceries and my bills. Still, I left that morning, after his comment, and went to my first day of classes; and I was hooked! I was excited to begin the Ph.D. journey. After I left class that day, I called my mother and excitingly told her how things went; however, I didn't part my lips to tell her about my earlier conversation with my boyfriend.

In spite of my personal values and the many lessons learned, I briefly experienced self-doubt when he spoke negatively against my pursuit of a Ph.D. At the time I thought if I ignored his comment that things would get better. As stated earlier, I decided against telling my mother about my boyfriend's negative comment. But, ironically, he beeped in on my phone line while I was still talking to my mom about my first day of classes. When I enthusiastically greeted him, and he replied, "I don't think that we are compatible. "I simply replied, "ok" and ended the call.

What was there to say? Was this the same guy I met three years ago? All I could do is cry in the car heading back to his house. I felt like a fool. The reality was, if I were not in school we would carry on as a couple. As I cried, I thought about how much I wanted to pursue my goals. How dare this fraud stand in my way?

By the time I arrived my tears were dried up. I made up my mind that I wasn't going to beg him to understand my position. I asked him to give me a week or two to figure out where I was going to live. He became irritated, emotionally abusive, and literally tried to make the next day's feel like hell. I called my mom a few days later and told her what occurred. She remained calm and was at his house in an hour with three of my male cousins in tow, and they began to move my items into the truck. The first thing my mother said was "You can stay with me, and we will figure the space issue out." Honestly, I did not want to move in with her because she was raising my three male cousins. I wanted my privacy, but I had no money for an apartment because I quit my full-time job. I reluctantly surrendered, but I felt like a failure that had lost so much in a short period of time.

My mother's experiences with men were very complex. I don't know her full story, but I knew she was a domestic violence survivor prior to meeting my father. I am her only child, and she always made it clear that I should not allow anyone, especially a man, get in the way of my dreams and goals. She was a tough and refined woman, who was purposeful in her teachings and interactions with me until her last breath. She exemplified and instilled the importance of self-love, purpose and a strong work ethic, which has directed my path in all aspects of my life.

REGROUP

Regroup became my new word after moving out and ending the relationship with my boyfriend. I moved some of my belongings into one bedroom and placed the rest of my items in my mother's basement. I adjusted to the living situation, and things were going well. I successfully completed the first semester of my Ph.D. program and was teaching as an adjunct instructor at local colleges.

Early in my second semester, I called my mom for my daily check-in. When I asked her where she was, she stated that she was in the emergency room. I responded, "As a patient?" because she worked in a hospital, so I was unsure. She told me that her foot was swollen, but not to worry. But, I was agitated because although we had a very close relationship, she did not bring it up when I saw her earlier that morning. Nonetheless, I trusted her response, but in reality, things were not ok. Although my mother was strong, from that day forth, I intuitively became even stronger for her, as her battle with right heart failure and sarcoidosis began.

POSITIONING OR PUNISHING

All I could think at the doctor's office was, "Why us?" I barely got over one hurdle when I was presented with the shock of my life. I instantly told myself that I would put my Ph.D. program on hold and figure things out! But my mother said, "Absolutely not!" She made such a big scene when I told her my plan that I decided to stay in the program. I am thankful she encouraged me to continue on, but at the time, I did not understand her perspective. I was her only child and was now the caretaker for my mother and, for a short period of time, my three cousins that she was raising. What was I to do? For a few months, I was able to maintain taking her to all of her doctor's appointments, teach three courses, drive to class and complete schoolwork. But I would often ask God why I was being punished and how could this happen to us? My mother was physically weak, and I couldn't do anything to help her breathe. The disease was taking over her body quickly, and I was scared; she was all that I knew.

I would act strong when I was around her, our family and her doctors, but privately I cried each day. As she declined, she had to unwillingly give up her power as the mom. I had to portray the strong woman that she raised me to be, and say no to self-doubt and yes to strength. I vividly remember the day that I had to really step up. She sounded like she was choking, so I went into her bedroom. Upon entering, I could smell an odor but could not pinpoint what it was. As I started to walk out of the bedroom, I saw a washbowl full of urine underneath her bed. When I pulled it out, some spilled on the floor, and she got upset. She screamed at me and said she would get it. But then, I saw more pans under the bed and began to cry and screamed back her "You can't do it, and it's ok! I will clean it up." We both cried, but I kept moving and cleaned it up. Her facial expression was unforgettable—she looked helpless and tired. I was scared at that moment but realized my resilience and purpose. Although I had a heavy load with school and teaching, it was a joy to get her ready in the morning, take her to her doctor's appointments and go out on lunch dates. I knew that God positioned me to take care of my mother and it was an honor to serve her in that capacity.

My path was necessary. If I had not moved in with her, I wouldn't have known the extent of her illness. She was prideful. A situation had to occur so that I could move into my mother's home, and someone had to test my faith so that I could emerge as an unwavering woman and scholar. My mom died the semester prior to my comprehensive exam. She tried to hold on, but it was not necessary. What was necessary occurred; I was positioned to be more powerful and grateful than I could have ever imagined. My mother's transition broke me for a while—I was depressed and at one point contemplated suicide. But eventually, I recognized that I underwent a transformation due to my adversities and blessings, and I earned my Ph.D. a year and a half after her death. During my commencement ceremony, I shed tears because of her absence, the many lessons she taught and her unconditional love.

Some clear lessons that I learned from this experience were to trust the process. I questioned so many situations along the way but realized that they had to happen to support my growth and build my personal and professional muscle. It prepared me for the next level and helped me to understand that there were multiple ways to get to an end. I wanted to quit school to take care of my mother because that's what we typically do in the African American community. My mom clearly knew my potential, and her resistance pushed me to another level of creativity to manage and tackle all of my responsibilities. In overcoming the many tests that I faced, I am more resilient, protective, persistent and confident. So, trust your process and endure in the face of challenges and obstacles. I embrace challenges as they come now and enjoy the process of taking them head-on.

In one of Pastor Sarah Jacob Robert's sermons (*Cold Season*, 2016), she asked a mind-blowing question—"If you feel that you can't stand the test of adversities, how are you going to hold blessings that come with being chosen?" This symbolic question brought it all together as I reflected on the challenges I've faced, as well as my many blessings. Through months of reflection, I realized my breakup with my ex-boyfriend steered me to my mother's doorstep. I was sent to take care of her, and she inspired me to complete my Ph.D. program and confidently walk into my purpose. Although the experience of taking care of my mother, her death, and completing my studies was not easy, it empowered me to trust the process and instilled in me the importance of self-reflection.

While trusting the process and participating in self-reflection, it is important to actively work toward finding meaning and fulfilling your goals. Think about your short- and long-term goals. Write them down. Consider posting your goals in a place that you frequent in your home and or workplace, or write them in a journal that you use often. Actively work toward your goals and know that challenges may come your way, but constant reminders of your goals will empower you to work towards your purpose. As well, begin the process of mindfulness as a form of self-reflection. Mindfulness is the capacity of being completely present, conscious of where you are in life and in the moment, and what you are actually doing. Consistent self-reflection and mindfulness are vital to growth and in understanding your obstacles and triumphs in the larger context of your circumstances. While practicing mindfulness, it is important not to become overpowered by what's going on around you. Create space and time to meditate about who you are as a woman, as it will help you see situations more clearly. I reflect daily, in my car, on my way to work and also in bed before I go to sleep at night; I've cried, laughed and had full conversations alone. It's essential to be intentional about self-reflection and to be open to feelings of doubt, confusion, shame, joy, and even "aha" moments. These emotions are part of the process and necessary for growth and having an understanding of who you are in the world and your purpose.

In addition to mindfulness and self-reflection, I had to be honest about my feelings and what I needed. Too often, people are not honest with themselves, which can be a major barrier to genuine mindfulness and ultimately finding purpose. Days after my mother's death, I told my family and friends that I was ok and didn't need loss and grief counseling. I even went back to school a week after the funeral. But I was not honest with myself nor with my family and friends. After multiple emotional breakdowns following my mother's death, I recognized that I needed to seek help. The misleading belief is that "strong" people don't need help and support to get through difficult situations. Today, I'm an emotionally healthy, strong African American woman; however, I didn't arrive in this space without support. My social supports are amazing, and they supported my growth. So yes, you have to do the work, but seek social and professional supports when needed. In moving toward purpose, count on people who genuinely support you and your process.

One key thing that I practice as a result of ending an unhealthy relationship and losing my mother is being unapologetic about who I am—meaning that my dreams, thoughts, actions, and experiences matter. So often we give up who we are to please others. Take time for yourself and protect your space because it is necessary for growth and alignment. After my mom died, I noticed that I was less tolerant of people taking up my time and energy. This was mainly because I was grieving and needed space, and unbeknownst to me at the time, I was being positioned to rebuild and meet my purpose. Be unapologetic and fearless in your pursuit to finding your purpose and meeting your goals. Take steps toward this practice, it takes time to achieve, but it can be done. Be encouraged and intentional about change, trust the process and remember that trials are necessary for growth, self-discovery and to be positioned.

REFERENCES

Jacobs Roberts, S. (2016). *Cold season* [Sermon]. Retrieved from https://www.youtube.com/watch?v=zw76G70B7uU

Reed, D. (2014). *Necessary* [Recorded by Dennis Reed & Gap]. On Water Walker [Medium of recording]. Twinsburg, Ohio: SBJ Anointed Productions.

CHAPTER 34

BIRTHING PAINS

How I Became a Theatre Director

Sharrell D. Luckett

Key Challenges: peer pressure, rejection, resilience

I am about to share with you my most humiliating and equally rewarding theatre experience which altered my career path in the arts —a time when I 'let go and let God.' It is my wish that this essay will serve as inspiration for young artists who have an interest in the arts but are not sure what area of the arts they should focus. As one will see, I trusted the process and the journey to becoming a theatre director. Though the path that would eventually lead me to my career was a difficult one, I would not re-work history. I now understand that struggle often leads to triumph.

I was born and reared in Atlanta, GA in a two-parent, middle-class household. Both my mother and father worked hard to provide a loving and stable environment for my two siblings and me. In elementary and middle school, I often excelled in English and mathematics, but it wasn't until high school that I discovered my love for the arts. At the age of 14, I enrolled in a performing arts high school in Georgia. This program proved challenging because it trained teens to have competitive, albeit humble spirits. Competition can be healthy, but my peers

A Second Helping of Gumbo for the Soul: More Liberating Stories and Memories to Inspire Females of Color, pages 149–151.
Copyright © 2020 by Information Age Publishing

and I wanted to be Broadway stars and movie stars. And we quickly understood that the road to stardom meant being cast in the school plays and musicals so we could sharpen our acting skills. At this time, I truly believed that I wanted to be an actress, but during my first year in the performing arts program, I often surfaced as a leader in theatre in areas other than acting. For instance, my classmates and I would hang out after school and perform some of the scripts that I had written, and they would allow me to tell them where to move on the stage and help them through their acting process. I enjoyed being an informal director but still also wanted to be an actress. However, it seemed that when I auditioned for theatre class projects or the season plays during my freshman and sophomore years, I was cast in the ensemble, or not cast at all.

Competition from the upperclassmen was fierce. They could sing, act, and dance all at once, while the newer cohort that I was a part of would often cower under their talent. Because the drama teacher, Mr. Henry, was directing a play with a very small cast, he asked an upperclassman to direct another play that the freshmen could audition for and be automatically cast in. After the required auditions for the upperclassmen play, the cast list was posted. Oddly enough, I was the only freshman out of about 25 students that were not cast. I was upset, to say the least.

Mr. Hendry did not force the upperclassman to put me in the play; rather he ushered me into the rehearsal space with him and instructed me to sit in the audience. He didn't know what to do with me, so he told me to simply sit. I was humiliated and embarrassed. All of my friends were in the upperclassmen play and I had to sit quietly in the theatre during the rehearsal period for the main play. Since I was upset about not being cast in the other play, I did exactly what Mr. Hendry instructed me to do and observed him direct a show. The painful incident of rejection actually led me on a journey where I further explored and accepted my passion for the arts: theatre directing. While my friends only knew of the art of acting, I learned the art of both acting and directing from watching Mr. Hendry work. I eventually emerged as a leader in my high school's drama program, directing short plays and co-producing a theatre talent show.

Through rejection, the universe isolated me with a great instructor working with and training actors who would eventually become Broadway stars. My young mind watched as Mr. Hendry blocked, re-blocked, and blocked some more. Blocking are the movements, such as walking and sitting, that actors do on stage. I also watched Mr. Hendry create stage pictures, conduct table work, and improve characterization. By age 17, I had experienced several shows from the page to the stage, directed by Mr. Hendry, and had also observed productions by the Freddie Hendricks Youth Ensemble of Atlanta, his professional theatre company for teens. An artistic visionary swept me away into a world of engagement and leadership.

When I was in the 11th grade, Mr. Hendry departed the drama program, so my peers and I wanted to produce our own show. I remember that moment so clearly. We were all sitting in the theatre and talking about writing a show and performing it—our eyes glossy, looking at one another, trying to figure out who could lead the rehearsal process. Finally, I raised my hand and said, "I can direct if you all are willing to listen to me." They agreed, and I officially became a director at 16 years old. I took my first risk in the theatre by declaring that I could direct.

Mr. Hendry continued directing and training actors who later came to be Tony-nominated Sahr Ngaujah (*FELA!*), Broadway actress Saycon Sengbloh (*Motown, FELA!, Wicked, Eclipsed*), and Kenan Thompson (*Saturday Night Live*); and scores more who have gone on to do great works in the theatrical and film arenas.

TRUST THE JOURNEY

This experience of rejection changed me. Because I chose to allow the universe to direct my path in what at first seemed negative, I found my 'calling.' My job as the audience member was the job that birthed the director in me. Because I did not act negatively when I was rejected by the upperclassmen, I was able to pick up a new skill that would prove useful in my immediate future. I was changed in ways that I am now aware of and ways I am still discovering nearly 20 years later.

Currently, I am a professional theatre director and a teacher of the craft, having directed and taught in Atlanta, New York, and Los Angeles. After I began directing in high school, I continued to act and direct in college. These leadership roles helped me land a job as a high school theatre director and teacher. After spending a few years in the classroom, I decided to pursue my doctorate in Theatre, receiving a full scholarship to the University of Missouri-Columbia (Mizzou). At Mizzou, I continued to direct and flourished as a serious artist and scholar. Directly after graduation, I was selected as the Guest Artist in Residence at SUNY-Potsdam's Lougheed-Kofoed Festival of the Arts, where I directed *Ruined,* a play written by two-time Pulitzer Prize winner Lynn Nottage. Soon after, I began a successful career as a college theatre and performance studies professor. I have had the privilege of presenting my research at Harvard University, Cornell University, Princeton University, Spelman College, and Marymount Manhattan College, to name a few. So, when one asks how I approach and respond to life's challenges, I reply that the way I react to life can strip me down and make me whole again at the same time. I have learned to trust myself and to sit quietly after I feel like I've done all I can to rectify an uncomfortable situation. Patience can often make space for the birthing pains of discovery; altering inhibitions and preconceived notions. In my case, 'letting go and letting God,' led to a stripping of myself to rediscover and reinvent a new self. Trusting the journey and the process is not always easy, but I encourage young artists to lean into the challenges that they encounter. Failure or rejection is sometimes the best teacher. It's what one makes of their experiences that determine where they will land. So leap, and trust that you will land firmly in the soil that is made especially for your growth.

CHAPTER 35

BLACK BERRIES, SWEET JUICE

Erasing Colorism and Embracing Dark Beauty

Tamera Malone

Key Challenges: bullying; colorism; dark skin; self-image

"Black roach. Tar baby. Black monkey." That is what it meant for me to be a dark-skinned girl growing up in Memphis, Tennessee. Those are just a few of the names I was called by my annoying little brother, by the neighborhood kids I often played hide and seek or curb ball with, and by my classmates that I did ballet and homework within after-school care. You see, being a dark-skinned little girl was not anything I was proud of. I did not want to be dark-skinned. I did not wear my skin like it was a badge of honor. I did not flaunt it. I hated it, and I mean that from the depth of my soul. I hated it because it made me feel dumb. I hated it because it made me feel ugly. I hated it because my elementary crush, wearing his Levi jeans and his Reebok sneakers, did not like it.

Instead, he liked my light-skinned, longhaired, hazel–eyed, best friend. Don't get me wrong. I know why he liked her. She was beautiful, funny, and smart. I thought I was too, but to him, I was not because I was dark-skinned. I hated it because I rarely saw dark-skinned little girls when I watched the Disney Channel, Cartoon Network, or Nickelodeon. I hated it because when I would listen to my

A Second Helping of Gumbo for the Soul: More Liberating Stories and Memories to Inspire Females of Color, pages 153–156.

favorite rappers, they would always talk about how much they loved redbones. I was not a redbone. In fact, I was far from it. I was a black roach, a tar baby, and a black monkey. I could totally relate to Notorious B.I.G when he described himself as "heartthrob never, Black and ugly as ever." Me too, Biggie. Me too. At least that's how I felt.

WHEN MY DARK SKIN BEGAN TO MATTER

I cannot recall the exact moment when I realized that, to some people, my dark skin was not considered beautiful compared to lighter skin. I do know that it was around the time when I was in the third grade. I remember playing with kids in the neighborhood, and whenever we would make fun of or insult each other, people would always use my skin tone as one of their "go to" insults. Everyone would laugh, and I would become extremely sad. I never really had any good comebacks, so I just had to take it. I was humiliated. I was embarrassed and, with each insult, I hated my skin tone more and more.

Interestingly enough, though, the kids that made fun of my dark skin were the Black kids. I went to a very diverse elementary school, and I had quite a few White friends. My White friends never made fun of my dark skin. It was always the kids that were the same race as me. That is what we call colorism—when people that share the same race as you treat you differently or discriminate against you simply because of your skin tone.

I remember talking to my mom about being made fun of, and while she would always come to my defense to the point of sometimes cursing kids out when they made me cry, she never verbally reassured me that I was beautiful—regardless of my skin tone. I do not believe it meant that she did not think I was beautiful, but my mother never said it. I wonder if I needed to hear it from her. My father was not around, so I was not going to hear it from him…you know how they say that a little girl's first love is her father and he is the one who instills in her that she is beautiful, inside and out. Well, I never experienced that. The closest man in my life was my brother, and he ran around the house wearing a t-shirt and power ranger underwear screaming "black roach, black roach, nah nanny nah nah." So, yes, I needed to hear it from my mother. I needed her to not only defend me but to say to me "You are beautiful. Your skin is dark, rich, and perfect in every single way, no matter what people may say." I needed her to say it to me because the world was saying the exact opposite.

AN ATTEMPT TO ERASE MY BEAUTY

As I got older and became more aware of the ways I was discriminated against because of my dark skin, I forced myself to seek out and become attached to people who looked like me but had been embraced by the world. That is when I fell in love with the television show *Moesha* played by the singer, Brandy. Brandy's character on Moesha represented everything I wanted to be. She was smart, beautiful, confident, funny, outgoing, popular, stylish and, most importantly, she was a dark-skinned girl. Moesha was not as dark as me, but she was close enough, and her character helped instill a little bit of the confidence that I was missing as a preteen. I loved watching her on television because I saw someone who looked like me that everyone loved. There was also Ashley Banks from the Fresh Prince of Bel-Air, Zaria from the Parent Hood, Laura from the Family Matters, and Lisa Turtle from Saved by the Bell, just to name a few. When I would see each of these characters and their different shades of a darker brown, it made me feel a little prouder of my dark skin. However, it still was not enough.

When I entered high school, things took a turn for the worse in how I felt about my skin tone. During this time, I really began to like boys and was trying to figure out who my friends were. I really wanted people to like me. I was a pretty likable person. I was smart, outgoing, and I had a great personality. But I just did not feel pretty enough, and I would notice little things about the type of girls that the majority of the boys liked, and those girls, of course, were all of a lighter skin tone than me.

One day, I was in Walgreens with my mother, and we were perusing the beauty department, and I noticed this purple box and written on it in big, bold black letters was "bleaching cream." I picked up the box and began reading the description. My mom had walked ahead to another aisle. I quickly ran away so that I could find her in order to convince her to buy this cream. "Mom, can you get this for me?" She asked, "What is it, Tamera? I told you not to touch anything in this store." She snatched it out of my hand and slightly raised her voice asking, "Bleaching cream? What do you need bleaching cream for?" I reluctantly replied, "Because I am too dark, and this will make me lighter. I just want to be a little lighter." She studied the box for a few seconds and finally said, with an attitude, "Tamera, this stuff probably does not work, but I will get it for you." That was one of the worst things, although I know not with ill-intent, she could have ever said to me. What she should have done was assure me that my skin was perfect the way it was and that I did not need to ever bleach my skin for any reason. However, she did not, and not doing so supported my want for the bleaching cream and she unknowingly reinforced what society had been telling me all along—that my dark and chocolate skin was not beautiful enough.

Over time, my mom bought me a few tubes of the bleaching cream and, of course, it did not work. I want to reiterate to you that my mother was phenomenal. She was not perfect (no one is), but she did the best that she could to raise my brother and me, along with the help of my grandmother. When I became old enough to understand colorism for what it really was, my mom and I were able to engage in conversations about why she supported my desire to be of a lighter skin tone, instead of working to debunk the narrative that I and society had created about dark skin being less beautiful and not attractive. She told me that she wanted to do whatever she could to make me feel better about my skin tone. She assured me that she always believed that I was the most beautiful girl in the world, but did not believe that simply telling me would be enough. She wanted to do whatever would make me happy, even if that meant cursing out bullies and buying me bleaching cream. My mother admitted and owned up to this mistake of parenting and has since worked her hardest to tell me how beautiful my dark and chocolate skin is as often as she can.

WE GOT THE JUICE

Colorism is real, and I often think people who are not dark-skinned do not understand the impact that it has on the confidence of women and girls in this world who are of a darker skin complexion. In the past and in the present, dark-skinned women are seen as less beautiful—if not totally unattractive. This is evident in the media, in Hollywood, in music, and just in everyday life. However, while this is still an issue, people have made it a priority to be more diverse in the different skin tones that are represented in the industries mentioned above.

I am 30 years old and I still have not overcome the insecurities I developed growing up dark-skinned. I am still learning the importance of self-love and self-validation. I get so excited when I see or hear dark-skinned girls and women being celebrated and recognized for their beauty because we are and have always been beautiful! I am going to celebrate dark skin forever because so many people do not. Becoming more accepting of my skin tone has made me more confident in all other areas of my life.

I want young girls and women across the world to know that, no matter what society tells you or shows you, you are beautiful, and you are worth it. It is important that we support and uplift each other as Black women—no matter the differences in skin tone, weight, height, hair texture, or any other physical characteristics that society uses to pit us against each other. We need to know that our Black is beautiful. We need to know that our Black is magic. We need to know that our melanin is poppin' and that we are all Black girls that rock. Biggie may not have embraced his blackness, but Tupac said, "the blacker the berry, the sweeter the juice." And to that I say, "What he said!

CHAPTER 36

ESCAPING THE WHITE GAZE

Courtney Mauldin

Key Challenges: abandonment, low income, survivor guilt, mask, substance abuse

When I consider my trajectory as a Black woman, the ways in which I've been racialized throughout my educational experiences and in social spaces, I am unable to recall times that I have not felt the pervasive presence of the White gaze. So often, under this gaze, I have either been the anomaly or deemed as disposable altogether. The phenomenon of the White gaze treks back to Toni Morrison's 1970 novel, *The Bluest Eye.* I read this novel, assigned by my AP English teacher, during my senior year of high school. With good intentions, she had us explore the main character, Pecola's story. However, beyond curriculum-scripted questions, we were mostly left uncomfortable having to deconstruct why Whiteness was the standard in a classroom where the Black to White ratio was 25:1. How were we supposed to explain to our White female teacher that she was the standard, that her values and the school's curriculum, reflected her as normative?

The gaze of which Morrison spoke went beyond an audience. Instead, it was a standard, a White approval that I have found myself wrestling with, internalizing and simultaneously resisting in my efforts to find liberation in my Blackness while also attaining a status that was vastly different than my upbringing. While the White gaze was at the crux of how I felt then, and how I still feel today, I have

A Second Helping of Gumbo for the Soul: More Liberating Stories and Memories to Inspire Females of Color, pages 157–160.

had to move throughout the world and society. But, there is an entire narrative of my life where I have sheltered shame. I have worn the non-desired labels of low-income, abandoned, and anomaly because I "made it out." However, in recent years, I have learned the power of embracing these parts of my truth because they have shaped and molded me into who and why I am.

In this chapter, I prioritize my upbringing as a young Black girl who was considered the poster child in school: A child who also carried a masked load that my teachers, friends, nor mentors knew about until I was further along in my adulthood. Even now, many are unaware and apply their own labels to who I am and where I come from. Concurrently, I speak about Whiteness and its pervasive gaze as I've traversed public education, higher education, and now the academy as a Ph.D. student. I break this chapter into my years of schooling, as they are markers for how I remember poignant personal, social, and academic experiences.

THE FORMATIVE YEARS (P–5)

I affectionately call these years the "good ones." My mom was a single parent, and I was far from concerned about my father's absence because I was so insulated by my grandmother and mother's presence. However, I do recall seeing my dad on sporadic birthdays. Each birthday he would show up late in the night and disrupt my sleep with a White doll in his hand. I never understood his role, why he brought White dolls, or why he continued to show up when I felt (at the time) that what I had with my mom was enough.

During this time, we were the single parent family who was able to donate money, gifts, and time to Christmas charities. We were also the single parent family who helped to provide for the kids in my classroom who were in need of extra snacks and food to survive over the weekend. But, I was oblivious to the fact that I was only a few years shy of being on the receiving end of the same assistance I witnessed my mother so dutifully give out.

In a matter of five years or so, our lives were altered by the delicacy of substance abuse that infested and destroyed many Black families, including my own. As more items around our house began to go missing and my mom seemed to move further away from who I knew her to be, school became my escape.

One teacher, in particular, took a special liking to me and began to affirm my academic and social strengths. It is important to note that experiencing schooling in a predominantly Black and lower socio-economic context informed how I navigated schooling from a young age until now. In the Black community, the instillation of being "twice as good" as White kids (who my classmates and I had never seen, by the way), crafted a narrative that I had to compete with a group of kids with whom I had never actually interacted in the flesh. This invisible, yet valid competition that was reinforced by my teachers and family bore an immense pressure that I carried and continue to carry with an understanding that says: to succeed, we have to be twice as good, period. I now realize there has been a thread of perfectionism for which I have aimed that is intricately linked to my upbringing and my socialization in school. From earning good grades so that I could earn free food coupons that would help my family out during rough months, to also believing that if I performed at my fullest potential, I would be getting something right for my mom; something that would make her happy again. Looking back, those years were good, but they were fleeting.

MIDDLE SCHOOL YEARS

After moving away from our home in North Memphis, an area known for its population of drug dealers, I knew that the dynamic of my family and living situation would never be the same. The substances and trauma that surrounded us had made its way into our home, which resulted in the relocation from the only home I knew for an extended amount of time. We moved to an apartment complex that seemed to be draped in darkness. I was so ashamed of our living conditions that I would not allow friends' parents to drop me off. The muddy brown complex, the smell of sewage nearby, and the butter knives sealed in the door as security—all served as a reminder that what I once knew as home and stability, no longer existed.

We lived in the apartment complex approximately two years. During our stay, a local gang burned the two units next door from us down in order to make themselves known in the area. I no longer knew whose life I was living, but I was certain that it wasn't my own. During this time, returning to school simply became a performance: one of secret addresses, half truths about why my mom was not able to pay for school activities, and lingering outside of the school building well after dismissal wondering who would show up. No one knew where I lived, or how I lived. I am still unsure of how I saved face so well that no one, not one teacher, not one friend really knew what I was masking, but I still prevailed, leaving middle school as valedictorian.

HIGH SCHOOL TO THE ACADEMY

After middle school, I had transitioned to living with my grandmother full-time. While we both pretended that it wasn't a full-time arrangement, we both knew that the likelihood of its permanence was inevitable. In accepting that hard truth, I decided that I would have control over my high school years. I had no understanding of how I was able to earn valedictorian status during my middle school years. There was so much that I knew I did not know, but I was determined not to let this be the case in high school. In doing so, I transferred to a different high school. I was able to do so because I asked a friend's mother to retrieve an optional school transfer application for me. I secretly filled it out and forged my mother's signature. When I found out that I was accepted, I was overwhelmed with both excitement and fear. But, I stood my ground, albeit shakily, with my grandmother when I explained that the school was a better option than where I was zoned, and hoped that she could sense my level of desperation.

Eventually, my grandmother conceded to allow me to transfer high schools but stated that I could go but would have to figure out transportation to and from school on my own. Needless to say, the city bus became my friend. While enrolled at the new high school, I was able to take AP and Honors courses, acquired access to tutoring and ACT prep, and was instructed by teachers who were willing to sponsor me for activities that I was unable to afford. These supports shifted my access to knowledge and shaped my schooling trajectory. So, the jokes and laughs from kids who saw me riding the bus were worth it! Also, by this time, I had perfected the art of performing that my home life was typical, so I was able to feel as if I belonged.

The White gaze was one that not only operated in my academic pursuits but also in my home life. I did not want to be the girl whose life reflected static conceptions of blackness. Instead, I wanted to be seen as more than my circumstance. Therefore, the notion of being an anomaly falsely allowed me to believe that others wouldn't categorize me as disposable. Too often, the narrative of the 'exceptional Black' has done harm within our own communities and hence continues to position White people as "the standard." As I matriculated from high school to a predominantly White institution for my undergraduate career, the recurring White gaze was omnipresent. At the time, I didn't realize how dangerous the myth of meritocracy was and how it had been instilled within me and many other students, including those of us who were Black and up against structural and systematic oppression. We had been taught to have our own investment in White systems of oppression if we wanted to advance or "make it out" of our own communities. "Making it out" somehow signaled that we were aspiring to do something else; but that "something else" never really renders itself as Black. All of the parts that were affirmed and praised about me in the university schooling system had very little to do with my Blackness unless it pertained to a diversity award or some type of financial support; these were minimal payoffs of having the identity of a Black Woman. Yet, existing under the white gaze meant that I was constantly up for White approval in a White system that had White values.

My current experiences in the academy as a doctoral student has revealed the same truths that I faced during my undergraduate studies. Within the vignettes that I have shared from my schooling and social experiences as a Black woman, I shared the hard truths and the ability to survive despite the truths. With those experiences, I have grown to realize that my survival is predicated on my ability to see the joy in living. Discovering myself outside of the applied labels of Black, woman, low-income, or even being considered an anomaly from my community, has given me permission to grow, accept, and find liberation in all of the parts that make me who I am.

"Me and you, we got more yesterday than anybody. We need some kind of tomorrow."

— *Toni Morrison*

CHAPTER 37

THERE'S STRENGTH IN MY STRUGGLE

Tonya McCoy

Key Challenges: betrayal, divorce, forgiveness, self-care

I realized that I had cultivated a spirit of resentment for my spouse before he asked for a divorce. He left six years prior without the courage to share his concerns with me. He called me awful names, and it was apparent that he preferred other women. My resentment of him stemmed from his rejection of me. Yes, I wanted to work on our marriage, but I had grown tired. I no longer felt secure with him. Yet, I did not leave because I did not want to be the one who gave up. I became aware of my dependency on him to meet all of my emotional needs. I wanted him to be my protector, lover, friend, and fixer. It finally registered that I placed undue expectations upon him. Especially, expecting him to respond to me as I would. Unfortunately, it was much later before I comprehended the selfishness of this desire.

BROKENNESS

Over and over again, he trampled over my emotions. I felt he didn't care about them (emotions). What did I expect? This was the dysfunctional pattern of our lives. He held things in; I talked yearning for resolution, but he huffed and puffed

A Second Helping of Gumbo for the Soul: More Liberating Stories and Memories to Inspire Females of Color, pages 161–163.

and avoided resolution. I wanted to do the "right thing" so I asked for forgiveness, essentially, out of guilt from my resentment. I was waiting for him to change. As I waited, I experienced pain while making great efforts to evade and elude it. However, my waiting had become a place of brokenness. I wondered, and I asked God why I was experiencing so much pain. I didn't feel loved. I felt worthless, non-valued, rejected, and invisible. These emotions were vast and over-powering. It seemed as if I was facing all of the hurt inflicted upon me by others, as well as the hurt that I was inflicting on myself. I thought I had a right to be hurt; after all, he left me. I was broken. I was weakened. I wanted to escape the injury and the associated agony, but I was unable to do so. I was protesting being the one who was suffering as I continued struggling to get away from the pain.

Nonetheless, in this place of brokenness, my will was broken. "Not my will Lord, but thy will be done" (Luke 22:42 King James Version). I had to stop my way of thinking so I could know God's will for my life. I had a choice to decide my will to be in control or surrender to the will of God. When I was guided by my will, I experienced lowered self-esteem and emotions of bitterness, hurt, and rejection. Whereas, when guided by God's word, I accepted the pain as a process leading to my destiny, although I didn't appreciate or welcome it (pain).

FORGIVENESS

I did not want to hurt, so I closed off portions of my heart to disallow access to others. Thus, my focus turned inward, and I was able to comprehend and gain an understanding of how a lack of personal attention contributed to my pain. I was disappointed in myself. I kept hoping and expecting that he would change, but I needed to change. I needed to change how I responded. Why was I pulled into his confusion? Why was I judging and criticizing myself based upon his betrayal and rejection of me? I had to make a decision whether to continue my attention centering upon his rejection of me or adjusting my efforts to becoming a better me; physically, emotionally, and spiritually. What made this decision difficult? I failed to recognize that I had experienced the trauma of betrayal that kept me in bondage to the opinions of my former spouse. But, the process of being broken instigated the healing process where the calluses of pain, rejection, bitterness, hopelessness, hurt, and low self-esteem were removed. My heart was purged and purified to not only forgive my spouse but to forgive myself. I was changed during the healing process.

MOVING FORWARD/LETTING GO

With the change, came isolation. I was at a place where I could only depend upon God. Friends and family had a very limited understanding. Trusting in the Lord was my daily focus, and it offered encouragement. I realized that I was actively grieving the loss of my best friend. In addition, I was grieving the person I was and wanted to be. Now, it became imperative that I let go. My concentration and focus had to be upon me. I had to learn to be with me, love me, and enjoy me. I knew it was time to let go of my spouse, the marriage, and the 20-year relationship. However, I didn't have the strength to do so.

Nonetheless, I had to choose myself. Otherwise, I would be consumed with the pangs of bitterness. It felt dark. Was this a test of my faith? I knew God saw my pain, yet when would He deliver me? When would the ache and unhappiness go away? When would the injuries heal? Eventually, I let go and allowed God's love to become my strength. Although I had been weakened by pain, God's love gave me strength. As I accepted God's unconditional love, I realized HIS love replaced the hurt, disappointment, and rejection that was lodged firmly within my heart. As I continued holding on to the love of God, the wounded areas were healed.

NOW COMES THE STRENGTH

When I embraced the hardships, I became stronger, and my faith deepened. I remember reading that individuals with great levels of faith are typically persons who have experienced great struggles. I knew if I had given up in the midst of the trials, I would have never experienced this kind of faith, growth, and love of myself. Just as a caterpillar is strengthened during the transformation phase, I became strengthened during the brokenness phase. It's at this phase that no one was able to witness my internal struggle. Others could detect movement, but they were unable to comprehend my struggle for freedom. Freedom from betrayal and rejection. The crisis brought about a change within me and the adversity initiated growth.

Suffering is universal…everyone suffers. It doesn't matter what educational, socio-economical, geographical, religious, or cultural experiences you have faced, everyone experiences pain. If you experience life without any obstacles, it will cripple you, similar to a butterfly released early from its cocoon that is never able to fly. You must remember that suffering is not an end in itself. I encourage you NOT to run from suffering. It is in the struggle that God can complete a profound work in your life. Just as flowers will not yield their perfume unless they are compressed, and diamonds can't be formed without heat and pressure, struggling comes to develop and cultivate you to be creative, artistic, imaginative, ingenious, and innovative. Remember, how you prepare yourself to deal with struggles determines your level of growth. It is in times of adversity; you can grow physically, emotionally, and mentally. Adversity brings you to your full potential. Don't run from adversity because there's strength in your struggle.

CHAPTER 38

THE EDUCATED IMMIGRANT

A Narrative

Marcelle Mentor

Key Challenges: resilience, coming of age, personal growth, thriving

ACT ONE: WHERE IT ALL BEGAN...

I am an only child who was raised in a home with two parents who aspired to give me every possible educational opportunity. My mother was an elementary school teacher, and my father, a sales representative. At the ages of 72 and 70, they both are retired and enjoy their lives to the full. They are still happily married and love and care for each other after their 48 years together. I loved our annual vacations, listening to my parents talk, sitting nestled in the backseat with my toys, books and snacks, and looking at the South African landscapes I grew to love so. My dad loved Elvis, and I knew every single song by heart and spent these times imagining myself on a stage singing "Are you lonesome tonight?" I love the part where he stops singing and speaks the part from Shakespeare's as you like it... "You know someone said that the world's a stage, and each must play a part." Even now, driving and just staring, sitting quietly is a solace to my soul.

A Second Helping of Gumbo for the Soul: More Liberating Stories and Memories to Inspire Females of Color, pages 165–168.
Copyright © 2020 by Information Age Publishing
165

My parents fastidiously went in search of schools that they considered the best for Colored children. To get to the high school I attended, I was forced to take a train at 5:30 am because I was not able to attend the "Whites only" school in my area that offered English as an instructional medium. The value of reading in English, stood out as my beacon, as it not only occupied me when lonely, but also took me to worlds where I knew I would travel when I was older and more accomplished.

Until my undergraduate years, I was brought up somewhat sheltered and was often vaguely aware of the harsh realities of life in South Africa and how it impacted the lives of my family' and friends. Many of my peers, by first-hand knowledge, knew the intricacies and atrocities of the South African society. They had been beaten, detained, and had lost family members to the struggle against Apartheid, but I was naive and uninformed on so many levels.

ACT TWO: EDUCATION FOR ALL...

I started teaching high school English in 1992 in a sub-economic area. South Africa still had its racial divisions, and as a Colored teacher, I could only teach at a Colored school. These students were fed the knowledge, from Apartheid television, film, and newspapers that told them that they were lesser citizens and that it was acceptable for them not to reach their potential. I found it necessary to impart on my students that they were so much more than academic prowess, especially in the light of the fact that many of their parents were uneducated and worked long hours, or were slaves to Apartheid mentality. There was a high rate of poverty and with it came alcohol and drug dependence, along with physical and sexual abuse in all its forms. It was a challenge to teach in this environment and often a hit or miss in that there were times when I reached my kids, and other times I had to watch helplessly as life was flushed.

It was true that Colored and Black teachers in South Africa were teachers of academic subjects. Moreover, we were and still are the pastors, the social workers, the guidance counselors, the judge and jury, the forgiver of sins and the bearers of all sorrows big and small. We were called to be superhuman sometimes, and all we often are, are human beings in superhero outfits made from rags, and other scraps of material.

In 2000 I applied to teach English at a previously all-White high school. This school was a bastion of Apartheid where many of the architects and forerunners of Apartheid had gone to school. I was afraid when I started teaching at this school—I was not afraid of my ability as a teacher, I was better qualified than so many of the teachers there—I was afraid of the racism that permeated the school, what the backlash of that would evoke in me. I felt I was the representative of my race, of the minority, of the struggle.

I was overwhelmed, yet threw myself into my new job with vigor. I literally ingratiate myself into a culture so foreign to me, yet in doing so, I exposed my culture and myself. I hope I showed that we were not as different as Apartheid would have liked us to believe.

I was astounded by the privilege of 95% of the students who were mostly White, and the poverty of most of the 5% of the students who were mostly children of color. How did I teach the kids of color to traverse these two worlds when I struggled with those issues myself? How did I show and teach the students of color to be unafraid, to speak up, to not cower and buckle and bend under the influences of White Apartheid indoctrinated and perceived dominance? How did I teach them not to buy in, not to sell themselves out? Was it necessary to teach them not to be dissolved in the sea of opulence and opportunity, so that they could hold on to who they were culturally? Teaching and learning these life lessons were my greatest challenges.

ACT THREE: BEING GROWN...

As a child spending time with my mother, it was inevitable that I would spend hour upon hour in the world of women. My mother is a paradox as she would always say "you are an individual," yet always acquiesced to my father's will. I was raised in a society of women where we are raised to be "good" wives and mothers. And this is what I took with me as I watched my aunts do the same things for all my life—I watched the women in my family and community do this, without fail, through abuse and adultery...they honored and obeyed.

In August of 2005, I came to New York with the man to whom I was married along with my sons, then aged 6 and 7. We had made a shift of life, in pursuit of his dream—and I was an obedient wife; what he wanted I would follow. At first, we were happy and adjusting to a time and place so foreign to our very beings. Yet it became apparent that he wanted more, or rather wanted less...of me. At first, I fought the breakup of the 15-year marriage. I had been with him since I was 18 and had sold my soul to him; give him absolute control of me. I was enraged, disillusioned, hurt and shattered beyond anything I could imagine.

I remember in December 2007, we had been arguing, and as I was yelling a response he stepped in and smacked me so hard across my face my spectacles went flying...nothing could have prepared me for that moment in my life...no amount of education or family love prepared me for this I remember calling my sons, my voice raspy from shock, asking my eldest to help me find my specs so that I could see what I was doing. I very calmly packed a suitcase, took the boys and called my cousin to fetch us. It was an odd moment because until then I had told no one that we had been having troubles—yet all I asked my cousin was "can you come fetch us now?" She said later that when she heard my voice, she knew immediately to get me. I now understood what people mean when they say that the emotional pain was so overwhelming that it hurt to breathe...

Later that night we spoke over the telephone; I was an obedient wife, I went home the next day; I continued not to tell, not a soul, not my parents, not friends...

how could I when I was smart, educated, funny, and outspoken? How did I voice what I was thought I was conditioned to be silent about?

Until the summer of 2008, he hit me again, and I, overwhelmed, fell to the ground—as I landed, he put his foot on my face! I heard my mom's voice that instant "get up!" she said, "get up!" And I did…I got up and left. I had no place to go, but I left. It's been nine years since…and the memory of it brings with it a mixture of awed anger and sorrow, but my silence is broken. And that alone is a release to that memory, as I will always remember myself as the winner here, as the victor, simply because I speak about it.

ACT 4: NEW PATHWAYS…

And here I am, a little more than nine years later—stronger, wiser and enthused for life. I completed my Ph.D. at Columbia University; I raised my boys by myself and fought the boys' father for child support and to sign divorce papers, which he finally signed nine years after I left him. His spite and maliciousness continued through a nine-year separation. We were evicted, and I had a credit score of 480 after he left us penniless. But yet I have survived and persevered; it wasn't easy, but my sons and my parents, and the family I built for myself here in this city has strengthened and fortified me, I feel safe and secure in myself and my abilities, just like I did when I was a little girl, snuggled at the back of the car, watching the landscapes pass my and being awed and inspired by everything I saw. I have claimed that back. I laugh, and I live.

This narrative is documented release from the silences in my life. I would caution other women of color when they are overwhelmed and despondent—like Audre taught us—that their silence will not protect them, Silences threaten to overwhelm us; silences threaten to box us in and shape us into something alien to our true nature, silences that would attempt to rob us of our very selves. Speak up, speak out—surround yourself with a sisterhood that will carry you when you can't walk. Believe in yourself—You are so much greater than you can imagine.

Our education is much more than the academic degrees we hold– our education is encapsulated in our being, combined with our life experiences into a melting pot—to create what and who we are. It will sustain and fortify us. It is our liberty.

CHAPTER 39

MY METAMORPHOSIS FROM CATERPILLAR TO BUTTERFLY

Karen J. Miller

Key Challenges: loss; self-loathing, shame, blame, family dysfunction; sexual, physical and emotional abuse; trauma; terminal illness

"What the Caterpillar calls the end of the world, the Master calls a Butterfly."

—Richard Bach

My earliest childhood memory was approximately four years old. As a child, I do not remember experiencing any hugging, embracing, words of endearment, or hearing "I love you" from any of my immediate family members. I felt no love, nurturing or acceptance. I lived in the home of my maternal grandparents with my older sister and my mother, who was divorced.

My grandfather was the patriarch of the family. He was a very authoritative, stoic, strict, closed, prideful, abusive, intimidating, and seemingly unloving gentleman. He earned his living as an excellent self-made carpenter. My grandmother was a kind, gentle, sensitive, compassionate, passive, unassuming and spiritual

A Second Helping of Gumbo for the Soul: More Liberating Stories and Memories to Inspire Females of Color, pages 169–172.
Copyright © 2020 by Information Age Publishing

woman who was a victim of emotional and physical abuse, perpetrated by my grandfather; she was a doting wife.

My grandmother completed Normal School, which was a two-year college for colored persons in the South. She taught school prior to migrating North with my grandfather where she worked as a presser in a factory. As children, my sister and I never witnessed the abuse that my grandmother endured because it was covert. But, my sister and I feared my grandfather. My grandmother provided care for my sister and me while my mother worked the evening shift at a community hospital, as a nurse's aide. My grandmother was the most significant person in my childhood; she raised me, and I truly loved her.

I felt different growing up because I was a child of divorced parents. I barely knew my father. He was a postal clerk and an alcoholic. I typically saw him on Thanksgiving and or Christmas; he was always drunk. I never bonded with him and never felt love for him or from him. I never received the validation from my father that I needed as a female child. He once said I was "homely," but I was getting "better looking," surely that added to my self-esteem! I did not grieve when my father died; because I had no emotional investment. However, I did grieve not having a father all of my life.

My mother only had one weekend off a month and one day off during the week. I saw her in the morning before going to school, and I was in bed when she came home at midnight. I missed my mother desperately. Her absence created a void that I could not fill, and although the time I spent with her was quality; it just was not enough. I always yearned for her presence.

I was taught to be polite, respectful, speak good English, not to use profanity (I never heard a curse word used in my home) not to engage in sex prior to marriage, pray and follow the Ten Commandments. I was always obedient, quiet, passive and helpful, and I always wanted to please, in hopes of receiving love in return.

What I did not know, at the time, was that the family secrets that were later revealed along my life's journey would significantly impact my life. As I grew older, I realized that my caregivers had difficulty managing their individual lives and therefore could not impart healthy ways to assist me in navigating my future adult life.

The family secret that I learned, at age 11, from my father, was that my mother at age eighteen became pregnant and had a baby boy. She was forced to give him up for adoption to family members who were childless. My grandfather, according to a family member was outraged, and told my mother "I don't want that bastard in my house." When I told my mother what I learned, she cried and had no response, but my grandmother confirmed the secret. My sister and I were told not to mention or share it with anyone, ever and our questions went unanswered. We were living in denial, shame, and blame, and we soon discovered that the boy that was introduced to us as our cousin was actually our brother.

My brother and mother reunited two years prior to her death. He never met meet his biological father. But, issues of attachment, shame, blame, alcoholism, and inferiority challenge him because of his adoption, and he has chosen not to be close to the family, and I continue to work on resolving my own issues around acknowledging that I have a brother (shame).

My mother remarried when I was nine years old to a man whom she had dated for seven years. He was a hardworking (he worked two full-time jobs for twenty years), kind, and devoted man, who loved my mother, sister, and me very much. He always referred to my sister and me as his children (never stepchildren), and although he never replaced my biological father, I loved him very much. But, due to his rigorous work schedule, I only saw him on weekends.

I began dating a football jock at age 16; my first boyfriend. We attended the same high school, but he was a year older than me. When we started dating, I was unaware that he was an alcoholic. I later learned that he drank daily, but he kept that hidden from me. I graduated from high school, and because my family valued education, I was scheduled to attend college in the fall. But, at age eighteen I began having unprotected premarital sex with my boyfriend. I was never educated, nor would I dare ask my family questions regarding sex education.

Prior to attending college, I discovered that I was pregnant, but I was persuaded by my family (mother and grandmother) to terminate the pregnancy. I felt I had no voice or choice. My boyfriend, who was not in favor of the termination, paid for the procedure. He and I never discussed it. My family told me that my grandfather would have a heart attack if he knew I was pregnant.

My mother located a woman, through friends, who performed abortions in her home for a fee (abortions were not legal at the time). I suffered a horrific, traumatizing, life-altering experience, and as a result, I would never be the same. I was directed to go to the local drug store and purchase a rubber catheter to take to the procedure. My stepfather, in silence, drove me to the procedure; he waited in the car. I lay on a porcelain kitchen table, and the catheter was used to begin the horrible experience.

The procedure was not successful, but the second time was a "success." The pain was excruciating, and I had no pain medicine. My mother was at work, and my grandmother stayed in her room while I went through the ordeal alone. I could have died, but I had no emotional support from my family. I suppressed the anger I felt, and although I had started college, the grief, loss, and emotional trauma I experienced negated my concentration and I left school after the first semester. No one in my family ever discussed the situation.

I married a year later after learning I was pregnant, again. I knew I was going to carry this baby to term, and I was not going to put myself through the trauma, and life-threatening danger, again. The marriage produced two beautiful sons. My husband joined the Marines and did a tour of duty in Vietnam.

He was physically, emotionally and sexually abusive to me (he raped me frequently during his drunken stupors). Once, he nearly choked me to death, but my oldest son stopped him. He was mean, nasty, and verbally demeaning. He bullied me to the point that I thought I was at fault for his abuse and he was never apologetic for any of his behavior. His redeeming quality was he provided well for our family. However, his alcoholism worsened after his return from overseas. My mother encouraged me to stay because she felt my boys needed their father! While working full time, I returned to college because education was my coping mechanism. I managed to earn a Bachelor of Arts degree in Human Services and a Master's in Social work as a full-time student and a battered wife. But, we finally divorced after 25 years.

I did not want to live alone, so I soon remarried a man who was similar in personality to my ex-husband. Yes, I managed to do that again! He was physically and emotionally abusive to me, and he was also a liar and unfaithful. He sexually groped one of my friends and made romantic advances to other friends. He mismanaged his and my money to nearly losing our house and similar to my first husband, he assumed no ownership for his behavior, always placing the blame on me.

I earned a second Master's degree in Education Administration while married to my second husband who was not supportive of my achievements. With three degrees, I still had feelings of failure, and two toxic and volatile failed relationships I began therapy to understand and resolve my issues of poor choices, and why I made the choices I did because I needed to learn how to love myself.

I experienced another traumatization, loss, grief, and thoughts of failure, as a parent when my youngest son was incarcerated and served eight years in prison. I was in a very dark place. I visited him in prison locations in various states and supported him emotionally and financially while he was away. His brother visited him when he could and after four years of being enraged, his father finally visited.

After my retirement in school administration/social work I applied and was accepted to the Ph.D. program at Howard University School of Social Work at age 62; a deferred dream comes true. I graduated with my Ph.D., and a certificate in Women's Studies. Two months later I was diagnosed with lung, ovarian and metastatic cancer in my large intestines, stage 4. I had chemotherapy and was told that 60% percent of the cancer had dissipated, and I would be on chemotherapy treatment for the rest of my life!

GOD had another plan! Eight treatments later my CT scan revealed NO SIGN of CANCER! God miraculously healed me! I have been cancer free for three years! I never gave up or gave in; I walked by faith and not by site, and I'm currently working as an Assistant Adjunct professor at Howard University School of Social Work.

The challenges, pain, disappointment, and loss that I encountered in life have prepared me to encourage and inspire wounded women to become healthy and whole; and to be self-loving, self-caring, and to always follow their passion.

CHAPTER 40

THE MASK GAME

Kiana Peoples

Key Challenges: domestic violence; self-image; abandonment; masking; deficit thinking; self-advocacy

"One of my earliest childhood memories is of me smiling! One such occasion was picture day at Head Start. I remember the outfit my mother purchased for me. It felt like she spent weeks looking for the right size to fit me. My mom would say. "True Southern women are always dressed appropriately, "for me, this included a pair of patent leather black Mary Jane shoes with an assortment of ruffled socks, but most often, white was usually the color chosen. On that particular picture day, my attire was no different. I wore a red knee-length skirt with white polka dots, a crisp white blouse with a drawstring collar and of course a pair of shiny black patent leather Mary Jane's. As I recall, although ashamed to admit, I had a few bad habits. Throughout most of the morning, the shoestring ties of my blinding white blouse were in my mouth. I guess I was nervous, but I remember the cameraman reminding me that I wanted a pretty picture, so that meant I had to stop chewing on my blouse and smile.

Another memory of me smiling was home in Alabama! Sweet tea with lemon, biscuits, and honey, and of course, fried chicken, which could be for breakfast or dinner. That combination always got (and still gets) a smile from! There was

A Second Helping of Gumbo for the Soul: More Liberating Stories and Memories to Inspire Females of Color, pages 173–177.

nothing like feeling the sun and a gentle country breeze on my skin as I pushed my sister as she sat inside my red wagon with white wheels, then after going a little distance, I would run to jump in with her and laugh when we flipped over, but then begging her not to tell momma.

Another smiling memory was of me and my sister, still very young, riding on the shoulders of our big brothers. Both of my half-brothers loved to play basketball. In the family albums, there are pictures of them looking like a young Wilt Chamberlin and Magic Johnson with those awful short basketball shorts and those extremely long socks with the ring around the top! I still laugh out loud when I run across those pictures! I felt so special when my brothers would take us with them. Later, I learned that they considered themselves to be lady's men and the only way they could go to the courts was if they took us with them, according to momma, but what momma didn't know was that our brothers used us to lure girls to the basketball courts so they could babysit us while our brother's played basketball.

These were the few early childhood memories I still can recall. That's because, during this time, when I was around five years of age, my mother was in a relationship with a man, like my father before him, who expressed himself in verbal and/or physical abusive behaviors. He often threatened to "whip us" for various incidents, and although he never did, I remembered feeling fearful even while I played the role of the protector of my baby sister. I never wanted any harm to come to her. I often even took her punishments though most of the time she rightfully deserved them. Looking back, I realize of course, that some of those lessons she needed to learn. I also realize what my godmother meant when she one day said, "Child, everyone has their own cross to bear, and your shoulders have enough to bear being female and Black without trying to carry two of them." Her words have stayed with me through my life travels.

THE MASKING PHASE

I was told often, I loved to smile, and anyone who knew me as a child often tells me the same today. Friends, and family would say, "That girl is always smiling and showing off those big deep dimples!" But little did people know that behind those cute smiling pictures, was a little girl, a young lady, and for some time a woman grappling with shame, fear, pain, and embarrassment. I call this time in my life "the masking phase and what I later learned from my mother was that she too had worn a mask made of the same chains of bondage that bound me.

School was a happy place for me. It was my escape. I did not find schoolwork challenging, and because of that, I was picked on by my peers. Although I was the tallest of all the girls and some of the boys, I had difficulty controlling my weight. This was partially due to a poorly balanced southern diet humbly provided by my mother while at the same time, retreating to sugary foods to deal with the stress of living in a home environment underlined with episodes of domestic violence, and a revolving door of men who, when my mother was at work, found me to be the object of unwanted attention.

My mother became pregnant at the age of sixteen by her 18-year-old boy-friend and because this happened in the 1950s they quickly wed. She soon became pregnant and gave birth to their second son after they married, and although he provided for his family, he attempted to pacify his frustrations of being a young husband and father by gambling and drinking, which quickly led to incidents of verbal and physical abuse between him and my mother. This behavior continued until she decided to separate from him with their two sons and later divorced in the early 1970s. Unbeknownst to my mother, a pattern emerged that seemed to have locked her into a life of victimization, and fruitless relationships including the one with my father who married my mother but seemed to have no desire to know his two girls. This was due mostly to the fact that he was locked in arms with and addiction to alcohol that eventually ended his gifted career as a welder, dissolved his first marriage and left my mother and us with promises and no real follow through.

I desperately wanted to be a "daddy's" girl, but that never happened. I also wanted a "normal home life." Despite my mother's attempts at stability, we moved around a lot. But when I was in school, I was able to pretend, and so the masks assisted me in excelling. I became involved in any activity that would keep from away from home just a bit longer. I repeated the second grade not because I did not understand the work, but because I thought it was "stupid" to repeat things I had already done. As I sat in the same classroom the following year with the same teacher, I was angry, hurt, and felt trapped. The second time around that same teacher took an interest in me holistically. She became concerned about my weight, so she started to monitor my snacks, and at lunchtime, she discussed with me about healthy food choices. She went as far as to inform the lunch staff not to allow me to have sugary dessert items or extra portions when I went through the lunch line. She also had the school physical education teacher encourage me to do extra laps or exercises, and when my mother came to the school for teacher-parent day, she informed her about the changes she put into place for me at the school and encouraged my mother to continue the practices at home. Sadly, Momma did not. Instead, she said that I was "big and beautiful," but I never felt that way.

CRACKING THE MASK

I continued to internalize the trauma I had been dealt well into my high school years, and although I continued to do well academically, I did not have a good positive body image. Fast-forwarding to college. I didn't want to attend the school my family wanted which was a historically Black college, but the oddest thing happened, and as fate would have it, that is exactly where I started my college experience. I was instantly enchanted. So many Black and Brown bodies, some who spoke different languages and seemed excited about learning, which was very different from the students in my previous schools. I continued to struggle with my weight, but there, I was no longer being teased. I began to understand that the home life I once knew didn't have to be the environment I wanted for myself and as I had done before, I joined as many organizations as my schedule would allow. But this time, something was different. I was busy because I wanted to be not because I was escaping something.

One day during my second year of college, I walked by the social work department where the Whitney Young Social Work Club was hosting a clothing and food drive for a family who lost their belongings in a house fire. At that point, something clicked—those years I spent every moment I could at school was not just because of the learning, but it was also because of the teachers who were there pouring a bit of themselves into me. I understood at that moment that God had indeed shown favor on me and that He divinely placed people on my path of life to fill in the holes that left me self-conscience and damaged.

I decided to seek a master's degree, but the environment was much different. I applied to a well-known predominantly White institution in the south made known to the world due to the governor's refusal to integrate in the 1960s. I studied in the building adjacent to where the incident took place. I believe that in an effort to remove guilt, the school removed the steps to that building. However, it did nothing to remove the lingering presence of racism felt among the campus halls. I will never forget the fact that I was initially denied admittance because one of the faculty members on the acceptance committee thought someone else had written my essay due to her belief that African-Americans did not have the ability to be scholarly writers.

Her opening address contained the phrase "you people" multiple times as she addressed the body of entering first-year master students during orientation. It was clear that her colleagues simply overlooked her behavior, and I was in disbelief. I also recall a conversation that I had with the Master of Social Work (MSW) chair of the School of Social Work. I was the elected president of the social work club, and within the first week of starting the program, I felt that I needed to address the matter since no one else spoke up. During that conversation, the chair stated that "Despite some issues and/or views, the school of social work consistently maintained the largest enrollment of African-American students on the campus." I thought to myself, "How does this response equate to what my peers and I experienced within just a few days of school starting?" As I sat and listened, I began to understand that there were many masks worn by people everywhere, and it forced me to address my own, especially if I planned on being successful in my career as a social worker and if I hoped to empower others.

THE AWAKENING

I have since learned that I had to forgive my father. I only saw him a few times during my adolescence and teen years. He did not attend any of my graduations, birthday parties, games or my wedding, but my godfather did. In fact, I did not speak to or of my father until I was well into my late thirties. It was my godfather who called me to tell me my father died. The news didn't upset me initially, but a few months later, while I was driving to work, out of nowhere, I began to mourn. I cried for all of the Father's Days, birthdays, and holidays that he denied me to celebrate with him. I cried it all out. I did not utter a word, I just cried and cried—hard. A few years earlier, I did a similar thing for my mother, although she was still living. She could not give me what she did not possess, but what she did have, she gave freely, which was the form of resilience that she demonstrated and lavished on me. She made me believe that I could and would make it anyhow. I visit whenever possible, and although our relationship is not perfect, I'm okay with it because I am not perfect, either. I learned to release what was not in my control and embrace what is. This is a lesson in life I believe we all should learn in one form or another because the most joyous thing happened of all after all that crying—I now smile because I am truly happy,—not because I'm masking.

CHAPTER 41

FROM COLORED TO AFRICAN AMERICAN

Growing Up in the Segregated South

V. Marlene Prater

Key Challenges: segregation; colorism; desegregation; community

I've spent 20 years teaching at the same junior high school, 19 years in the same classroom. However, last year I was told that I would be changing from teaching seventh-grade science to teaching eighth-grade science. Of course, I was hesitant about changing grades, but I had no choice. Choice has come up often during my lifetime. As an African American female, I've had to make many choices and sacrifices. I've been the only teacher of color in this school for my entire career. Transitioning from my teens to 20s in the 1970s was a treacherous journey, but I like to think that I helped create pathways.

I've told it many times before, and my story will never change. I grew up in the segregated South and attended a segregated elementary and junior high school. I was taught by colored teachers and colored principals, and I wanted to attend a Black college. The summer after graduating from high school, I made a last-minute decision to forgo Tennessee State and instead, enroll at Kentucky State.

A Second Helping of Gumbo for the Soul: More Liberating Stories and Memories
to Inspire Females of Color, pages 179–182.

I'm sure my life was similar to most young Black females during that time—the typical summer job was babysitting, or light housekeeping because we were not allowed to work on the front line at theaters, or restaurants. While at college, I was shocked to learn that some of my classmates were hired to work at a few of the local businesses off campus. But, this was during the time of the "Black Power Movement" and apparently the times were a-changing.

Kentucky State College became a university shortly after I graduated, and I received my Bachelor of Science degree in the last class that graduated under college status. I'm proud of my roots and feel privileged to have graduated from not one, but two HBCUs. I eventually attended and graduated from Tennessee State University with a Doctor of Education degree in Administration and Supervision. That is the beginning and end of my story; I hope that while reading the following paragraphs, you can envision some of the changes that occurred during my life. I also hope that you can visualize some of the obstacles I encountered that helped to shape me into the person I am today.

My mother gave birth to four girls, and she was protective of all of us. Mother was aware of what people would do to us, herself included, simply because of the color of our skin. She had shared stories of the atrocities that happened to colored people when she was younger. She cried when Dr. Martin Luther King, Jr. was assassinated in Memphis, but afterward, she was fearful. She feared that violence might erupt in this area, and we watched protests, marches, and riots on television. The fear my mother had was real because she knew how our people were treated.

Mother loved her family. Our Sunday visits to my grandparent's house were memorable. We would sit around and talk to my grandparents, aunts, and cousins. My grandmother always had a pot of hot coffee for them drink. The older folks would laugh and talk for hours, while the kids played outdoors. I experienced fun times during youth and adulthood.

I recall when I noticed that people of color were treated differently. For example, I remember riding the Trailways Bus and asking my mother why we were passing all the empty seats in the front of the bus to get to the back of the bus. I also remember my mother pulling me close to her and being told to be quiet. I remember the Colored water fountains on the streets of my hometown and asking mother what Colored meant. I remember entering the side doors of the movie theaters because we weren't allowed to enter the front door. My junior high students cannot believe that at one time in history, Black students weren't allowed to attend schools with White students. There aren't any good things about this type of discrimination, but one positive thing is that I never encountered violence in my home.

As a young Black woman, I had to work harder and smarter to get ahead and to stay ahead. I believe that the White man created a mold in order for non-White people to fail. So, it is our job as people of color to break that mold and succeed. Opportunities for success were not readily available for me in my town. I knew that I had to go further and do better or else I would fail. So, I traveled away from home and started on a journey to continue my education and to develop a career.

My first job took me far from home, to a cold climate, in an inner-city school. Needless to say, my time there was short lived. I found another job at home in a nuclear facility. Working conditions were not quite as bad as the females in the movie Hidden Figures, but it was a similar environment. One supervisor called me a recalcitrant female (once or probably twice) for reasons that I won't mention. My thoughts were that he should treat me like he wanted to be treated. The people that I worked with understood that I had an opinion, and I expressed it! Kowtowing to the man wasn't something I planned to do. I knew that I wasn't treated fairly, but I didn't quit that job, and my work at this facility continued for nearly 25 years although I changed positions and worked in different departments. A plus is that while working there, I earned a Master of Science degree, and early on in my degree-seeking process, the company helped me pay a large portion of my tuition. By the time I was halfway through the program, the company was paying the full tuition. I finally left the company to become a school teacher, and I earned two additional educational degrees that were fully funded by fellowships. It was a blessing to receive funding for my advanced degrees.

Nonetheless, racial discrimination did exist during my youth, and Blacks were the recipients of that discrimination. I was so used to being treated badly that I felt this was how things were supposed to be. You know the old saying "when you know better, you do better." After arriving at college in a t state different from my home, meeting, and interacting with other students from across the United States, I finally "I knew better." I also knew that there were students that would speak out about the inequities.

I experienced some firsts in college. This is where I had my first drink of Kentucky Bourbon—I can recall the smell of it drifting from the distilleries up to the hill. Other firsts included wearing my first afro and dashiki, and I also marched with a group of my classmates to crash a gubernatorial inaugural ball. I also attended my first national championship basketball game while attending Kentucky State. For this trip, I traveled in a car with some friends for a long weekend to Kansas City, MO, with only $5.00 in my pocket for the entire trip! My college days were a great experience because I was surrounded by people who looked like me—Black! They were visible in both my classes as classmates and instructors. I felt comfortable in this setting.

The classic soul song *Young, Gifted, and Black* was popular during my college years. However, I realize that being Black was an obstacle. Being uneducated was an obstacle. Being female was an obstacle. The odds were against me, but I was determined to beat the odds. My parents gave all four of their daughters an opportunity to attend college, and three of us took advantage of that opportunity. My other sister got married and had a family, but I still feel that she would have been happier with a career. I could have chosen a different path, but I felt that furthering my education would be more beneficial to me, so I chose the path that suited me.

Yes, discrimination still exists. It exists in our government, schools, and businesses. There are instances of nepotism and acts of collusion occurring within local, state, and national agencies and institutions. As an older Black woman, I can see some progress being made with regard to racist attitudes. I was recently nominated and elected to be the first African American and the first female chairperson of the Democrat Party in my county. This is progress!

Additionally, I am a single parent of a son who got married and fathered two beautiful daughters. As I write this, they are making a move to a state that is nearly 3000 miles away. The absence of my only child and his family will be another obstacle in my life that will require some adjusting and adapting, but I will make the adjustment. Their move will start another chapter in my life.

The obstacles I overcame involved the time period of segregation. In the 1970s, I was a Black female in a White male-dominated workplace. It was difficult because White females had more rights and privileges; however Black females were gradually given more rights. A Black woman had to work harder and longer to receive recognition for doing the same things a White woman did. During my lifetime, I have learned that having family support or a supportive person is important, having a vision and goal to work toward is important, and having the means to accomplish those goals is necessary. Never give up on your dreams; one of mine was to earn a Doctoral Degree. Seeing my younger cousin working toward her degree inspired me to pursue mine, it just took me a while to start. I was fortunate to earn three degrees after becoming a single parent, and I'm proud to say that I worked a full-time job while doing so.

My past shaped me, hindered me, and inspired me. A combination of all of my experiences shaped me into the woman I am today. The period of time into which I was born also hindered me because I lived in a racist society, yet it inspired me to try to achieve more for myself. I have a wall plaque that reads "They told me I couldn't, that's why I did." When I saw this plaque, I knew that it would be my mantra for life. I suggest that you find a mantra for your life, keep working on your goals, and don't give up on your dreams.

CHAPTER 42

ON THE ROAD TO LEGACY

Daring to Dream

Erica Reid

Key Challenges: generational disparities; parental death; breaking chains of a history of failure

Dare to Dream 1ˢᵗ Generation Queen

As I stand first in the space of the unknown.
There is power in the first step
Step to high school graduation in 3 years
Step to going to college regardless of the financial woes
Step to a world that does not look like me
Step into a career that originally had no place for me
As I stand now modeling in a space that has become the familiar
I tell my students, someone's 1ˢᵗ generation baby
Step past the societal viewpoints that you ain't nothin but a criminal
Step past your acceptance that the power of your brain is only associated
with your ability to procreate
Step past the stereotypes formed around the beautiful color of skin
    you were birthed into

A Second Helping of Gumbo for the Soul: More Liberating Stories and Memories to Inspire Females of Color, pages 183–186.

Step past your own doubts of self-hate
Enter into a place of forced diversity
When they see you they will begin to think differently
Never be afraid of the conversation that is waiting for you

—E. Reid (2017)

The year I turned 26 was the beginning of a shift in my life. I was in my second year of teaching, living out my dream every day, and pouring into the lives of young minds that would shape my tomorrow. Being a first-generation high school graduate and then, a first college degree earner for both a bachelor's and master's degree made me feel like life was as good as it would get. I had done what both of my parents did not do. At this point in my life, I had lived beyond food stamps, baby daddy hiccups and took a detour to a road unknown to my entire family. I was living a dream. March 9th, set the course of my actual destiny in life. I was in my classroom when I got the call, my step-sister from New York, who was on the phone saying words that a 26-year-old person should never hear "Your mother is dead, your mother is dead." March 9th, was the day of my mother's 45th birthday and the day my life stopped moving. I went home, immediately. The days that passed were filled with sorrow, disbelief, and a sense of being lost that I am still unable to put into words. Life stopped moving for me at 26 because I had lived my life thus far ensuring that I made my parents proud by doing all the right things and now my favorite person on the planet had left me.

Purpose and drive seemed blurred for the rest of the year because I was numb. I went back to my role as a teacher. Each day, I tried to fill the lives of my students with joy and happiness. Their happiness gave me joy and just for a second; I could forget the moment, the news, and the day where life stopped moving for me. I thought as long as I stayed active, that life was going forward. It was not until my father died two years later when I realized my life had really changed. I was in my fourth year of teaching, in a new school district. I changed schools because truthfully, my previous principal, by no fault of her own, reminded me too much of my mother. The change was great and made things seem as if they were progressing. However, the phone call from my stepmother stopped me in my tracks. Immediately I left and began an "oh so" familiar process of preparing for the end of a life so young that ended so quickly. My father was 46 when his life came to an end. It was after his death that I begin to think about the essence of a life.

My father's death took me back to the story of my beginning. I remember my grandmother telling me the story. My mother and father were fighting during the last month of her pregnancy, and after my grandfather found out that my father had hit my mother, he was banned from the delivery room. My mother named me and forecasted the delicate part of my personality through my first name Erica, which means born leader. My mother didn't know at the time that she was creating a change in our family history with my birth. My father's death made me reflect on my mother's life and choice to be a single parent with five children from five different fathers within a village who never stopped helping her raise her children. She made choices situated in pursuit of love and ended up at the end of her journey with our five, beautiful budding smiles and her family. Ironically, having no father around was never something I thought about as a child because my uncle's and my grandparents helped fill any voids that may have gone unseen.

During the week of preparing for his cremation, I thought about our first meeting, when I was 14 years old. My parents always wanted the best for me, and I thought about the privilege and honor of taking care of my parents in their elderly years. I wanted to repay them for what they did for me by taking care of them. I thought about my father's life, as a hardworking Black man, with one child. He had suffered from an enlarged heart that robbed him of his late 30s and early 40s. He spent the years leading up to his death, recovering from a heart transplant and dreaming of his younger days and a return to his sense of being normal. He dreamed, and so did my mother. My father's last dreams reminded me of my mother's desires for my life. One day while leaving the grocery store she said to me, "Erica I want you to do everything I have never done." It was during the week of my father's death, in his apartment on a cold November night that I realized something extraordinary about my seemingly final road reached kind of life. I had survived! I beat the odds of seven generations of women who had several fathers to their children, seven decades of women with no high school diploma, or only a GED (General Education Development). Seven generations of women and men who never completed a single degree in college. A family history of lost dreams they didn't dare to live.

Both my mother and father had become a part of a tradition of unfulfilled destinies. An unfulfilled life purpose had saturated generations on both sides of my family. It wasn't that they stopped dreaming or had no ambitions, it was more of them getting caught up in daily life challenges. Poverty created a need to survive mentality for most of my family especially, my parents and grandparents. If you were lucky to get a job with benefits and avoid abusing drugs, alcohol or the world of prostitution, life was good.

My mother made her children her top priority. She was challenged with maintaining a decent job without a GED and feeding us. She worked one job for several years to make sure we had what we needed. My father's challenges were not different, as he also struggled and worked in a hospital buffing floors to pay bills, maintain his bachelor style apartment living, and to support his teenage daughter. The saying "The Struggle is Real" was a constant reality for my parents, my grandparents, and their parents. Their generations suffered as the result of poverty, and they never lived out the fullness of their dreams. I had survived and beat the odds.

As I prepared my father's remains to send to my grandmother, I made a choice to live beyond my wildest dreams because I had begun a change. This shift was co-constructed by each of my parents when they both instilled in me the essential tools of success; resilience, integrity, and loyalty. When I struggled with a mild form of dyslexia, it was my mother who spent several hours teaching me the difference between the letter "e" and the number three. While I accompanied my father during take your child to workdays, he showed me how to work hard. My grandparents demonstrated the vitality of an education GED. My family provided the internal aspects of character that equipped me to face the rest of my life.

When I returned to my school, I returned to a team that supported me like family; I started to wonder how my life would be if I truly lived like I was a shift of change. With sadness in my heart and a new outlook on my life, I decided to be the best educator I could be, love my students more, treat my colleagues even better than before, and teach at a level utilizing my capabilities. I encouraged my students to dream, and I dared them to be a force of change. It was a few years after my parents' death that I stepped into the next cycle of being a change. After ten years of teaching, patterns in education began to bother me, and I began to wonder how I could change the way our students were and how our families were served, especially in urban and inner-city schools.

My answer to these thoughts was applying to a Ph.D. program. I decided that I needed to be in higher education, the area where future teachers were trained, where conversations about best practices become the research articles that dictate instructional practices within the classroom of tomorrow. I was nervous about this dream, as the thought of venturing into this level of education shook me. I didn't think I was smart enough; and although I didn't have enough money, my mother's words and my continued family support came back to my mind and I decided to apply. This course of action led to my acceptance into the Teaching and Learning Department, and the start of the shift of change for my life, and the legacy of my family began. Although the road ahead is not easy or familiar, I have dedicated the rest of my life to being the change that destinies my family on a path toward a new reality where dreams are lived and not buried, and where people live out the destinies of their legacies.

CHAPTER 43

FROM THE SCHOOLHOUSE TO THE UNIVERSITY AND BACK

Applying Lessons from My Mother to Empower Others

Consuela Robinson

Key Challenges: poverty; single-parent; neighborhood violence; educational access; school transitions

It wasn't until college that I realized my family was considered the "working poor." In fact, terms such as socioeconomic status and "working poor" were unfamiliar to me until I began to study Ethnic Studies in college. Looking back, the fact that I was unfamiliar with these terms was a positive factor because it also meant that I was unaware of the odds against someone from my background taking the path that I did. Fortunately, neither my parents nor my school counselors ever treated me as if I could not achieve anything that I set my mind to.

Though neither of my parents attended college, both parents placed a high value on hard work and education. My mother, who immigrated to the United States from Trinidad before my birth, stressed the importance of education as a means to help others and improve the circumstances of life. My father, a career

A Second Helping of Gumbo for the Soul: More Liberating Stories and Memories to Inspire Females of Color, pages 187–190.
Copyright © 2020 by Information Age Publishing
187

military man, emphasized the importance of hard work and preparation. One of the frequent messages my mother conveyed to me growing up was that regardless of where you live or the negative influences around you, your environment does not dictate your possibilities.

My mother did her best to protect me from the potential hazards of my environment. Until late elementary school, I'd lived in military housing and attended schools with students whose parents were also in the military. My classmates and I were all from similar military familial backgrounds, and there was no obvious distinction in social class. I recall having a healthy dose of childhood innocence. However, after my father retired from the military, my childhood took a turn. My parents divorced, and we moved from military housing and

My mother, now a single woman with limited financial resources, was forced to make difficult decisions. She moved the family into a community that was very different than the quiet, peaceful, orderly and somewhat sheltered military community that we were accustomed to. The community was composed of hard-working families; a few who owned their homes, but most who struggled to make ends meet, and others whose primary source of income was government assistance. My mother, who probably could have qualified for government assistance as a single woman with five children (four of whom were school age), had too much pride to apply for or accept welfare. She chose, instead, to work and divide her meager income amongst the family.

My new neighborhood was riddled with violence. During the late 1980s and early 90s in Southern California, it was not uncommon for me to see crime tape near the bus stop on the way to school due to a young person in the neighborhood becoming a victim to gang violence. It was also not uncommon to see young female peers pregnant before the end of high school. At night, the sound of "pop, pop, pop" in the neighborhood, followed by the reflection of red and blue police lights shining through the windows, became almost routine. As a household, we became trained on "duck and cover" strategies and staying away from windows. My mother "handled" this by keeping us in the house as much as possible and not allowing friends from the neighborhood in the house. She would often say, "Your books are your friends...go read something." As a result, my siblings and I were accused of being "stuck up" and "acting and talking White."

Books and school became my refuge, and I actually began to prefer staying indoors and reading, rather than going outside, even during the summer months. A change of residence also meant a change of schools. This began, what I refer to as my "education on education." My mother did not want my siblings or me to attend the neighborhood school because she didn't feel that it was a quality school. She wanted to keep us from neighborhood influences as much as possible. My older sister, who was recognized in the community for her talent as a singer, was recruited to attend the local performing arts magnet school. My younger sister, my younger brother and I, each talented in our own right, followed suit and were also enrolled in the performing arts school as well.

Attending a magnet school exposed me to a more diverse peer group and helped me to see a vast set of possibilities for my future. I connected with peers, teachers, and I had a special connection with my school counselor. For a woman who was not college educated, my mother was educated enough to know the value of connecting with individuals in schools who would help her to navigate the school system and who would nurture her children's educational pursuits as much as she did. My mother became a frequent caller to my school counselor's office. My mother and my school counselor became my dynamic duo and most vocal educational advocates. In elementary, middle, and high school, I was always told by educators and family members that I was smart. Although I was told that I was smart, I was unaware of how these individuals defined "smart," and it wasn't until high school that I began to believe them. My school counselor introduced me to the college application process, college visits, and scholarship opportunities. I thrived academically and was able to apply and gain acceptance to several colleges. Since I had done very well academically throughout high school, I believed I would do just as well in college. My thoughts could not have been further from what I experienced in college.

The first year of college was a rude awakening, academically, socially and emotionally. I felt as if I was living a double identity. I was unsure of myself, and I felt as if I did not fit in with students who did not look like me, came from more affluent families and attended more prestigious high schools. The population of African American students was extremely small compared to the magnet high school I previously attended and I soon learned the unspoken practice of greeting other African American students with a smile or a wave, whether we knew each other or not, as if to say, "I am glad to see you, and you are not here alone." Although not ashamed of my beginnings, I was reluctant to share anything about my background with classmates for fear of being judged. This was further compounded by the fact that a close family member was incarcerated while I was pursuing my education. This loss impacted my entire family, and we all felt the despair of no longer being able to experience life as we knew it before the incarceration. I felt that I had two identities: one with my family and one in school. During the week I studied hard and kept up the façade of a happy, carefree college student from a "stable" family, while on weekends, I visited my family member in prison. I began to wear an invisible, psychological mask to hide my anxiety and the pressure that I was feeling as a result of trying to keep up a façade. I didn't want my classmates to have any indication that the person sitting next to them experienced life "issues" that I often heard them speak about in derogatory terms.

I struggled academically, particularly in the areas of math and science, and wondered why some students breezed through these courses, while the coursework seemed like a foreign language to me. Though family and educators always told me I was smart, I definitely did not feel smart at the time. I soon realized that as much as my mother and my school counselor supported me furthering my education, they could not have prepared me for the fact that I was now in a university setting with students who had opportunities and access to courses and educational experiences in high school that I did not. While taking college courses in Ethnic Studies, I had an epiphany—despite feeling academically underprepared for college, my life gave me a wealth of firsthand experience to contribute to the class discussions. I was able to contribute and engage in meaningful discourse with others on issues of educational disparities, social hierarchies and race, class, and power dynamics of various ethnic groups in the United States. For the first time since entering college, I experienced academic success, became more energized and established relationships with a group of peers and trusted educators who understood my journey and encouraged me to continue to pursue my studies. I eventually graduated with my degree in Ethnic Studies and became the first person in my family to graduate from college.

After my undergraduate experience, I continued my educational path by pursuing a Master's Degree in Social Work in order to empower disenfranchised individuals to fight against the negative "isms" (e.g., racism) in the world. Like my mother, I believed in the transformational power of education, and I chose to utilize my social work degree in the school system. What better place than K–12 education to empower children and families? Throughout my career as a social worker in education, I worked with many families and students who had faced challenges similar to those I experienced in my own life.

I've gone from the schoolhouse to the university and back to the schoolhouse. The difference now is that as an adult, I have the life experience and tools to assist parents who, like my mother, want the best for their children despite family challenges. I am deeply humbled every day to have the opportunity to assist students and families with navigating educational settings, that can be daunting, unfamiliar and unwelcoming, especially to individuals who are immigrants like my mother. My background and challenges, which I was reluctant to share in college, is now shared as a vehicle to support, encourage, and motivate others to achieve their educational goals.

Though I struggled through my first several years of college, I made it through, and I am now pursuing doctoral studies in Educational Leadership. I've learned that my background and experiences have made me the advocate, survivor, and achiever I am today, and should not be hidden from others. Hiding your background leads to self-inflicted stress and pressure and denies others the possibility of being encouraged by your path. Throughout my educational journey, I kept in mind the lessons from my mother: regardless of where you live or the negative influences around you, your environment does not dictate your possibilities. Be encouraged!

CHAPTER 44

ALWAYS PUSH FORWARD, NEVER LOOK BACK

Cristina Rodriguez Chen

Key Challenges: familial pride; faith; English as a second language

From the time I could remember or even rationalize thoughts, I knew that I had a great calling on my life. Although it has taken me more than half of my life to figure out this calling, looking back, I can see that God's divine presence has always guided my steps. I am the youngest of 7 children born to Cuban immigrants. My parents, Consuelo and Servando Rodriguez, fled to the United States in 1966 to escape the communist oppression of Fidel Castro. Along with them, they brought their young children, their culture, and the clothes on their backs. Although their intent was never to stay in the United States, sadly that was their destiny. Many Cubans of their era believed, their move was temporary, and someday they would be able to return to the place of their birth. But for my parents, that was not the case.

When my mother had her sixth child, she had a tubal ligation. Two years later, I was born. For many years, I struggled with the thought that I was not wanted. However, what I grew to understand years later was that I was meant to be here on this earth. Nothing, not even medical technology, could keep me away. During the first three years of my life, we lived in the projects of Tampa, Florida. My

A Second Helping of Gumbo for the Soul: More Liberating Stories and Memories to Inspire Females of Color, pages 191–194.
Copyright © 2020 by Information Age Publishing

father worked at a shipyard in the evenings, and my mother was a stay at home mother. When I turned three, my parents bought a two bedroom, one bath, wood frame house in a low-income area of Tampa for$7,000 and they lived in that home until their last days. This. Needless to say, it was too small for all of our family members.

My parents were both uneducated. My father had at the most, a 6th-grade education. My mother sadly never learned to read or write in Spanish, let alone speak English. However, my mother was one of the smartest and strongest women I have known.

The greatest gift my parents ever gave me was the ability to speak Spanish. In my home the rule was "if you don't speak Spanish, you do not eat." Let's just say I was a pretty chubby child. They instilled a sense of pride in me. To them, being Cuban was something to be very proud of. They taught me the music of their homeland, the traditions, and customs of their people.

During my elementary school years, I went to an inner-city school. Although my first language was Spanish; I was taught English. But, from the time I started school, struggled academically. By the time I was in 4th grade, I not only had difficulty with being able to read, but I also became a very sad child. I was dealing with a deep sadness and low self-esteem. I remember being a very unhappy and not having the skills to express or even understand what was happening to me. School was difficult and my home life was difficult as well. We did not have many luxuries. I even remember my parents reaching out to community resources for assistance with things such as Christmas presents.

It was not until I was in the 7th grade that my grades improved. Looking back, I now realize that the reason I struggled so much in my elementary years was because not only did I lack a strong foundation in my first language, I was struggling to learn a second language at the same time. It typically takes second language learners approximately 5 to 7 years, sometimes 10 years to develop the cognitive academic language proficiency to be successful in school, which is why I struggled so much during my early years in school.

Like many Cubans of my parent's era, they never learned to speak English. I never really understood why they chose not to learn the language of their new country. It wasn't until later in my life, when both of my parents had passed away, that I finally understood why they never learned English. I read a book called Next Year in Cuba written by Gustavo Perez-Firmat (2006), a first generation Cuban. In his book, he explained that his parents, like mine, were Cuban Refugees, exiles. They were forced to come to the United States to flee political persecution. As exiles, this meant that their intention was never to stay in the United States. Their stay was supposed to be temporary. After reading his book and reflecting on my life, I finally understood so many things that my parents did not have the words to communicate. I recall as a child hearing my parents say things such as "Well, next year we will be in Cuba." Or "When I die, I want to be buried in my homeland of Cuba." All while, keeping their traditions and customs and making sure that their children spoke the language of their motherland. This is why many Cuban communities in places such as Miami, continue to speak Spanish and maintain their culture.

My parents instilled a strong, incredible sense of pride in me. My father always told me to be proud of where you come from and to never forget who you are. Thanks to him, I have always hung on to what I know to be true. I am the proud daughter of Cuban immigrants. I am Cuban-American. I am proud of my heritage, the struggles I faced in my life and the successes that I have obtained are because of my strong sense of self.

Growing up as the child of immigrant Cubans who did not speak English, I had to grow up pretty quickly. From a young age, I learned survival skills that many children never have to deal with. I had to serve as an interpreter for my parents, and some of the conversations I assisted them with were not appropriate for children. But, my parents had no other option. The other thing about being raised by immigrant parents was that we did not have the resources other families had. Whatever clothes I wore were bought from thrift stores or hand-me-downs from neighbors or relatives. I remember going to school with a striped shirt and checkered pants. To a young, impressionable girl, this was quite difficult, as I did not understand the rules of putting clothes together, and without understanding why, I was made fun of a lot in school.

When I was thirteen years old, I remember that my father had open-heart surgery. That was a pretty scary time for my family. From that point on, he could no longer work at the shipyard. To make ends meet, my parents began selling fruits and vegetables outside of a local Cuban bakery and in local areas 7 days per week. I recall that my father bought an old pickup truck and in the bed of the truck created an attachment that looked to me much like a house. It had a roof and was lined with rows of wood so that they could showcase their goods. When not in school, I would accompany my parents to different neighborhoods to help them sell their produce. I remember my father using this cowbell to get the neighbor's attention when he came down the road. Over time that cow bell became so well known in different neighborhoods that people would come out of their homes to shop my father's produce. If working 7 days a week wasn't enough, I recall my sister and I would have to wake up as early as 1:00 am or 2:00 am to accompany my parents to the local produce market. They would get there early so that they could buy the freshest produce for their customers.

For a thirteen-year-old girl, being taken to school in my father's work truck was quite embarrassing. I recall that as we would approach the school, I would duck deep down in the seat. My father threatened me by saying that if I hid in the seat, he would ensure that everyone saw me coming by making the loudest noises. I learned very quickly to stay seated, but just hurry out when he dropped me off. I started working at a very young age. At 13, I was not only helping my parents with their produce business, I also began working at the bakery. I saved my money to buy my school clothes and supplies. Being able to do so gave me such pride and a sense of independence from the poverty I had known all of my life.

My parents had taught me work ethic, pride in self and a desire to do better. As I grew up, I was determined to change the outcome of my life. I wanted to be better and do better. I knew the only way to accomplish this feat was to get an education. I graduated from high school and went straight into college, becoming I am the first one in my family to receive a college education. I decided to become a teacher. Once I finished my Bachelor's degree, I continued my education and earned my Master's degree, and although it took me approximately 23 years, in May of 2017, I finally completed my Ph.D.

Unfortunately, both parents have passed. Neither one of them was alive to see my graduation day. I feel that the day I graduated with my Ph.D. was the day that I broke all the chains and curse of poverty in my family. Moving forward my children will never struggle in life the way I did. Sadly, my parents were never able to fulfill their dreams of going back to Cuba as their final resting place. But, what I can say is that thanks to their strength, I was given an opportunity to change not only my life, but the life of other children like me—those who come from homes of poverty, where English is not the dominant language.

Today, I work as an educator. I am an advocate for children like me. I strive daily to educate teachers about Culturally and/or Linguistically Diverse (CLD) children of poverty, like me. Those who choose to hear my story forever change the way they see these students. I also strive to let my story be known by others like me. If I can just help one child change the course of his/her life, then my struggles have been worth it.

What I share with these students are the words that still ring in my ears from my parents. "Always push forward, never look back. To be better yourself, you must work hard and do better. Never forget who you are or where you come from. Be proud of your roots. Your future lies at your feet. Follow the steps God places in front of you. Those steps will take your further than you ever dreamed." Thanks to my parents, I am a fighter, a survivor and an advocate for all children.

REFERENCE

Perez-Firmat, G. (2006). *Next year in Cuba: A Cubano's coming-of-age in America.* Houston, TX: Arte Público.

There is nothing better than feasting on a "trial turned triumph." As you feast on the triumphs of these stories, let them feel and feed your soul!
—*Michelle Frazier Trotman Scott*

CHAPTER 45

LIFELINE TO SUCCESS

Tia Scott

Key Challenges: family issues; alcoholism; low teacher expectations, perseverance, student voice

I believe that the challenges I have faced are not intended for me to hide, but to
share with other women for ministry, growth, and enrichment. My life challenges
began at birth. I was born the oldest of three girls to a clinically depressed mother
and an alcoholic father. My parents separated before my third birthday; thus I
have no memories of living as a family with my father. Most of the stories I have
heard about him surfaced when I was an adult, and many of them were not good
stories. However, I want to be clear that the one thing I never doubted was my father's love for us. He unconditionally and consistently proclaimed his love for us
whenever we saw or talked to him. I partially credit my success to the love of my
father. Tragically, he died in April 1978, just before my 15th birthday, succumbing
to the woes of alcoholism, cirrhosis of the liver, and some unknown person who
beat and murdered him in his hospital bed.

Now, I cannot tell any story without mentioning the two women in my life who
nurtured and watered the seeds of love that my father had planted in me. My aunt

A Second Helping of Gumbo for the Soul: More Liberating Stories and Memories
to Inspire Females of Color, pages 197–200.
Copyright © 2020 by Information Age Publishing
All rights of reproduction in any form reserved.

and my grandmother were always there for me, even before I recognized that I needed them. They challenged and inspired my belief system, encouraged me to always do my best, and delivered powerful messages of perseverance.

On the outside, I battled community and teacher judgment, a visual handicap, and the pressure of my peers who wanted to know how I could hold my confidence while facing so many personal and family challenges. In the neighborhood where we moved when I was 10, all of the families were intact with both a mother and father, except ours; it was not a comfortable existence for us. Well beyond what I could ever articulate, my village was made complete by my aunt and grandmother who gave me words of wisdom and a healthy perspective.

Whenever I faced adversity, anybody who knew me well asked, "What did your aunt say?" because they quickly learned that growing up, she was whom I immediately sought for advice. My grandmother showered unconditional love on all of her grandchildren and built her life around us. I admiringly admit that she was my college roommate because I moved with her when I went to college to create a little separation from my mother.

I grew up in the city, attending public schools, and moving from school to school as my mother changed her course of life. We first lived in a couple of small apartments in the southeast quadrant of the city, then settled for a few years back at home with my maternal grandparents and my aunt. By my 17th birthday, my mother met and married her second husband, a man who adored and cherished us as his own children. He too, showered us with his unconditional love and protected us as if his life depended on it. Also, an alcoholic, when he and my mother separated, back to my grandmother's house, we moved. By this time, my grandmother was single too.

I remember feeling obligated to remain home for college because I thought that my mother needed me to protect her. I had assumed the role of family protector because of my mother's early relationships. My father and stepfather would lash out at her but seemed to keep a low profile whenever I was around. I heard stories, but never witnessed firsthand their bad behavior toward my mother. I played this role with my mother and my sisters—no one was going to be hurt or disrespected in my presence.

In school, I remember some teachers asking me, "Did you know that you write well?" while others disbelieved my work and asked to hold my papers until I produced more work of the same quality. It was a repeating theme throughout my education. I do not know how it came about or even how I found my voice, but my voice has a long time. To others, there was nothing about my personality that would make people believe that I had that voice.

Despite all the changes in my life and attending several schools, I managed to develop my gift. Although I never wanted to be a writer, my path just carried me there. Unfortunately, I faced the obstacle of ME. I carried hurt and anger, and sought to be heard and understood at every turn. Although I was meek and soft-spoken, my attitude spoke volumes when I thought I was being wronged.

Teachers told me, "Your mouth is going to get you into trouble," and "You'll never amount to anything." People scoffed at me and looked down their noses at me when I lashed out at those who I perceived treated me unfairly; I was the little girl with a big mouth.

In high school, my aunt told me about an internship in the Federal government that would follow me from the summer after high school graduation through my senior year in college. When I went to my high school counselor for my transcript, she calculated my grade point average and declared, "Why, you're in the top ten percent of your class!" She was shocked, but I wasn't. So, in April of my senior year of high school, my school counselor made sure that I completed an application to Howard University, and she followed up with them until I received my acceptance.

Over the next four years, I was emotionally battered along with the other Black writers at the government newspaper, where I interned. At some point, I even decided that writing was not for me, but I had never done anything else. During the summer after college graduation, just after being offered a permanent position at the newspaper, I cashed the check that everyone had warned me about. I had arranged to meet with the Public Affairs Officer, who ran the newspaper where I was interning. I wanted to address the way he had been treating the Black staff writers and ask about how things would change if/when I accepted the permanent position. Needless to say, that position never became mine. The conversation was impossible, and the response was worse than the treatment I had experienced throughout my internship. Wounded and embarrassed, I learned a lesson about diplomacy that I carry even today.

Still, I forged ahead with determination and vigor. I transitioned to a career as a writer and editor at another governmental agency before moving on to private industry and later, a large corporation. After marrying and then giving birth to my second son, I decided that I needed to call it quits. I was burning both ends of the candle and was finding it difficult to keep up with corporate demands and be a good mother.

After three children and some time, I decided that I needed to re-enter the job market, but I had not kept up with the industry. A lot had happened since I last worked—the Internet and technology—and I was not sure what I could do. A neighbor suggested that I try a family friendly career—teaching. After substitute teaching for half the school year, I realized that was not the answer. However, I noticed that the school counselor was always smiling and after meeting with her, I made my decision to go back to school to pursue a master's degree in counseling and combined my two loves—writing and children.

As a high school counselor, I wrote hundreds of recommendation letters while talking to kids to help them make good choices. Again, I assumed the role of protector and later immersed myself in an alternative program where I could be the voice of the children with little exposure. It was my turn to help students find the right path and lead them to the resources that they did not know existed. As much as I loved the kids that I "protected," I cried for them so much that I had to protect myself by returning to comprehensive schools to work my plan from another angle. I have a girlfriend who told me and still believes that I always find the hardest, most resistant student. She cannot figure out how I find them, but I always wanted (and still want) to be there to help those kids develop what I wish someone had helped me to develop—decorum.

As I reflect on my path, it is interesting to note that I cherish loyalty and truth. I believe that the best gift you can give to anyone is yourself through loyalty and support. If my own children question anything about me, it is never my unconditional love and support for them. I love kids and believe that, as adults, we must protect them at all cost. They are the future; thus, we are the lifelines to their success. It must have passed through the genes because each of my children (now adults) turn into different people when it comes to kids. It is amazing to watch.

As for me, I am doing something that I never expected of myself; I am enrolling in a doctoral program. I have enjoyed a successful writing career and a successful school-counseling career. I can at least say that, although my mother did not always know where or how to lead me, she insisted that I would not have to walk in her path. She connected me to the people who could and did help me—my aunt and my grandmother. I have three great sons that I have been able to watch grow, nurture, and support, despite and through various obstacles and challenges. I am capable of providing the unconditional love and support that was given to me by the village of my father, my stepfather, my mother, my aunt, and my grandmother. Create a village for your family. We did, and because of that village, despite the odds, deficits, challenges, and obstacles, I am a winner!

CHAPTER 46

AN AFRICAN AMERICAN'S EXPERIENCE OF THE TALENTED-GIFTED-STEM ROLLER COASTER

Terrell Shockley

Key Challenges: low teacher expectations, gifted and talented education implications

AN AFRICAN AMERICAN'S EXPERIENCE OF THE TALENTED-GIFTED-STEM ROLLER COASTER

My talented and gifted education and STEM interests began like an ascending rollercoaster. At the age of 18 months, I accompanied my grandmother to work where she was the director of the early learning center. My love for learning began there, with the three and four-year-olds. At the age of five, I enrolled in a science and technology pullout program. The teacher created a problem-based, multisensory environment, for kindergarten through second-grade students. I remember many of the tasks; we grew vegetables, disassembled computers, and dissected fetal pigs. This is one of the reasons that I support STEM in early childhood programs.

A Second Helping of Gumbo for the Soul: More Liberating Stories and Memories to Inspire Females of Color, pages 201–204.

Mirroring the research, my STEM learning reached a peak after grade 2, and the rollercoaster began to decline. In third grade, I experienced a shift. I officially received the "gifted" label, but the pullout sessions ceased with the decision to integrate our group, and my mainstream classes bored me to tears. Literally. The only memorable lesson for me was a field trip to a local prairie. Every other part of science took place mostly indoors with a focus on reading and writing (which I found boring). The roller coaster did not move in third grade, not even a micrometer.

In fourth and fifth grades, the roller coaster descended. Although the TAG pullouts began again, this time we met with a different teacher and for mathematics; I liked that it challenged us, but I was not as engaged as I was when I was participating in the problem-based K–2 science pullouts. I also landed on the receiving end of my first incident of bullying in 4th and 5th grade. The girl who decided to bully me (because she said I always talked White), and she continuously called me the names of my White friends. I remember her threatening me, calling me scared, and she was right. Although I was not scared of her, I was scared of my mother—who taught at the school.

Unfortunately, the name-calling and threats became too much, and the bully and I ended up fighting in the bathroom. The bully said that the reason I went to the other class with the "White people" every year is because I talked White and because my mother worked there, not because I was smart. What I learned from that experience are the implications of code-switching and what people may think when you do not code-switch. All of my school friends advised me to simply ignore the bully. After the bathroom incident, she ignored me too.

In seventh grade, the TAG/science roller coaster moved in an ascending direction again. I soared in science classes. I attempted and completed every science project, both the required ones and optional ones. For one of my projects, I brought in an aquarium, a piece of a hose that my dad cut for me, and some dirt to create a geyser for a physics demonstration on pressure and volume. I wanted to learn more in math as well, but my math teachers provided mostly worksheets, which I would finish very quickly, and then work on assignments for science.

In eighth grade, I visited the International Baccalaureate (IB) classes at one high school and the Advanced Placement (AP) classes at another. I chose the AP route, which required reading novels from the summer reading lists before ninth grade. Unfortunately, that summer there were not any Black authors on the English and History Reading list, so I protested. Students were to choose three books that summer. When I inquired about other options, the only other Black author on the curriculum for the entire year was Maya Angelou. I had already read all of her books, so the teachers assigned me the six books in the Roots series by Alex Haley. Not only did I end up reading double the number of books, English and History also required double the work to stay focused. Rosa Parks and Martin Luther King, Junior were the only Black people we studied that were uplifting, so I had to find my own books to read if I wanted a text from a Black author, and when we were required to present and embody a speech by a famous person, there were not any Black people listed to choose from. I had to add to the list again, and I presented a speech by the late U.S. Representative, Barbara Jordan.

In addition to a lack of historical or current options of optimal interest and cultural relevance for a high performing Black female student in advanced courses, I also encountered alternative facts. I remember the lessons of my 11th grade American History teacher, very well, although I have tried not to. He began the unit on slavery by saying something like this: "You know when you do something that you feel bad about, and you wish you didn't do it but, it happened?" He maintained that slaves were too expensive to be whipped and beaten, so they were not. I remember arguing with him about slaves being whipped and beaten, and his reply was that my argument made no economic sense. He then asked the class if we would go outside and key our own cars. He also taught us that if slaves wanted to go back to Africa, they could (he was referencing Liberia of course) and that is how he knew that being a slave was not so bad because they stayed. My teacher and I continuously debated revisionist accounts of American history. Even though I already hated history, I considered this a low teacher expectation. There was no way that he thought that I was smart if he thought that I should believe this. I had the prior knowledge from other classes and from reading Roots during the summer before ninth grade to participate in an accurate debate about slavery. Also, I became the Black History Brain Bowl Captain for my service organization the year that I took his class. I declared war against him and his revisionism. That year, the roller coaster ascended and descended, and I officially crossed off History from the list of "likables."

I remember my classmate asking my history teacher where he attended college. When he told us, I knew that regardless of the close distance and the offers made to me, that I would not even grant them an application fee. I knew that I would definitely attend an HBCU, which I was unsure of before my experience with this teacher. One of the reasons that I considered attending the local university and not an HBCU was because I saw people of different races at the local university. I knew that I did not grow up in a largely diverse school environment and I wanted to learn more about other cultures and other people; however, I decided I would have to delay those diverse learning opportunities until graduate school (fortunately my undergraduate science courses were ethnically diverse). There was only one Hispanic student at my high school who was from Colombia, and there were a few Asian American students. One Asian American student, who identified as Chinese enrolled in my High Honors Chemistry class, where I learned even more about low teacher expectations.

The first day of High Honors Chemistry class, the teacher turned around and stretched her brows at me in a look of what I saw as surprise. "This is High Honors Chemistry," she said. I smiled and informed her that I was aware. She said it twice more, which confused me. So, I stood up to show her my schedule. Also, my friends (the same crew from elementary school) had saved a seat for me, which made her look even more confused.

Chemistry was easy for me, very easy. I knew The Periodic Table very well and was able to teach it without hesitation, but I did not perform well in her class. I also did not take the AP Chemistry Exam the next year, as she was the only Instructor; instead, I helped other students study for the exam. I was uninspired by all of what she taught and by her astonishingly low bar for me. She would ask me questions about my hair texture, etc. and that was the most we ever discussed. Over those two years, people who I outperformed or performed equally as well as, since kindergarten, miraculously became smarter than me. Something started to change regarding my interest and performance in school.

During the same year of High Honors Chemistry, I also enrolled in High Honors Physics. I was the only person of color in both classes. My Physics teacher, who was highly skilled in Physics, did not apply his mathematics skills to my tests. There were errors in scoring, on every-single-test. Interestingly, none of my classmates experienced these grading errors. After each test, I recalculated the points, handed the test back, and he revised the grade. This happened on lab exams and lab write-ups as well. I made an "A" every semester, and on every test once corrected. At the end of the year, the teacher finally thought that I was able to learn and apply Physics. I remember that he told the class that if they ever wanted to learn how to write a Physics lab, that they should ask me. I had nothing left to give schoolwork; I felt like all interests in academic subjects went on a sabbatical. The roller coaster descended in science from that year until my freshman year of college Chemistry, at an HBCU, where it reached one of its peaks.

I still read about top performing students losing interest in science courses. I watched students that tested into TAG in elementary school lose interest by the time they arrive in middle school. I struggled to convince TAG students to enroll in advanced science courses when I taught high school biology. I wondered, had a teacher turned them away?

Although some learning experiences are a roller coaster filled with monocultural curricula, and historically inaccurate information, these descending points are only a few segments of any roller coaster. I hope that generations of Talented and Gifted students remain on track, focus on the peaks, highlight the ascending points, and continue upward.

CHAPTER 47

UNDER RECONSTRUCTION

Ariel Smith

Key Challenges: insecurity;, self-esteem; self-image; imposter syndrome; poverty

For years I wore my academic achievement as a mask. It gave me a form of confidence that waxed and waned in between whenever I would make a perfect score on a test, to having my peers and even my family ridicule my looks. I was proud of my brain, but I hated my face. Through elementary and high school, I felt proud that teachers and administrators constantly chose me to represent the school and be the recipient for several academic and service awards. Yet deep down, I felt empty and worthless because I was rejected from activities with my peers and especially when it came to dating in high school. I used to look at the girls in my class and wish I had their style. I wished I was as pretty, as feminine, as agile, as outgoing…as perfect as they were.

I tried as best as I could to fit in, but it would always result in an epic fail. I stood out like a sore thumb. Adults who would meet always said I had an "old soul" and they were right. My great grandmother, great aunt, and grandmother raised me because my mom dropped out of high school and had me at age 17. There were no kids on my block I could play with; even if there were my family kept such close tabs on me I would have never been allowed to play with them. I never had a birthday party with friends my own age growing up, and my family

A Second Helping of Gumbo for the Soul: More Liberating Stories and Memories to Inspire Females of Color, pages 205–208.

made up the majority of my contact and in-depth engagement with other people for relationship building. Because the students in my class often had developed negative behavior reputations, my great aunt made it clear she didn't want to find me hanging with them. She had no need to worry though –they didn't want to be around me either. I was too much of a nerd and a teacher's pet, so there was nothing about me that related to them. It was much easier for them to exclude me than include me.

I wanted to pretend that the rejection I felt with my peers didn't hurt, but I was lying to myself. I wanted to be accepted, and I never felt that acceptance beyond academics. The problem didn't fade when I got home, either. One moment I was being praised for bringing home straight 100s on my quarter two report card in the fourth grade, and the next moment I'm being told by great aunt how ugly I looked with acne on my face. I can't tell you how many times I used to look at myself in the mirror and tear myself apart, but I can tell you it was daily. I looked at myself and saw someone no one wanted. I started with my looks and would go on to other things I didn't like about myself: too awkward, too nerdy, too tomboyish, too in-nocent. I looked my list of things I saw in myself and compared to the popular girls at school, and it easily became a no-brainer why I didn't fit in elementary or middle school. Why would anyone want to be around someone like me?

I carried this toxic and degrading view of myself into high school. This time though, more challenges surfaced. Before high school, I attended a predominant-ly Black private and Christian school for economically disadvantaged students where I was the star student. Nearly everything came quick and easy to me. It was the one thing I felt I could better than the girls I envied. But now, at a predomi-nately White, Catholic, and middle to upper-class private school I fought to stay on top. I knew what it was like to feel inferior in comparison to my other Black peers, but I never had to face imposter syndrome and exclusion like I did when I got there. Those feelings intensified when I fought my way through all honors and AP courses. There were times where we had to work in groups, and I was the only Black person (or person of color) in the class. My partner(s) would say the bare minimum to me while having full conversations with the other White students.

Perhaps they said little to me because we had little to nothing in common. My life had been molded and shaped by things they would only ever read about. They always had friends over at their homes, and I never did because we were embar-rassed that our living conditions were far below sub-standard. In high school, my peers knew what it was like to ride horses, go on family vacations, dining out with family, or preparing for their driver's license exam in the car their parents just bought for their sixteenth birthday. I knew what it was like to go YEARS without ever having a bathtub to bathe in and use buckets to fill with water. I knew how to use home hospice toilets because the actual toilet wasn't safe to use. I knew what it was like to spend my high school years with no running water, buying jugs of water at Walmart and catching rainwater to flush the toilet. I knew what is like to not have a bed of my own; we took two ancient beds and pushed them together for me, my great aunt and great-grandmother to sleep on. I made an art of crawling in the right way to avoid scrapes and cuts from the springs. If I failed at being skillful enough to dodge the wild metal coils, I knew to take rags and wrap them. I also knew to try my best to stay on my great aunt's good side whenever she was angry, no matter how near impossible that was. And, I knew how important finances were after watching my great aunt cry after filing bankruptcy or going through unemployment. My classmates learned on TV that poverty left people with no money to buy whatever they wanted. I learned that growing up in poverty and dysfunction can leave a person broke and broken...and I was that person.

Between feeling inadequate because of my looks, personality, or background, I found myself desperate to align myself with anyone who called me a friend or anyone who said I was pretty. That's a mistake I made through college. I felt like if I had friends that were pretty, popular, and seemed to have all the things I didn't, I would eventually "arrive to their level." I thought if I were able to date attractive guys, it would establish that I am beautiful and deserving of love like everyone else. It was as if I had created a list of prerequisites before I thought anyone, including myself, thought I was good enough to be seen as beautiful and lovable. I equated people using me and giving me even the slightest bit of attention meant that I was accepted and most of all wanted and valued.

I thank God for giving me wake up calls. There certainly was more than one because I needed several. It took several friends using me for money and connections. It took several guys ghosting me because they didn't want to put in the commitment I desired by waiting until marriage. And it took listening to what my friends, who I thought had everything going for themselves, were actually going through behind closed doors before I was able to realize a few things. I realized that because I had cast such a lowly, degrading image of myself long ago, I had accepted it as my truth. Not only did I accept inferiority as my truth, but I also gave others permission to accept it as their truth of me. I looked at myself wrong; all my life I was trying to do things and be things that would qualify me to be good enough for other people. But they didn't get to determine my value. I did.

Realizing that I control my value has been scary and liberating. It can be scary at times because sometimes, I still find myself seeking approval. Yet, it's liberating because I don't have to wait on anyone or anything to validate me. Waiting on others and opportunities for some of my desires stifled me. For example, I was too afraid to try new things such as going natural because I was afraid I would look ugly. After doing the big chop myself, I felt a little apprehensive at first, but now I love it. For the first time, I can look at a picture of myself and compliment myself...even with a few acne scars. Embracing myself has actually allowed me to grow and develop. Since starting college and moving away from home, I have been able to explore what my style is and what I like. While my style is totally different from friends, and I'm still a nerdy, awkward Black woman, I own every last one of those adjectives.

One exercise that has helped me embrace myself is about exposing all of the lies I have internalized about myself; whether they were projected on me by others or by myself. I take a notebook, and in pencil, I write down all the negative things about myself that I perceive to be true. I skip three lines between each. Then in red ink, I find three positive statements to counter each of the negative "truths" I've written. I then read the red, positive truths out loud each day, even if I don't fully believe them. Over time, I start believing them, so I erase the negatives I had written in pencil. In time, only the positive affirmations about myself that are written in pen remain. I still do this exercise I learned from motivational speaker Lisa Nichols who said this, "What people say about you and what you say about you isn't true until you accept it as your truth." Her statement has stuck with me since! Each of us have the power to either build ourselves with love or tear ourselves down with insecurity, comparison, and self-hate. After years of demolishing, I chose earlier this year to rebuild.

CHAPTER 48

DON'T LET THE JUMP SUIT FOOL YOU

Inmate Mothers Reclaiming Power from the Inside, Teaching, Learning, and Parenting

Mattyna L. Stephens

Key Challenges: Incarceration; loss of power; separation; resilience

Boom! Boom! Boom! It all starts with a balled fist pounding on the door, or the door being kicked by a member of a special task force either in the middle of the night or early in the morning. The children watch as their mother is being arrested and, then, hauled off in a police vehicle. Sometimes, the arrest may occur on the job. They lay and wait for you to exit the building to make their arrest. You see, for centuries African American women have been chronically neglected from the protection of the justice system.

To understand the context of the narrative, one must understand my beginnings. Anyone who has ever searched for a job knows that it is a grueling process. After learning that I was in search of a job, an associate advised that I should attend a job fair hosted by a local community college. I took the advice of my associate and attended. Out of desperation, I agreed to take the instructor of busi-

A Second Helping of Gumbo for the Soul: More Liberating Stories and Memories to Inspire Females of Color, pages 209–212.

ness position with the assumption that my appointment would be on campus. As the conversation progressed, I discovered that my appointment would be at the Women's Federal Prison. At first, I was a little reluctant about accepting the assignment because of the media portrayal of incarcerated women. It was fear of the unknown. Nonetheless, I took the job.

When I turn into the entryway of the facility, inevitably, I read the huge brown sign posted off to the left—Women's Federal Prison. Each time I read the sign, thoughts of fear and long-suffering seemed to resonate. The women's Federal Prison of Ketchum (pseudonym), Texas is a minimum-security facility that rests on 37 acres. While the term minimum security can be misleading, there are facts that remain. You are confined. You eat when they say you can eat. You sleep when they say you can sleep. And, you shower when they say you can shower.

As an instructor of business, the women enrolled in my course to meet the requirements of earning a certificate in business administration. Developing an autopictography is one of the projects the women are assigned. During class, each student is given the opportunity to tell her personal story based on the pictures each woman provides. As such, the autopictography is a window to the women's experiences. Without minimizing the experiences of the other women, whenever the African American women would share their stories, I leaned in just a little closer. The more they shared, the more I inquired. Progressively, I learned that some of their life experiences mirrored that of mine. When, I shared my experiences, they too had come to recognize some similarities. The more comfortable the women became, the more they wanted to remain after class to share their stories. Despite their circumstance, these women were my sisters and they needed to be heard. So, I created a safe space to share their experiences. As I had come to know these women, fear of the unknown turned into compassion.

The experiences of four African American women, Bobbi, Leslie, Shayla, and Melba, seem to resonate with me. As the mother of four boys under the age of 10, Bobbi was sentenced to eight years in federal prison. Although her place of origin is the state of Texas, she did not receive visits from her children. Leslie has two children. The place she calls home is the state of Georgia. She was sentenced to over five years in federal prison. Leslie did not receive visits from her children. Shayla was sentenced to three years in federal prison. She is the mother of three sons who are all under the age of 10. As a resident of Texas, Shayla received visits from her children only once a month. Melba has two children. She was sentenced to over six years in federal prison. Mable is also from the state of Georgia. She does not receive visits from her children. While the women acknowledge the role they played in their circumstances, they did question the unfair treatment by the justice system regarding the decision making that led to their sentencing.

Some of the women were arrested in the presence of their children. In some instances, the children arrived home from school only to find their mother missing. For all of them, they were forced to defend themselves from a structural force, namely, the justice system that perpetuates racism and sexism, and where people are often treated unfairly, especially Black women. To make matters worse, they were placed in a facility that was almost 500 miles away, making visitation with their children difficult. Some of them experienced feelings of loneliness and depression because of their inability to see their children. All of them expressed concern for their child's learning and development. Especially, the mothers with children under the age of 10. Since mothers are their child's first teacher, this means the learning, interacting, and parenting of their children was disrupted. Even more, the women were working in jobs within the facility where they earned far less than minimum wage. Little by little, these women had been stripped of their power.

As they recounted the harsh realities of incarceration, my lips rested silently as I remained mentally in a nonjudgmental space. Eventually, I became the learner as they transitioned into the role of teacher. When mothers become powerless, the impact stretches far beyond the prison walls to include the children that have been left behind.

Through technologies including, video conferencing and video recording the women began to reclaim their power by tearing away those invisible borders that were keeping them separated from their children. To utilize the video conferencing services required a fee of $6.00 for a 25-minute session. Turning trials into triumph, the women developed a micro-economic system where they pooled their earnings so that each of the group members could share in the usage of video conferencing services. By using the services, the mothers were able to interact with their children, which helped to maintain an attachment bond. Video conferencing also allowed the women to participate in birthday celebrations, take part in their child's morning routine, and engage in the exchange of dialogue with their children. The services afforded Mabel the ability to interact with her son to help manage his behavior. Shayla, on the other hand, was able to engage in birthday celebrations with her children. Although she did not acknowledge the learning taking place, during birthday celebrations, interactions between the mother and child involved singing, counting, dancing, and playing making it possible for learning to take place. By using the services, Leslie was able to offer her daughter advice in regard to college admissions.

Many of the mothers often worried about their child's learning during their incarceration. Through the usage of video recording, the women were able to engage in a shared book reading experience. During this process, the inmate mothers selected a book and read it aloud to their child. The session was recorded and then downloaded to a compact disc (CD). The mother is then able to mail the book along with the CD to her child. The children are then able to engage in a shared book reading experience with their mother in her absence. While engaging in the shared book experience with her sons, I discovered that Shayla impersonated characters in the book while including the names of her children in the story. By doing so, these actions contributed to the development of the children's expressive and receptive language skills along with vocabulary. While reading to her children, Bobbie often pointed to and named objects in each of the books. This behavior contributed to the vocabulary development of her children. Instead of reading storybooks, Mable read the bible to her children. By doing so, Mable contributed to her children's faith literacy and moral development. Moreover, as the women engaged in shared book reading experiences, they were also modeling literacy to their children.

Hearing the women's stories was transformative. I came in as the teacher, but instead, I became the learner. I listened to how the women had overcome their obstacles, and I learned. The aha moments helped me to realize that nothing could or should be taken for granted...our freedom; life; formal education; experiential knowledge; specific roles (mother, sister, friend); our jobs...absolutely nothing. Although this is probably one of the oldest maxims in history, are we really hearing and taking heed? From these women, I learned that, if there seems to be no way, you have to make a way. In order to interact with their children and engage in the learning and caretaking of their children, the women pooled their resource, so that each group member could utilize the services. From this, I learned what it means to build trust, loyalty, accountability, and group cohesion. I also learned that despite someone's circumstance, you can always learn something from them, and in this case, the learning is self-empowerment. I hope that when you read this narrative, you will come to know that educators are not always packaged in the normative black skirt, white shirt, heels, and glasses. Sometimes, they are packaged in an orange jumpsuit and boots.

CHAPTER 49

LIFE AFTER DEATH

Ruby J. Stevens-Morgan

Key Challenges: dysfunctional family; abuse; rural poverty; alcoholism; family violence; death; low academic achievement

Life in the home where I grew up was good at times and bad at other times. As a child, I didn't think about how well I was coping with growing up in a dysfunctional household. Other people I knew were in similar circumstances, so I didn't realize dysfunction wasn't normal. I also didn't realize that something would happen before I was a teenager that would change the course of my life.

I was number eight of the nine children in my family. Neither of my parents had a high school education, but that was common at that time for Black people in small rural towns in the South. My parents worked full-time factory jobs and raised us on a farm as a way to feed and clothe us. We grew a variety of crops, raised hogs and chickens, and had plenty of fruit trees on 40 acres of land, and yes, we had a mule. I was young enough to miss most of the hard farming labor, but my older siblings did a lot, including planting and picking cotton.

During the farming years, we planted many crops—corn, peas, cabbage, string beans, peas, turnip greens, okra, cucumber, tomatoes, pepper, white potatoes, sweet potatoes, cantaloupe, watermelons—you name it, we grew it. After crops were planted, we had to hoe and pull out the weeds until harvest time arrived. We

A Second Helping of Gumbo for the Soul: More Liberating Stories and Memories to Inspire Females of Color, pages 213–216.

then harvested the crops and prepared them to be canned or frozen. These were our main sources of food throughout the year, and although there were 11 of us, we never went hungry. Thinking about it now, I believe that even under those circumstances, we could have had a good life if not for the violence that waited patiently for routine release. My parents took us to church on Sunday, and they worked Monday through Friday, but on Friday night, it was on! The corn whiskey from local bootleggers and old man Jack Daniels (the whiskey) reigned every Friday and Saturday night to the extent that I have very few memories of the first 12 years of my life, except those two nights.

I spent many weekend nights hiding under a bed or on the floor in a basement "side room" holding my ears as tightly as I could to muffle the sounds of shouting, slamming doors, and gunshots that sometimes rang out in the dark. I couldn't cover my ears enough to block the sounds. Sometimes, the police were called but, as I remember, they seldom did anything about it. As I'm writing now, the fear I felt as a young girl—not yet a teenager—doesn't seem that far away, since it happened almost every weekend more than 40 years ago!

THE NIGHT THAT CHANGED EVERYTHING

One weekend in the early 70s started like so many others. Some of my older siblings were out on dates, and the four younger ones, including me, were home with my parents, my oldest sister and her husband. I have no idea how or why the fighting started, but it did. Like always, I felt scared and sick to my stomach. My dad (we called him Daddy) always had a gun handy and often threatened to use it. He had carried out a threat once a few years earlier when he shot my oldest brother with a rifle loaded with buckshots. I can remember being in the "side room" that night, crouched in a corner holding my ears. Daddy was hiding outside. When my brothers came home to try to calm things down, Daddy started shooting. I could hear footsteps running and suddenly heard my brother say, "He shot me y'all"! Man…that was a sickening feeling! My brother was okay after a few days in the hospital, but I don't think they ever removed all the buckshots from his thighs.

If only the violence would have stopped there. It escalated to the point where my mom kept a gun handy also. My dad hadn't shot her before, but he repeatedly threatened to do so. She had been hospitalized on a few occasions because he had beaten her pretty badly, and I remember he kicked or stomped her at least once. He often threatened to kill her when we (the children) weren't around. For me, that was Monday through Friday when we were in school, and I believed he would make good on his threats. Because of that, I skipped a lot of school so I could be there until my mom left for work and when she came home. When I was in school, I couldn't concentrate for thinking about what he might do when nobody was around.

Then it happened…the night that all hell broke loose. I was under the bed in the "middle room" with two of my siblings. My parents were arguing in the front room. We could hear yelling and cussing and what sounded like fighting. I can't remember if one of my sisters was in the room then or whether she went in later, but as I recall, my mom came out for a few minutes and quickly went back. After that, I remember more loud thumps and yelling, and then a gunshot or two rang out. My sister was yelling, and I heard her say, "Shoot!" Another gunshot or two immediately followed. Then silence.

My mother came out of the room, and all I could see were her feet. I was afraid to move. I didn't hear my dad or my sister. My mom called the police, and when she turned to go back to the front room, I peeked out and could see blood streaming down one side of her face. I just knew she had been shot! Time stood still… then it went by quickly. The police were there, and my sister came in and said my oldest sister and her husband were driving my mom to the hospital. We would follow in another car, and the ambulance was there to take my dad. As we headed to the front door to leave, we had to walk past my parents' bedroom. I briefly glanced, and I saw my dad kneeling beside the bed with his upper body slightly on the bed. He had been shot, but that's all I knew. I was trembling uncontrollably.

At the hospital, we sat in the car in the Emergency Room parking lot. I remember thinking, God, please don't let my mom go to jail. The ambulance hurried into the parking lot, and they rushed Daddy in on a stretcher. It seemed that a really long time passed before the doors of the Emergency Room opened again. The man that came out first seemed to have a pleasant look on his face—a smile really—so I figured everything was okay. That feeling quickly changed when a stretcher with a body completely covered, followed him. The body was that of my dad. The man in front of the stretcher was the local undertaker, what we now call a funeral home director. I felt sorry for my little brother because he loved Daddy so much, but I don't think I cried. I felt such a sense of relief. I knew at that moment that I didn't have to be afraid anymore.

LIFE AFTER THE VIOLENCE

I was in early middle school when my dad died—maybe 6th grade. Life changed for me after that. I didn't realize until I was a high school senior collecting report cards for my senior book what an impact those early days had on me. My report cards told the story of a young girl who missed 1–2 days of school every week and was barely passing any subject with most grades, except conduct, being C's, D's, and F's. Then, I noticed something else. After my dad died, everything changed. My attendance changed to missing only a few days a year and my grades were mostly A's and B's, maybe three C's, and one D in Biology because my mom had mistakenly thrown away the frog that was my science project. That was the moment I realized the impact of being in a dysfunctional household. For the first 12 years of my life, I wasn't living…I was surviving. In essence, my life began when the violence ended.

My mother passed away in 1987 from medical complications, but she lived a pretty good life after the violence. My parents didn't have much formal education, but they taught us three important values—a relationship with God, hard work, and love of family that became obvious after my dad died when, even as adults, we all met at my mom's house for Sunday meals and played softball or volleyball until after sunset. Those were good days! We still have our annual Thanksgiving Dinner at my oldest brother's house in the country with most of the immediate family in attendance. Still good days! As for me…I'm happy and no longer afraid. I love my family, and I love being with family. Alcoholism and physical and verbal abuse no longer have a suffocating grip on the Stevens family.

Since my father's death, I live life to the fullest, and I'm not done yet. I've made up for lost time. I graduated high school ninth in my class, as the top African-American student, and I earned an associate degree with plans to work my way to the top as an Administrative Assistant…NOT! I went back and earned my Bachelor's degree…later my master's degree, and finally my doctoral degree at 47 years old. I am a long-time educator whose teaching methods and love for children were shaped by my own experiences of being an invisible, well-behaved little Black girl despite excessive absences and nearly failing grades. I am the founder of a nonprofit education organization, mid-level university administrator, adjunct instructor, and an aspiring entrepreneur.

When people see me now, they see Dr. Ruby Jewel Stevens-Morgan, but I am always willing to share my story. I don't come from a family of educators, and my life hasn't always been easy. I work with young people and have shared my story many times to let them know they are not defined by their past or by their parents. Regardless of what has happened to you, how people have treated you, or what you've done, you can overcome, whatever your age. The key is to focus on what's right and not what's wrong. Despite our past, all of us have what we need to become what we want to become, deep inside of ourselves. I am not a product of my past; rather, I am a forecaster of my future! I believe that one day, people around the world will know my name.

CHAPTER 50

A MEDITATION ON
JUST BEING ME

Valerie Taylor

Key Challenges: peer pressure; acting white accusations; racial identity; self-esteem; sexism; discrimination

"Girl you know you ain't Black." "You think you White?" "You think you better than me?" "Black folks don't do that?" "You uppity." "You an Oreo." "You aren't really Black!" are but just a few of the many of taunts I have heard whispered and shouted to me during my life journey. While I awake each day and to see my Black skin covering my female body, I have been constantly told that because I am a vegan, beach-loving, Buddhist, bookworm, passport carrying, animal-loving, free-spirited woman, that I am not Black.

I was born to Black parents, had Black grandmothers and grandfathers whose fore-parents, were for the most part Black, although now that my father had his ancestry DNA checked, I can say that a few other races and ethnicities also pepper my DNA mix. But I Am Black. I am like millions of other African diaspora people in America whose complicated ancestry makes them Black. I am not, nor do I look "mixed" or biracial, which would have probably entitled me to some it-is-okay-for-her-to-"act White" passes. I look Black, so how I talk, my interests, and how I engage with people has always been highly scrutinized and criticized because I supposedly do not sound or act like what has narrowly been defined as being "Black."

I am also a woman—so I am a Black American woman who knows that society has understood my life to be synonymous with "complicated" from the very moment that I was born. Neither my gender identity nor "femaleness" is questioned –just my blackness. I have always had to prove it. I am a Black woman who has had to battle racial bullying by Black, White, Latinx and Asian children (way before there was a term for it); combatted the danger of stereotyping at school, work and play and carry my blackness" card (love of watermelon, black-eyed peas and old school hip hop) which I must be prepared to share at all times. I have had my hetero dating preference (Black men only) and my "authentic Black experience" questioned in public spaces by all kinds of folks. I have been excluded, demonized and harassed just for being me. I have struggled much of my life to be accepted by my own people.

I pause here to say I love myself, although what I will share is that my life journey and the shaping of my identity as a Black girl and woman has not always been easy to navigate and, at times, has been incredibly painful. I have learned to embrace authenticity and love of adventure. While I know that I am by no means the only Black woman to struggle with racial identity and acceptance, it is the persistent silence that continues to surround this issue that is troubling. NOTHING HAS CHANGED—the media still portray Black women as Jezebels, Mammies and Sapphires, and many Black folks everywhere still unknowingly continue to embrace these tropes, and uphold the narrow definition of what being "Black" is supposed to mean.

Beginning with my rejection of the television show Good Times as a child, I was told that even my media choices meant that I was not "really Black." I dislike the many negative portrayals of Black folks found on television– especially Black women—that still persists today in the mainstream media, even in shows with positive storylines. (However, I did love Living Single and Girlfriends that disrupted the negative stereotypes of Black women—they were friends who were smart, creative, college-educated, employed, professionals). Most Black television shows do not amuse me nor represent my experiences and worldviews.

I am a chocolate-skinned, just-over-the-tall-height-line with a medium-sized build, natural hair wearing sistah. Since my early 20s, I have rocked natural hairstyles—first braids, then a weekly barber shave-down-low look, and now I just let my hair grow happy and nappy from my scalp. When I was a girl, my battle with my short, permed, just their hair was also part of my inner battles with not being "Black woman pretty."

I was a child who received love and encouragement from my parents. They broke the "Whites only" barrier to become the first Blacks to buy a home in a suburb in San Francisco Bay. That meant that I was the only Black child in my predominantly White elementary school classes for years. It was California so, yes, there were a couple of Latinx and Asian students, but we did not know we were our own potentially powerful tribe of "children of color," we just knew we were not White.

Academically, I excelled and had no problems making friends. I went to my White friend's homes, and they came to mine. However, they constantly reminded me that I was different. They defined my distinct otherness by my full lips, dark skin and my hair—for which I was teased. I was not White, which was viewed negatively. Being Black was always something to overcome. Their view of blackness continued to be defined by the White media, so they told me "I was not really Black"—not like what they saw on television. My response was, "Yes-I am Black." I knew this because I liked to read Jet Jr., Essence and Ebony every month, my family watched television shows with Black actors and actresses, we cheered every time a Black person won an award or recognition, my parents took me to Black cultural events. I had an extended Black family through my parents' friends and, occasionally, attended a Black church. I knew I was Black because we did these things precisely because my family was Black.

But I struggled with my self-esteem because my identity was constantly challenged. Often in conflict were the dominant Black narratives I saw daily in the media and what others believed was the authentic Black experience versus my own life experiences. I just wanted acceptance.

My parents were not new to breaking racial barriers, so they quickly recognized the complicated challenges of raising a Black girl in an all-White community. (Interestingly, it was my love of the sun and swimming that made them amp up the cultural lessons on blackness. Ironically, I was not "trying to be White," I just liked to feel rays of the sun on my skin which, of course, was not what Black folks were supposed to do.) But, I love chocolate skin—always have, my own and especially dark-skinned brothers. I still love swimming and feeling the rays of the sun on my skin, and they still frown at my time at the beach and time in the sun.

At a young age, I knew I was Black and a girl child and was facing a lifetime of discrimination, so I was an early adopter of Black feminism, although I did not have a name for my beliefs. I just called it fighting injustice. I am a voracious reader and became fascinated by the many diverse women and men who fought against injustice. I was often the first to hold various positions as a girl and or Black student, so I thought I too was fighting against injustice. These positions further complicated my acceptance by Black peers who were often mean and critical, so my self-esteem was always fragile.

I attended Mills College, a women's college—where I faced racism and Howard University, an HBCU—where I faced sexism. While in college, I was fortunate to find many other Black sistahs and brothas like me who I could vibe with and who accepted me as I was, but I still struggled to find my way and make peace with being different.

My professional journey began when I combined my communication and political skills. In my community building and social justice work, my nontraditional Black identity had both opened doors (I've been bestowed with not sought honorary Whiteness) and made it difficult to build trust and acceptance with Black community members. While working on environmental justice issues, Black women's health issues, at a Black museum and other projects, my blackness was constantly questioned by everyone, including community elders, politicians, youth and business leaders. I was never sure if it was my "nontraditional" blackness that made them wary or my strong passion and advocacy of the various issues. I often had to jump through extra hoops to be accepted. I was always forced to "splain" my Black pedigree –who I knew, my Howard degree, previous work in communities of color and even, occasionally, have a "true" Black person vouch for me.

My many years working in social justice communications and political advocacy and the many lessons that I learned working with communities of color both guided my doctoral research and continue to be the foundation of my interdisciplinary teaching. I currently teach what I have always had a passion for—Gender and Sexuality Studies, African American Studies, Education, and Leadership. I am a living testament to my students that there is no singular "Black woman" identity.

I encourage everyone to live an authentic and adventurous life. There are already so many challenges in our individual life journeys, especially for women of color. I believe people should work to be their authentic, adventurous selves. I advocate for trying new things daily. I know that my Black identity struggles stem from the narrow definitions that Black folks and the larger society have imposed. Living an authentic and adventurous life does not mean packing and moving to Timbuktu –although I would applaud you if you did—but it does mean being open to new experiences and people and supporting others on their own journeys no matter how much they may differ from your own. It means trying a new fruit or vegetable at the grocery store each week, driving a different way home twice a month, taking a different class at the gym, eating at a new restaurant by yourself, and supporting others that do the same.

Identity is fluid, so we should embrace that fluidity. Being Black and a woman is hard enough—the rigidity that is often imposed around that identity just adds challenges in what is often a rocky journey. I am thankful; in my journey, I have met others, so I am no longer the only water and sun-loving Black woman my family knows—my closest friends all love the beach and sun too.

CHAPTER 51

LOST IN TRANSLATION?

Elsa Villarreal

Key Challenges: ELL; translating; familial pride; tracking

Imagine not being able to speak the language in a foreign country and relying on a five-year-old child to accurately translate the transactions of a bank teller, doctor's orders, and grocery store labels. I was that five-year-old who had not yet discovered words such as deposit, withdraw, and medical dosage. I only knew how to write my name. My mother depended on me to stretch my vocabulary in both English and Spanish to get the job done. I recall telling the bank teller, "My mom says you have her money, and she needs some money right now (withdraw)." I recall the neighborhood pharmacist staring at me nervously as I explained to mom how to take her medicine in Spanish because she knew that one mistake in translation of prescription medication could have serious consequences.

And where was my father? My father was working long hours and providing for the three of us. He was the sole provider for the family, and was a first generation Mexican American who worked his way up from being a golf caddy at the age of 13 to a golf course superintendent. I mostly saw him at dinnertime. My father's new job position enabled my family to move out of our mobile home on my grandparent's property into a newly established suburban neighborhood where I met my first White friend, Kristi, a blonde haired Kentucky girl who was

A Second Helping of Gumbo for the Soul: More Liberating Stories and Memories to Inspire Females of Color, pages 221–224.

ten years older than me. She was my first best friend. Kristi taught me the English alphabet, numbers, nursery rhymes, and music. I remember getting irritated with my mother when she would pull me away from playtime with Kristi to run errands and translate. I learned that Kristi's mother never asked Kristi to run errands with her, so I began to see how our families were different. I had to grow up faster than my peers. In my young age, I started to resent my mother for not being able to pick up the English language as fast as I did. Why hasn't she learned English by now? I had learned more words, but mom was still speaking Spanish. Would I have to translate for her the rest of my life?

When I started Kindergarten, I earned a break from my translating responsibilities, until the new Spanish-speaking student enrolled in my class. Here we go again. I was pulled from socializing with my kindergarten classmates to translate for the new girl from Mexico. She stuck to me like glue, and I hated it. She was with me during story time, recess, and lunch. Even though I was a five-year-old kindergartener starting my academic journey, my parents would have told you that I was an independent soul. I needed my freedom. The new girl was needy, and I began to resent her and my teacher for putting me in this position. I felt like I was held behind in excelling at my work because I was the only student who spoke Spanish in the class, and I had to stop working on my tasks to help someone else. Translating at school and translating at home felt like a full-time job, and I did not sign up for this job! Translating was a burden, and I begrudged those who could not speak English, including my mother with whom I often clashed over misunderstandings in language communication.

College was my first formal education in Spanish. I learned to read, write, and speak with confidence. My Spanish vocabulary was catching up to my English vocabulary, and I found myself communicating with my mother without misunderstandings. Suddenly, I was finding the right words to say to her. We were bonding, and my perception of the Spanish language and being bilingual had shifted. I had developed pride in who I was. I accepted both my U.S. and Mexican identities, and I used them to achieve my personal and professional goals. I was not ordinary; I was extraordinary.

My translation skills were sharp enough to earn a bachelor's degree in Spanish. I taught Spanish to high school students for seven years, and I proudly exposed my students to my home language and culture. At that time, the majority of the Latino teachers on my campus were the Spanish teachers, and I felt the Latino students, who were the majority student population at my campus, needed a role model. I became a high school assistant principal and served the students at my graduating high school for eight years. With the support of my head principal and central administration, I was the first administrator to pilot the Optional Flexible School Day Program (night school) in my district. Students enrolled in the program were dropouts; young parents; former gang members; special education students; English language learners (ELLs); economically disadvantaged; homeless; and over-aged freshman. As a product of my school district, I was hired to reconnect and reach out to my community in reducing the high school dropout rate. My knowledge of the community, my own cultural background, and my ability to speak Spanish enabled me to create critical partnerships with my community and ensure student success.

At this time, my mother applied for a job serving food in the school cafeteria. The cafeteria manager was hesitant to hire her over the language barrier. She offered to work for two weeks without pay to demonstrate her work skills. The cafeteria manager was so impressed with her persistence that he offered her the job. I was exceptionally proud of my mother for going out of her comfort zone to advance herself. I don't think she'll ever understand how my resentment for her transformed into admiration. All of this time, translating, what I believed to be a burden, had developed into a strength. I used this strength to force open doors of opportunity beyond my imagination—I am currently working on my Ph.D. in Educational Administration at a Tier I university.

OUTSMARTING THE ACADEMIC TRACKING TRAP

Throughout elementary school, I depended on my father to help me with homework (spelling tests, long division, and grammar). My father's presence and guidance were critical to me navigating the public school system. In my transition to junior high, I almost fell victim to an academic tracking trap. I was instructed to bring a letter home for my parent to sign. This letter requested parental approval of my academic schedule for the next school year. My father was not home from school yet, so I asked my mother to sign it. This letter was in English, and my mother hesitated to sign the letter. She suggested that I wait for my father to come home from work to sign the letter. My father was upset that my academic schedule was pre-programmed for the regular academic track. He was disappointed that I was set up for regular academic classes, and no one (teachers or counselors) recommended me for anything more challenging. In fact, no one called my home to justify why I was pre-programmed for this track. I was not aware that academic tracks existed. Instead of following the regular academic track, my father enrolled me in advanced academic track (college-bound). At that point in time, I did not have to prove my academic potential, so I was granted the change simply because my father requested this move in writing. The problem was that the school counselors had assumed my intellectual abilities without obtaining parental feedback. As a student, I assumed everyone was in the same playing field, and although I was one of the few students of color taking advanced high school courses, I was motivated to work harder and fight to stay in these courses. If my father believed in my potential, I was determined to prove it to everyone else. My determination paid off. I was one of two Latina high school students who graduated in the top ten percent of my class and earned an academic scholarship to a four-year university.

SHARING WHAT I LEARNED WITH STUDENTS

No footprint is the same. Each of us has a duty to leave our individual footprint and impact our world. Therefore, celebrate your individuality. Take pride in your family and culture. If you are bilingual, trust in a respected teacher or counselor to have you navigate your educational pathways. Throughout our lives, people will evaluate your ability potential based on their notions and assumptions. Here is a newsflash: notions and assumptions are based on individual biases. Question your academic rigor and seek out multiple mentors to help you navigate through your academic journey. Become an advocate for yourself. Don't be afraid to ask questions.

ADVICE FOR EDUCATORS

Whether you are a teacher, parent, or student, do not underestimate the power of a determined mind. Reflect on your biases. Consider mentoring students in your school/community and support mentorship programs for first generation college students. If you are an educator, it shouldn't just be your job—it should be your calling!

ADVICE FOR PARENTS

Your level of education does not define your ability to parent or advocate for your child. Follow your instincts and question teachers and administrators. Do not be intimidated. Seek out school staff, other parents, and community leaders for guidance on maximizing your child's learning!

When students, educators, and parents work together, we can make a difference in the lives of students.

CHAPTER 52

SUZY SNOWFLAKE

The Tale of a Brown Girl Dancing

Rachelle D. Washington

Key Challenges: colorism; hair politics; overweight; academic expectations; microaggressions

EPIGRAPH

There I was, Suzy Snowflake, Head Snowflake, the tutu-adorned, chocolate-dipped ballerina, *cambré*, little chubby brown sugah leading the troupe. We were dancers—twirling whirling hues of *deep sun-kissed, mocha-laced, blueberry dotted, purple grained, high yellow shades* of a soulful kaleidoscope. Each step was more determined than the first, glissade. I was the first deep chocolate girl to lead. What a prideful moment it was for me—landing the role over at least ten other girls. My Daddy said was the Blackest and beautifullest snowflake he had ever seen. Suzy Snowflake danced Free. I recall others whispering that I was too dark or too chubby when Miss Elma Lewis selected me for the role of Suzy Snowflake. My sister, nick-named Skinny-Minny, who wore light blue cat-eyed glasses against her caramel-colored self, rooted for me: You can do it, Rachelle!

A Second Helping of Gumbo for the Soul: More Liberating Stories and Memories to Inspire Females of Color, pages 225–228.

The above excerpt from my dissertation demonstrates how stories, old and new, accompany us along our life journey. Lewis, an activist, and business owner opened Boston's first cultural center to serve its Black community—the Elma Lewis School of Fine Arts (ELSFA). With Lewis heavily involved in the community, the addition of a cultural center brought hope and hearth against a backdrop of Boston's racially segregated neighborhoods, bussing, and White flight. Boston's Roxbury and Dorchester communities, along Blue Hill Avenue, were reminiscent of Atlanta's Auburn Avenue or Harlemesque where Black businesses were born, thrived and died. Willful and audacious at the height of Boston's busing, Elma Lewis often provided her center and other spaces along Blue Hill Avenue for community gatherings. Miss Lewis was mindful of how hard it was for chocolate girls, for she, like me, was dark-skinned and full-bodied. She wore a signature bun atop her head and had a voice like smoked glass. People would listen.

Since taking that stage as Suzy Snowflake, I have encountered many stages—through acting, dancing, singing, presenting, preaching and teaching—and have often recalled how my experience at ELSFA led to embodiments of loves and liberations. Thank you, Elma Lewis. I got this, and I am going to dance. From a once young girl to now, I have had to make decisions to sit it out or dance, and I chose to dance, even when there were those who questioned how a chubby chocolate girl from Boston could become a teacher and, ultimately, a college professor.

Africanist communities remain steeped in color issues. I was born into a family of kinfolk hovering at the Mason-Dixon Line and beyond whose skin tones range from melanin-etched crème to indigo. Fortunately, my familial experience is not laced with colorism. I left Boston to attend an HBCU in Atlanta and embraced the beauty of Black folks, our history, and our future. Ironically, the colorism issues were more acute at an HBCU, I observed. I was relegated to the margins or valorized: "She's from Boston . . . too smart and good-looking to be dark-skinned." I shake my head even now over those memories. I am a woman who once danced on her literal toes, during childhood. Now, I take center stage, moving away from the edges, disrupting the world. The whisperings have not subsided inside me, even as I trouble our world; I hear a cacophony of colorist words spoken aloud: "I can see you are not exactly a 160-pound White woman, and you have natural hair" . . . "You sure are pretty for a dark-skinned girl/woman" . . . "Have you thought about pressing your hair?" . . . "You are unlike any Black person I know, and I do not know what to do with you." These comments come from within university settings (both PWIs and HBCUs) across 12 years—where Black women (professors and administrators) who looked and projected cool, confident and comely, like me, were an anomaly. Many of the Black women professors and administrators defied stereotyping; which led me to ask, "Who set those for me?" However, agency embedded early on pushed me out onto the stage (again and again) and led me to dance and twirl into a world where little chubby chocolate girls learned that we were gifted, talented and beautiful; and I took Elma Lewis with me.

Prior to teaching in universities, I had come to teach Brown and Black girls in an urban elementary school in Atlanta. I remained mindful of how intra/micro-aggressions could crush spirits. I was mindful as Black girls entered the classrooms with fresh ideas, fresh mouths, and freshly pressed hair or trendy natural tresses. They arrived at school the first day embellished with barrettes, bountiful and boastful braids, and bravada. They navigated the classroom and hallways with a certainty that rivaled adults maneuvering in a new setting. They took charge of classroom discussions. They took charge as helpers. They took charge on the playground. They were purpose-driven in physical education class, even as their pressed-back plaits gave way to unmanageable tresses. These little girls had a purpose. Yet, the notion of valorizing faces of color took shape. I watched and balked as lighter or darker-skinned children were placed in front as line leaders—depending upon the adult. After all, this was kindergarten. I recall the memories at every juncture because the spirit of these young girls was in me. Indeed, it led me to continue to learn about the experiences that propel girls like them and me to become doctoral students.

During graduate school, professors encouraged me to use narratives, storytelling and/or oral history to learn more of the voices and relevant socio-cultural needs of Black girls and women. How affirming to explore and include a rich array of works—non-academic and academic alike—that expanded the narratives of monolithic and essentialized experiences of Black women! I turned to my stories and the mediums that held them—napkins, diaries, journals, church bulletins, theatre playbills, matchbooks, and more. The deeper I explored, the deeper my commitment grew to use stories to answer questions about schooling narratives of Black women before they arrived at the doorways of PWIs. The metanarrative or larger story included the cultural influences that shaped us along the way. I include my story as a once upon a time ballerina as inspiration from a lantern like Elma Lewis who lighted my way.

Lewis's influence stayed with me on a pathway that includes faculty and administrative positions in P–20 educational settings. My foci are advocacy, artistry, and activism; they enable me to aid in the creation of new and improvement of existing academic, community and home partnerships related to literacy and social justice. I am the co-founder of Camp Read-a-Rama (established in 2009), a themed literacy-based camp that uses books as a springboard for all camp activities. I am a daughter, sister, niece, cousin, aunt, and mother of many. Mostly, I live brokering dignity and respect by decreasing distances between those who judge and those who are judged. Recently, I ran across a card from a colleague bidding me farewell as I left a highly visible job to pursue doctoral studies, full-time. Her words (excerpted):

> I must admit that I was a bit intimidated by you when we first met. You have a way about you that I've never encountered before. I was in the presence of a strong black women...with an air of confidence...you are indeed the embodiment of what Maya

Angelou meant when she wrote, Phenomenal Woman. I thank God for having the opportunity to have met you. Your strength and presence will be missed.

I had saved the card unbeknownst to me, which was in a box marked personal along with this note: *Today I actualized my new Black me.* I wore my afro to work like an accessory, like an amulet. Funny, I recall the occasion. I was in transition from tamed, bone-straight relaxers to coiled, spiraled natural tresses. I had been at the beach, and no one wanted to do my thick, oily hair. Yet, my godson's curly locks? All hands were raised. The next morning, I chose to go to work with an afro and recalled walking from the parking lot to the office, rocking freer and lighter. This recollection gives me pause and permission to delve into boxes—literally and figuratively—marked 'personal, do not open.'

Write. I encourage young women of color to use stories to expand the binaries and boundaries that can restrict their lives. Write. I encourage Black girls and women to write their stories to enable them to dance and celebrate our history of resistance, our diligence in womanish ways, and the revealing of ourselves, if only to ourselves. Oh my, write, write, write.

"When I leave here, the body of my work will be all of these wonderful people out there in this in the world, doing great things."
—*Elma Ina Lewis*

CHAPTER 53

THE VALLEY MOMENT OF LIFE

A Lesson in Resilience and Faith

Jillian Whatley

Key Challenges: domestic violence, single-parent, resilience, post-relationship trauma

On Saturday, February 11, 2012, I sat in a cold auditorium taking the LSAT Test for the second time, wondering if this was God's plan for my life; or was this a battle between His desires for my life and my own personal desires, which may not align with His. Initially, I thought going to law school was the completion of my career journey, and that would be it. Wrapped up in a tiny little bow my purpose would be fulfilled. But, I have since come to learn much more about God's multi-layered purpose in my life. Later that same evening, the awful news of the death of Whitney Houston, a lady whom I deeply admired and known as 'The Voice' died.

My heart literally dropped as uncontrollable tears fell down my face. Out of fear and love for my new baby girl, I grabbed her and held her closer to my chest taking in breaths as my prayers bellowed for the grieving mother and daughter. As the news rolled in on various networks, it was confirmed that our beloved Whitney had died by drowning in a bathtub full of water, after a long battle with drug

*A Second Helping of Gumbo for the Soul: More Liberating Stories and Memories
to Inspire Females of Color,* pages 229–233.
Copyright © 2020 by Information Age Publishing
229

addiction. As I reflect on that day, I was not only mourning the loss of Whitney, but for her visible struggle to find her purpose, and how that image mirrored many of the women I knew, including myself. Many of us may say, well she found her purpose in singing melodies that we fondly relate to events that occurred in our lives. However, her ever-present struggle to perform, to be a superstar, or to stand on a superficial stage, set in motion a downward spiral to seek God.

One week later, my family sat anxiously awaiting her funeral, as we joined with the world to mourn the life of a fallen star. While several superstars, politicians, family friends, and many others spoke at Whitney's funeral, there was nothing like Kevin Costner's speech. His speech not only spoke to the many grieving family members, friends and fans; it resounded ever so loudly in my soul as a new mother, someone searching to hear God's voice, a faithful daughter, a protective sister, dedicated friend, and a psychologist for many adolescent girls to countless women. In essence, Kevin spoke to the issue that many young girls face every day…. That not good enough feeling. In his words, "and so to you, Bobbi Kristina and to all those young girls who are dreaming that dream, that may be thinking, are they good enough? I think Whitney would tell you, 'Guard your bodies, guard the precious miracle of your own life, and then sing your hearts out,' knowing that there's a lady in heaven who is making God himself wonder how he created something so perfect." That day God spoke to me like never before, and it seemed that with every breath, God continued to speak louder to me about my purpose here on earth.

While holding my daughter tightly, my spirit reflected on my "not good enough" feeling. Within the last few years, I had fallen in and out of love, had a beautiful baby girl, discovered my strength and my weaknesses, experienced God's goodness in a valley moment of life, and began a journey to find my purpose in life. Something happens when you have a child. Some mothers call it worry, others anxiety; despite the descriptor, we assign to that feeling none of us can deny that an awareness that is birthed out of our psyche about ourselves as mothers, daughters, individuals and our role in society. Now take a step further— something happens when you give birth to a child that is of your same gender.

As women, we embrace the happiness of being a girl, the anxious autonomy of our adolescence, the giddy freedom of young adulthood and the emerging confidence of being a young woman optimistically embarking on all of our hopes, dreams, and desires. On the other hand, we are well aware of the struggle to intimately know God while conforming to society's norm, the struggle of falling in and out of love, the struggle of being independent or dependent as we transition through relationships, the struggle to find boundaries, the struggle of learning that beauty goes beyond the physical, the struggle to find a self-esteem that is not reliant upon unrealistic expectations, and the struggle to not lose yourself in people, situations, and life transitions. As a new single mother, these thoughts circled my mind regarding my own precious daughter. Thinking about the profound words of Kevin Costner and reviewing the life of Whitney Houston I pondered, "What tools do I need to give myself and other mothers to raise strong girls"?

On October 25, 2011, I gave birth to a bouncing 8 pound, 3 ounces baby girl. For months, we had anxiously prepared for our daughter to enter the world and our family. The relationship between my daughter's father and I was surprisingly erratic. My initial impression of him was favorable, though it quickly morphed into disgust and disappointment. Two weeks after having a cesarean section, my daughter and I were nesting at home, and I was adjusting to being a first-time mother. As a part of the medical restrictions after a cesarean, patients cannot drive. One day during this time, I asked my daughter's father to pick up some items from the grocery store. In my mind, this was a typical request considering my condition. He abruptly turned around with anger in his eyes and threw me to the floor. My head and back hit the floor, and the worry rushed in concerning my daughter. After that incident, I was determined to end the relationship. However, he advised that we work to restore our relationship and go to couple's classes at our church. For the next two months, I went to church, but my spirit was telling me to run. A few months later, I had to do just that.... I had to run. Another incident occurred after we came back to my house after attending a celebration for my friend. He and I began to argue, and a physical altercation occurred resulting in him choking me. To this day, I remember seeing my daughter in her car seat. At that moment, the relationship was over, and in the months to follow, a restraining order was implemented, we were in court to determine custody, and court-ordered counseling was scheduled.... all within my first year of being a mommy. What happened?

I hit rock bottom emotionally. I felt as though I was losing, and the towel had been thrown in for me. I also hit rock bottom financially, and I questioned the love that I once knew. I questioned my decisions, and I questioned my future. As a mother, the most aggressive action a person can do is to threaten the livelihood of your child. It rips your hearts to shreds, and you can barely breathe. During my custody case with my daughter's father, my emotions vacillated between wanting him to be involved in our daughter's life, to trusting her in his care without my supervision, to feeling violated by his many attacks on my safety and well-being, to hoping that he loved her unconditional, to trying to figure out his reasoning for putting us through a difficult situation, to questioning his authentic love for me, to hating his guts, to accepting my situation on a Monday, to punishing myself on a Friday. My emotions were everywhere. I was operating in a state of emotional and physical confusion, so it was best for me to be still. I just needed to stand.

My rock bottom day came on a Friday. I cried to my number one confidant, my mother. My tears were about my feelings of being tired, angry and not knowing what to do. I screamed I pulled my hair, and I wanted to run. While this was occurring, my mother sat on my bed with her arms folded.

As the respected matriarch of our family, I had grown accustomed to her physical and emotional comforting. However, in this situation, she just sat there. She did not say a word. She watched me cry, and she did not touch me. For 10 minutes she sat. I was tired of fighting, but I knew I had to fight for my daughter. She deserved all things good, fair, and consistent. After I finished emotionally depleting myself and allowing fear to encircle me, I abruptly stopped crying and lay there while my mom just sat. It was as if she was saying in her spirit to my spirit, "Have you got it all out? Now it is time for round two of this fight. Get up, Jill!" Through my tears, anger, despair, hopelessness, fear, and desperation I got up and stood to my feet. From that day, I made a decision to continue the fight, though this time around I would not be fighting alone and left to my own defenses. God would be fighting this battle, and I felt and knew that I was totally relying on God. God had and will always have the final say.

It is important for you to find the strength to walk blindly in faith while trusting God and standing on His promises. One woman that displayed tremendous strength in the bible was Jochebed, the mother of Moses. At that time Pharoah declared that every Hebrew baby born was to be killed (Exodus 1:16). Imagine for a moment if someone in authority declared that your child was to die, or to be stripped from the vulnerable hand of the mother and sent to his death. Her heart must have skipped a beat, or even stopped for a moment thinking of the unthinkable. She had to act quickly. So, she hid Moses for three months (Hebrews 11:23). What is the significance of three months? At three months of age, a baby's activity level increase. They may sleep less, personalities start to emerge, and they began to react and relate to their world. It is an amazing experience and transformation, but it is very difficult when you are trying to preserve the life of your child. At three months old Moses was sent down the river, while his sister Miriam watched him. Pharaoh's daughter was out bathing and saw the baby and had compassion on the crying baby. In an effort to console the baby she asked her maid to draw the baby out of the water. Pharaoh's daughter sent Miriam to get a maid to take care of the baby, and Moses's mother was the maid who was selected. Jochebed was paid to take care of her own son. When the child got older, she brought him to Pharaoh's daughter who named him Moses. From the very beginning, Moses' parents decided to provide Moses with protection, and Moses was raised in Pharaoh's house.

On a sunny Friday in April, my 17-month-old daughter and I were walking into a hair salon for my appointment. My darling daughter enjoyed holding mommy's hand while talking and giggling as she trotted along. However, once we reached the door of the hair salon, she abruptly paused. She grabbed my leg, stopped singing, and she came to a dead halt. Once she assessed the situation and the people in the shop she proceeded carefully and very closely to me. Minutes later my darling daughter returned to her cheerful personality, and she continued to sing and eat her snacks. My daughter may or may not be aware, but her P.A.U.S.E meant something and should mean something in terms of her life. It is imperative to know when you encounter certain people or experiences in life, you must P.A.U.S.E. Behold, I am sending you out as sheep in the midst of wolves, so be wise as serpents and innocent as doves" (Matthew 10:16). My dear daughter, you must listen to God's voice. You must learn to discern the character of man and measure the spirit by the promises of God.

P- Pray for a discerning spirit and for God's wisdom in every decision (James 1:5)

A- Ask God to reveal anything in the situation or with the person that is not of you (Psalm 139: 23-24).

U- Trust in the LORD with all your heart and lean not on your own understanding (Proverbs 3:5)

S- Stand firm on God's word and rebuke any and everything that does not align with God's Word. (Psalm 119:105).

E- Expect God to answer and move in your life swiftly. (1 John 5: 14-15)

In summary, hurt comes in many shapes and sizes. When people are hurt, many think the obvious is to drink, engage in sexual promiscuity, or do drugs. However, what about the majority of us in the world who are hurting? Those of us who are hurting and do the following: continue to obtain more graduate degrees to avoid time to get to know a person in fear that we may get 'hurt" again. Or for those of us who delve ourselves into the church and inundate ourselves with church ministries, only to find out that church folks 'hurt' you too. Or the people who never sit still in life to enjoy, they are constantly hopping from one successful task to another, only to know that they are avoiding love or the potential for love because they are afraid of being 'hurt.' Or the single mother or father who was 'hurt' by their child's other parent. There are many ways we mask our hurt that can range from physical to emotional. Covering up our emotional wounds helps people cope with undesirable or uncomfortable feelings for the sake of our pseudo-image that "others see." The feelings relate to feeling or being made to feel: invalidated, not listened to or misunderstood, unworthy, unloved, taken advantage of, humiliated, weak, guilty, or feeling like a failure. Over the last few years, my purpose has been to work through the hurt and live in my God-given purpose. Amen.

The authors of this volume shared their highs, lows, and even their times of "simmering" in between. As you cook gumbo, one must adjust the temperature to their needs. We invite you to do the same!

—*Nicole McZeal Walters*

BIOGRAPHIES

EDITORS

Dr. Michelle Frazier Trotman Scott is the COE Director of Graduate Affairs and Professor of Special Education at the University of West Georgia. Dr. Scott's research interests include the achievement gap, special education over-representation, gifted education under-representation, dual exceptionalities, creating culturally responsive classrooms, and increasing family involvement. Dr. Frazier Trotman Scott has conducted professional development workshops for urban school districts and has been invited to community dialogs with regard to educational practices and reform. Michelle has written and co-authored several articles and has made numerous presentations at professional conferences. She is the co-editor of five books, *Gifted and Advanced Black Students in School: An Anthology of Critical Works and Young; Triumphant, and Black: Overcoming the Tyranny of Segregated Minds in Desegregated Schools; Gumbo for the Soul: Liberating Memoirs and Stories to Inspire Females of Color; R.A.C.E. Mentoring through Social Media: Black and Hispanic Scholars Share Their Journey in the Academy,* and *Faculty of Color Navigating Higher Education.* She is on the editorial board for *Multiple Voices Journal* and the *Education and Urban Society Journal.*

A Second Helping of Gumbo for the Soul: More Liberating Stories and Memories to Inspire Females of Color, pages 235–248.

She has also served as the guest co-editor for two editions of the Interdisciplinary Journal of Teaching and Learning (ITJL), as well as the guest editor for the Illinois School Journal. Michelle has reviewed for journals in such disciplines as gifted, special, and urban education and is a NAACP Image Award subcommittee member. Professional development includes membership in professional organizations, including the National Association for Gifted Children, Council for Exceptional Children, and American Educational Research Association. She currently serves as the Chair of the Special Populations Network of the National Association for Gifted Children, and is a past-president of the Division of Culturally and Linguistically Diverse Exceptional Learners of the Council of Exceptional Children. Dr. Frazier Trotman Scott is also the co-creator of an on-line, Facebook mentoring group called R.A.C.E. Mentoring, which was created by Dr. Frazier Trotman Scott and two of her colleagues to "…support, nurture, and advocate for Black and Hispanic doctoral students, junior/untenured faculty, and tenured faculty—too many of whom are under-represented in higher education."

Dr. Nicole McZeal Walters presently serves as the Associate Dean of Graduate Programs at the University of St. Thomas in the School of Education and Human Services Department, and is also an Associate Professor of Educational Leadership. In her role as Associate Dean, Dr. Walters is responsible for the academic leadership and coordination of all graduate academic programs, including strategic planning and resource allocation. As a leadership professor, Dr. Walters' research agenda includes developing leaders to embrace servant and moral leadership, social philanthropy, and integrating culture, language, and leadership to support academic achievement in historically underserved, marginalized students and families. She is a former school teacher, specialist, and principal. Dr. Walters has written extensively on urban education, women in higher education, and special education as well. Her academic work has been published widely in many book chapters and journals including the *Women, Gender, and Families of Color Journal*, the *International Journal of Educational Reform, Wisconsin English Journal, Gifted Child Today*, and *School Leadership Review,* to name a selected few, and has lectured widely at national and international conferences, universities, and local school districts. She also serves as a guest editor for Taboo: The Journal for Culture and Education. Dr. Walters holds a Bachelor of Science in English and Interdisciplinary Studies from the University of Houston, and a Masters and Doctorate of Educational Leadership from Texas Southern University. She can be reached at waltern@stthom.edu.

Dr. Jemimah L. Young is an Associate Professor in Multicultural & Urban Education, Department of Teaching, Learning, & Culture in the College of Education at Texas A&M University. She holds a doctorate in Curriculum and Instruction from Texas A&M University. Her areas of expertise include Multicultural Education, Urban Education, and the Sociology of Education. Her research interests are

(1) the academic achievement of students of color, (2) intersectional research of Black girls, (3) educational outcomes for marginalized and minoritized populations, as well as (4) culturally responsive pedagogy. She teaches classes at both the undergraduate and graduate level related to culture, identity, diversity, social justice, foundations in education, and qualitative methodology.

In addition to her faculty role, Dr. Young currently serves as the co-founder and co-editor of the Journal of African American Women and Girls in Education. Dr. Young is the co-editor of the book *Cultivating Achievement, Respect, and Empowerment (CARE) for African American Girls in PreK-12 Settings: Implications for Access, Equity, and Achievement* (2017) and has over 70 published works to include articles in *Urban Education, The Urban Review, The Journal For Multicultural Education, Roeper Review, Teachers College Record,* and *The Clearing House*. She can be reached at jemimah-young@uiowa.edu.

Donna Y. Ford, PhD is a Distinguished Professor of Education and Human Ecology, and a Kirwan Institute Faculty Affiliate in the College of Education and Human Ecology at The Ohio State University. She has authored a few hundred publications - books, articles, and chapters, along with numerous presentations and professional development workshops. Her scholarship focuses on recruiting and retaining Black, Hispanic, and economically disadvantaged students in gifted and talented education and Advanced Placement. Professor Ford is the creator of the Bloom-Banks Matrix. She has received dozens of awards, including being named one of the top 200 educators in the US.

CONTRIBUTORS

Haile Bennett is a creator, educator, entrepreneur, and student at Columbia University's Spirituality Mind Body Institute. As a scholar, she has explored art, critical communication, storytelling, and media literacy education as tools of self-exploration, resistance, and advancement. Professionally, Haile has worked as an independent marketing and outreach consultant, and with education-focused nonprofit organizations. Above all things, Haile believes that everyone should be comfortable in their own skin, free to express their truth and have access to the resources needed to thrive. It is this impassioned principle that Haile aims to channel in all her work.

Ansley A. Booker is a native of Eatonton, Georgia. She attended Georgia Southern University and earned a BA in biology. In 2007, she was selected for the Ronald E. McNair Post Baccalaureate Program. In addition, she has earned a Master's degree from the University of Georgia in science with an emphasis in pharmacy. Ms. Booker currently is a doctoral candidate at Mercer University in the Higher Education Leadership program. Lastly, Ansley is the Interim Director for the Mercer University Educational Opportunity Center (TRiO Programs).

Robin Brandehoff is an educator, Ph.D. student, and theatre arts practitioner-driven to work alongside students and emerging teachers in communities facing conflict and marginalization using drama to educate, play, and liberate. Her research focuses on examining the oppressions and traumas of marginalized communities of color through mentorship, theatre education, and performance to support and educate gang-affiliated youth and the educational leaders that work with them.

Dr. Lisa Bratton received her M.B.A. from Atlanta University and M.A. and Ph.D. degrees in African American Studies from Temple University. She is an Assistant Professor of History at Tuskegee University. Her upcoming book, "I am the Forever," chronicles the lives of Green and Malinda Bratton, her great-great-grandparents who were enslaved at Historic Brattonsville and became the first freedmen to purchase land in the York County.

Janice A. Byrd, an Assistant Professor in the Counselor Education and Supervision program at Kent State University, earned her Ph.D. in Counselor Education and Supervision from the University of Iowa. Dr. Byrd has previous experience as a school counselor, career counselor, and with teaching and mentoring youth. Professor Byrd's scholarship seeks to situate the lived experiences of students of color within the broader ecological context to systematically examine how their personal, social, academic, and career success is interrupted and/or enhanced by school, family, community settings, relationships, and policies throughout all stages of the educational pipeline (i.e., K–12, post-secondary, and advanced degree attainment).

Dr. Theresa J. Canada is a Professor in the Education and Educational Psychology Department at Western Connecticut State University. She served as chairperson of the department from 2007 to 2011. Research interests include cultural diversity in teacher education and counselor education programs; multicultural education; early childhood/adolescent development; equity and urban education. Her educational background includes a B.A. and Ed.D. from The University of Rochester, an M.A. and M.Ed. from Columbia University, Teachers College. Certifications and licenses include N, K 1–6 Teacher (NYS—permanent), School District Administrator (NYS—permanent), National Certified Counselor, Board Certified—TeleMental Health Provider and Licensed Professional Counselor (CT). Dr. Canada has presented papers and conducted webinars and workshops at national and international conferences. Her television credits include Dateline NBC, The Discovery Channel, and local cable television stations. She is a member of several professional organizations. She has been a board member of several national and local organizations.

Akilah R. Carter-Francique (Ph.D., University of Georgia) is an assistant professor in the Department of Health and Kinesiology at Prairie View A&M University. Her research seeks to explicate the intersections of race/ethnicity and women in the contexts of sport & physical activity, education, and health. As a former collegiate athlete in track and field at the University of Houston, she has a specific emphasis on examining the experiences of Black female college athletes. Examples of this work and others can be found in her co-edited books Athletic Experience at Historically Black Colleges and Universities: Past, Present, and Persistence and Critical Race Theory: Black Athletic Experiences in the United States. Carter-Francique is the 2018-2019 President of the North American Society for the Sociology of Sport (NASSS).

Dr. Cristina Rodriguez Chen is currently a Director of Special Programs for a North Texas school district. She holds a Ph.D. from the University of North Texas (UNT). Her area of expertise is in evaluating Culturally and/or Linguistically Diverse (CLD) learners for special education. She is a native Spanish speaker. Prior to serving as a director, she served as a bilingual educational diagnostician, as well as a resource teacher.

Dr. Adrian Chanel Clifton is a wife and mother of four beautiful children. Her community activism has led her to become a Co-founder of the Worley Street Roundtable, a non-profit organization that threads a network of support around marginalized families in the Columbia Public School System. Currently, she serves as a postdoctoral fellow at the University of Missouri-Columbia in the College of Education and as an educational consultant with Clifton Consulting, LLC.

Raven K. Cokley, M.Ed., NCC, is a third-year doctoral candidate in Counselor Education at the University of Georgia. Originally from Sarasota, FL, she received her B.S in Psychology from the University of Central Florida and her M.Ed. in Professional Community Counseling from the University of Georgia. Raven is a nationally board-certified counselor, with clinical experiences in P-20 settings, including charter/public schools and college counseling centers. Raven is a McNair Scholar alumnus and a 2018-2019 NBCC Minority Doctoral Fellow, awarded for her commitment to providing access to mental health services for members of underserved communities. Her research interests include experiences of giftedness among Black girls from lower-income families.

Dr. Alexandria Connally is a school administrator in New York. She is a lifelong learner who is a student of equity, diversity, and culturally relevant pedagogy. Her mission in life is to prepare the next generation of leaders.

Dr. Gwenetta Denise Curry an Assistant Professor in Gender and Race Studies at The University of Alabama. Current areas of study include Africana Womanism, Black Family Studies, Black Male Studies, Medical Sociology and Food Insecurity. My previous research investigated the relationship between educational attainment and body mass index among Black women.

Dr. Kelly Bullock Daugherty is a passionate educator who has worked in the urban school classroom setting for close to 20 years. In this capacity, she is not only a classroom teacher, but also a teacher leader who supports, mentors, and represents her colleagues and school in several different leadership roles. Additionally, Dr. Daugherty is an Education Advocate/Consultant for Transitions Educational Consulting, LLC, her personal business, where her scope of practice includes providing professional development in the areas of teacher efficacy, student engagement, and student motivation. Prior to that, she was a facilitator and member of the National Leadership Team for the Delta Teacher Efficacy Campaign in Washington, D.C. She currently resides in Northeast Ohio with her husband, Leroy, of 19 years and their three children, Blair, Steven, and Kylee.

Rebecca OluwaToyin Doherty, a researcher, an educator, and an entrepreneur at heart, is passionate about addressing access and equity issues with a special interest in the interconnectedness of research, policy, and practice. In the last 16 years, she has consulted on education, youth development, and international development related projects within government, nonprofit, private sector, and preK–16 organizations. Rebecca earned a Bachelor of Arts degree in English (Pre-law) with a minor in Political Science from Howard University; a Master of Arts in International Education (program implementation & management) from the George Washington University; and a Master of Education in an interdisciplinary/special study of the U.S. Education System (law, business, and learning) from Harvard University. Rebecca is the founder of ALVAINA, a nonprofit committed to addressing education access and equity issues through research-based programs, advocacy, and technical assistance. Rebecca is also the lead consultant and founder of Vous Parlez Consulting LLC, a company that addresses social problems with people-centered business solutions. Fondly known as Rebecca and Toyin, her hobbies include acting, singing, and traveling.

Latasha Drax, writer, teacher, advocate, holds the "...pen of a ready writer." (Psalm 45:1). A self-published author, Latasha has contributed to several literary journals, specialty magazines, and newspaper publications. She has taught secondary English, reading, and writing in the United States for more than 10 years and also taught postgraduate academic writing in China. When she is not teaching, writing or traveling, she helps champion the causes to end sex trafficking of minors, the school-to prison-pipeline and mass incarceration.

Donna M. Druery is a doctoral student. She serves as the Accelerated Preparation of Leaders for Underserved Schools (APLUS) grant coordinator for Components 3 and 4. Donna is in charge of recruitment and training of practicing (MISSING something).

Rev. Dr. Leslie Duroseau is an ordained Elder of the United Methodist church. She is a sacred arts minister of dance, with over 25 years of experience as a liturgical dance director and she is also a certified Holistic Health Counselor. She is married to Mr. Eddy Duroseau, and they have four children and two granddaughters.

Stashia L. Emanuel is the Director of Distance Education and Assistant Professor at Kentucky State University in Frankfort, Kentucky. Her research and academic interest are in the areas of academic and social adjustment of minority students at predominately and traditionally white institutions, organizational leadership at Historically Black Colleges and Universities, first-year initiatives and student retention. Dr. Emanuel received her Bachelor of Arts in Criminal Justice from Stockton University (New Jersey), a Master's of Public Administration from Albany State University (Georgia), and a Doctorate of Education in Educational Leadership from Argosy University (Atlanta).

Shandis English, MHA is a Doctoral student studying in the College of Health Sciences. Her research interests are identifying a gap in healthcare access, as pertaining to the veteran. She is currently attending Walden University in an online program as it allows her the flexibility to earn a Doctoral degree while focusing on her family and a sound career at the VA hospital in Madison, WI. She is a wife and mother of two Kania, and Kamron of whom she gains her motivation. She has a Master's and Bachelor's degree in Healthcare Administration from Phoenix University and hopes to soon become a director of a Veterans hospital.

Chiara Davis Fuller possesses 13 years of experience in international education with a focus in English as a Second Language education. She has taught English language courses, coached, organized educational seminars and developed curricula for students and teachers in Japan, Ecuador, Nepal and the United States of America. In the fall of 2018, she continues her academic journey as a first-year doctoral student in the Curriculum and Teaching Department at Teachers College, Columbia University. Her professional passion as a Harlem Education Activities Fund (HEAF) middle school Parliamentary debate coach, global teacher educator, and education event coordinator allows her to design inclusive, culturally responsive and diverse educational spaces for diverse learners.

Rhoda Myra Garces-Bacsal is now serving as the Associate Professor with the Special Education Department at the United Arab Emirates University. Prior to moving to UAE, she served as the Programme Leader of the Masters of Education Program in High Ability Studies at the National of Education, Nanyang Technological University Singapore where she also served as the Coordinator of the Diploma in Special Education and the Professional Development Leader and Pedagogical Development and Innovation Leader of Early Childhood and Special Needs Education Academic Group. She served as the Chair of the Programme Committee of the Asian Children's Writers and Illustrators Conference for the Asian Festival of Children's Content held annually in Singapore for 9 years. Myra shares her passion for reading and book hunting in her website gatheringbooks. org

Renee L. Garraway is a doctoral candidate at Bowie State University and is a recipient of the Culturally Responsive Educational Leaders in Special Education (CRELSE) Grant, which is sponsored by the U. S. Department of Education. Ms. Garraway has over 25 years of diverse work experience in clinical social work, special education, and school-based administration. Ms. Garraway believes that her teaching, social work, and leadership experiences have provided fuel for her purpose and she is committed to ensuring that all students, regardless of race, socioeconomic status, or exceptional abilities receive rigorous, engaging and relevant instruction in a safe and nurturing learning environment.

Judith Gil, DSW, LCSW-R is a licensed mental health practitioner/clinical supervisor in the State of NY. Dr. Gil attained the Doctor of Social Work degree from the University of Pennsylvania and serves as an adjunct assistant professor at various social work graduate programs in NYC, including Columbia University's Graduate School of Social Work. Dr. Gil's research places an emphasis on educational attainment among Black and Latina teenage mothers, in addition to resiliency and positive life outcomes for this special population. Her passion for this topic stems from her personal experience as a teenage mother and her ability to overcome challenges and obstacles associated with this life-changing event. Her lived experience served as a motivator to attain a doctorate and conduct research that would give a voice to women whose voices often times go unheard. Dr. Gil is a native New Yorker of Dominican descent.

Dr. Tyra Good is an Assistant Professor of Education at Chatham University, where she also serves as the Pittsburgh Urban Teaching Corps Liaison. She is the founder and Chief Academic Consultant with GOOD Knowledge Connections, LLC and the Black Educators Network of Greater Pittsburgh. Her research interests focus on building school, family and community partnerships for culturally and linguistically diverse students and their families. Dr. Good graduated with a Bachelor of Arts degree in Business Management from Howard University, a Master of Arts in Teaching degree from Chatham University and a Doctorate in Educational Leadership and Evaluation from Duquesne University.

Chasitie Sharron Goodman graduated from Tennessee State University with a Bachelor's degree in both Psychology and Africana Studies. After being heavily inspired and influenced by professor, and Oxford Roundtable scholar, Dr. William Hardy, she fulfilled her grandmother's prophecy by following in her grandmother's footsteps and answering the call to teach. Ms. Goodman went on to earn her teaching certification and a Master of Arts degree in English, also from Tennessee State University. Ms. Goodman currently teaches at the high school and collegiate level, and has taught, middle and pre-school. She has taught a full range of students from Exceptional Education, English Language Learners, and Adult Learners in a non-traditional college setting.

Dr. Pamela Grayson received her Doctorate in Educational Leadership from Dallas Baptist University. She currently serves as an online instructor for various educational organizations. She is currently collaborating on a study that will further assess the impact of unloving mothers on daughters within different ethnicities. Dr. Grayson currently resides in Dallas, TX.

Dr. Jasmine M. Hamilton is currently an Assistant Professor in the Health and Kinesiology Department at Prairie View A&M University. She teaches undergraduate and graduate courses and Assessment Coordinator to the College of Education has become an intricate part of her duties. Her research interests include socio-cultural issues, social identity, and social capital within physical activity, sport, and physical education. Dr. Hamilton received her undergraduate degree from Xavier University of Louisiana, Master's degree from Sam Houston State University, and doctorate in Kinesiology from Louisiana State University. She is the mother of one daughter.

Jamesha Hayes is a native Memphian that graduated from Rhodes College with a BA in English. She also studied at Oxford University Lincoln College in Oxford, England; earned her Master's in Education from Christian Brother's University and is currently working on her doctoral degree in Educational Leadership at the University of Memphis. Jamesha was a 2011 Teach for America corp member in the Memphis region that taught for four years at her placement school. While at her placement school, she founded the cheerleading program and the after school all girl enrichment & leadership program: Girl Talk. She is currently a director at Teach for America, where she coaches 2nd-year teachers around leadership, vision, and instructional skills.

Dr. Tiffany Hollis is an assistant professor of Special Education at Coastal Carolina University. Dr. Hollis has written several book chapters, articles, and briefs. She has presented at numerous conferences from Washington, DC to Montego Bay, Jamaica and facilitated professional development workshops for teachers locally, nationally, and internationally including in Jakarta, Indonesia. She has a clear and strong commitment to diversity, equity, and social justice with over 14 years in the education setting as a social justice educator with a special education background; ten of those years were spent working with students with emotional and behavioral disabilities and mental health concerns. Dr. Hollis has a special place in her heart for children who society labels "challenging," and who have been abused, neglected, experienced trauma, and/or have been placed into alternative settings outside of their homes.

Ms. Keena D. Howell earned her Bachelor of Science and Master of Education from Howard University. She is currently a doctoral candidate at Bowie State University in the Educational Leadership Program. Her research interests include chronic absenteeism; disproportionality of minorities, and restorative justice practices. An educator of 20 years, Ms. Howell has served in academic settings from kindergarten through post-secondary as a teacher, school counselor, administrator, discipline hearing officer, college advisor, and most recently, pupil personnel worker.

Javetta Jones-Roberson is a high school Dean of Instruction in North Texas. She is currently a Doctoral Candidate in the Educational Leadership department at Texas A&M University-Commerce, where her research focus is Culturally Responsive Leadership towards diverse populations in Advanced Academics. Javetta has been a teacher, elementary Gifted campus coordinator, high school Advanced Academics coordinator, and district professional development facilitator. She serves at the state and national level in various organizations dedicated to the advancement of students of color in Education. She is happily married to her high school sweetheart, LaDarrin and resides in North Texas.

Tammy Lane is a doctoral student in the Educational Leadership program at Prairie View A&M University. Ms. Lane's research and scholarly interests include exploring diversity, equity and inclusion issues related to marginal LGBTQ students, women, and men of color in the academia, and examining financial aid access at historically Black colleges and universities (HBCUs). Specifically, Ms. Lane's dissertation will explore the academic successes of resilient Black transgender students in a historically Black college and university (HBCU) context. Tammy holds a Master of Science in Higher Education and Student Affairs from Kaplan University in Chicago, Illinois and a Bachelor of Science in Early Childhood Education from Kennesaw State University. Also, Ms. Lane is an Administrator in the Office of Financial Aid and Scholarships at Prairie View A &M University. Ms. Lane's robust scholarship agenda comprises several publications and a host of educational conference presentations.

Tiffany Y. Lane is a native of Chester, Pa. Dr. Lane is a Social Work professor in the Ethelyn R. Strong School of Social Work at Norfolk State University. She is the co-founder of Phenomenal Young Ladies, Inc., which is an empowerment organization that supports healthy youth development.

Sharrell D. Luckett, Ph.D. is Director of the Helen Weinberger Center for Drama and Playwriting and Assistant Professor of English, Drama and Performance Studies at the University of Cincinnati. She is lead editor of the award-winning book *Black Acting Methods: Critical Approaches* and author of *YoungGiftedandFat: An Autoethnography of Size, Sexuality, & Privilege*. In addition to working as a director, playwright, actress, and dramaturg, Luckett is the founding Director of the Black Acting Methods® Studio, a training program in performance theory and practice.

Tamera Malone is an instructional math coach in Memphis, Tennessee. She is a doctoral student at the University of Memphis studying Instructional Curriculum and Leadership with a concentration in Urban Education. Her interests include mathematics, social justice, and educational equity.

Courtney Mauldin is a third year Ph.D. student in K-12 Educational Administration and Leadership at Michigan State University. Her research interests center leadership frameworks that sustain students of color with multiple stigmatized identities in schools. In addition to her doctoral studies, Courtney serves as Junior Representative for Division A of AERA and is a UCEA Jackson Scholar.

Tonya McKoy is a Licensed Professional Counselor in the state of Tennessee and a Licensed Associate Minister. In these roles, she has realized challenges many minority women face in maintaining healthy relationships. While she is passionate about women's relational issues, she continues to provide counseling and consultation services empowering women of color to love themselves.

Dr. Marcelle Mentor, a South African native, is an assistant professor of education at The College of New Rochelle. Her academic interest focuses on Critical Race Theory, with an emphasis on Black Masculinity. Her teaching philosophy is based on the concept of Ubuntu which is a Southern African ethical or humanistic approach which focuses on the fact that we are people through the existence and interaction with and from other people.

Dr. Karen J. Miller is a licensed clinical psychotherapist, grief specialist, Trauma Informed Care trainer and educator. She has a Ph.D., a certificate in Women's Studies, and a Master's of Social Work from Howard University, a Masters of Education Administration and a BA in Human Services and certification in elementary education. Her doctoral research focused on the effects of childhood sexual abuse and PTSD on self-efficacy among female offenders. She has presented at local and national conferences on her research. She currently teaches at Howard University School of Social Work in Washington, DC.

Dr. Cynthia Alexander Mitchell has served in public education for the past two decades as a teacher, assistant principal, district staff development coordinator, principal, instructional leadership director, assistant superintendent of academics, family and community engagement director, and currently manages leadership development for the 21st largest school district in the USA. Dr. Alexander Mitchell was also the President of the Memphis Public Schools Principal Association and was one of 30 Founding Principal/National Participant in the National Institute for Urban School Improvement LEADScape, sponsored by the U.S. Department of Education. She has also served as a district, local and national presenter. Her research interest includes leadership development and identifying the primary tenets of culturally responsive urban school leaders.

My name is Viola Marlene Prater, Ed. D. I'm a mother, a grandmother, and a teacher at a rural junior high school. Except for brief periods of time, I've lived in the same community. Since writing the Gumbo chapter, I've entered the local county commissioner's race, and hope to become the first African American female to serve on the board. The election is this week, and I'm focused on the future. Perhaps I will be able to write about another chapter of my life.

Erica Kristina Reid, originally from upstate New York, earned her B.A. in English from the University at Albany and an M.S. in secondary education from the College of Saint Rose. She served as a secondary English and language arts teacher, licensed to teach grades 6–12. Reid is working on her Ph.D. in teaching and learning, in the curriculum and instruction program with an emphasis in multicultural education. Her research areas and interests include online instructional design and curriculum development that prioritizes the needs of diverse learners in K–16 online settings.

Kiana Webb Robinson is Assistant Professor of Social Work in the College of Liberal and Performing Arts at Southern Arkansas University. He has 14 years of social work experience in diverse settings across four states. Kiana is a member of the National Association of Rural Social Workers, National Association of Christian Social Workers and the Licensing and Regulation National Taskforce for CSWE.

Tia Scott holds a bachelor's degree in journalism from Howard University, a master's degree in counseling from Johns Hopkins University, and is currently pursuing a doctorate in educational leadership at Bowie State University. She has spent the better part of the year presenting at professional conferences in Tampa, Washington, DC, and Richmond. Tia worked for over 13 years as a writer and editor then changed careers after being a stay-at-home mother. She has worked in the field of education for over 18 years as a student services professional, counselor, department chair, and site center director in a local Saturday school program. She is passionate about her work with children and advocating on behalf of students whose voices might otherwise go unheard.

Dr. Ebony Terrell Shockley researches STEM, Literacy, and Exceptional Education contexts for culturally, academically, and linguistically diverse groups. Her research occurs primarily in the United States and Cuba. In the United States, she serves as a Diversity Officer, Associate Clinical Professor, and Director of the Office of Teacher and Leader Education for the Department of Teaching and Learning, Policy and Leadership at the University of Maryland College Park. In Cuba, she provides guest lectures at the University of Camagüey and is the only U.S. citizen to serve on the Editorial Board of the university's journal, Transformación Journal. Dr. Terrell Shockley is a counter-narrativist, academician, and practitioner, her coursework and scholarship are rooted in social justice and multiculturalism.

Ariel D. Smith, M.Ed. is a second year American Studies Ph.D. student at Purdue University. A native of Birmingham, Alabama and 2018 Ford Foundation Honorable Mention recipient, Ariel's research positions Black-owned food trucks as the most recent iteration of the underground hip hop movement. She is the founder and host of Le Foodie Noir, a series dedicated to sharing the stories and experiences of Black food truck owners across the United States. You can follow her work at TheFoodTruckScholar.com.

Dr. Mattayna Stephens is a Post-Doctoral Research Associate at Texas State University-San Marcos. She received her Ph.D. from Texas A&M University. Dr. Stephens earned a bachelor's degree in Health Education from Johnson C. Smith University. She also earned a master's degree in Health Education from The Ohio State University. Dr. Stephens' research centers on: (1) human and social capital development; (2) women's studies; and (3) distance education.

Ruby J. Stevens-Morgan, Ph.D. holds a B.S. degree in Business Education from Auburn University, and an M.S. in Curriculum and Instruction and Ph.D. in Educational Psychology from the University of Kentucky. She is an educator with secondary and post-secondary teaching experience, served as a statewide consultant for the Kentucky Department of Education, and a mid-level administrator at Prairie View A&M University. Dr. Stevens-Morgan is the Founder and Executive Director of Achievers by Choice, a non-profit community organization with a mission to empower individuals with the social and academic skills to achieve personal and educational goals. She established nSPIRE Education Consultants, LLC to provide continuous improvement training and education support services to school districts throughout the United States, and she is a Tutor Doctor franchise, an Ontario-based company providing one-to-one in-home tutoring services in local communities worldwide. Dr. Stevens-Morgan is very active in her community and in her church and values her faith, family, and friends.

Dr. Valerie Taylor, Ed.D., teaches African American Studies, Gender & Sexuality Studies, Multicultural Education and Leadership and is passionately engaged in global social justice, celebrating the arts and protecting Mama Gaia. Dr. Taylor is a Black feminist, scholar-activist committed to the liberation of our oppressed minds, bodies and spirits. Her research interests include the leadership development of African American women and women of color in the media and she currently serves as a co-investigator on the University of Nevada, Las Vegas Abriendo Caminos/ Opening Pathways for Students of Color into Teaching as a Career action research project.

Elsa Villarreal is a doctoral student in K–12 Educational Administration at Texas A&M University, College Station, TX. She served 15 years as a high school teacher and a high school administrator in Texas public schools. Elsa' research interests include Latino/a leadership, K–12 Principals, and leading English learners.

Dr. Rachelle D. Washington is a first generation Ph.D. holder and champion of equitable education. For the past 20+ years, she has held faculty and upper-level administrative experiences in P–20 settings. She combines her dedication with a delicate, yet, intentional meld of advocacy, artistry, and activism to provide innovative, culturally relevant teaching, programming and projects. Dr. Washington is published in the area of language and literacy, teacher education, narrative research and schooling narratives and sociocultural aspects of children's literature. From academic journal articles to chapters, napkins and shaped-notebooks— among other mediums—her passion for writing, critically and creatively, is evidenced. Dr. Washington's constant companion is beloved rescue Cocker Spaniel, Zora, named after Zora Neale Hurston, who is one of Washington's favorite writers and researchers.

Dr. Jillian Whatley is the former Coordinator of Psychological Services for Atlanta Public Schools. She is an adjunct professor at Georgia State University. Dr. Whatley currently services as the school psychologist for Georgia Network for Education and Therapeutic Services. Dr. Whatley is the founder and owner of Lissie's Voice, Inc. and education consulting firm.

www.ingramcontent.com/pod-product-compliance
Lightning Source LLC
Chambersburg PA
CBHW050417280326
41932CB00013BA/1892

* 9 7 8 1 6 4 1 1 3 8 7 0 3 *